THE MAN WHO WAS
GEORGE SMILEY

THE MAN WHO WAS GEORGE SMILEY

THE LIFE OF JOHN BINGHAM

MICHAEL JAGO

Biteback Publishing

First published in Great Britain in 2013 by
Biteback Publishing Ltd
Westminster Tower
3 Albert Embankment
London SE1 7SP
Copyright © Michael Jago 2013

Michael Jago has asserted his right under the Copyright, Designs and Patents Act
1988 to be identified as the author of this work.

All unpublished material is taken from the John and Madeleine Bingham Collection,
Howard Gotlieb Archival Research Center at Boston University and reproduced by
kind permission of the Hon. Charlotte Bingham.

'The New Snobbery' reproduced by kind permission of Punch Ltd.

Every reasonable effort has been made to trace copyright holders of material
reproduced in this book, but if any have been inadvertently overlooked the
publishers would be glad to hear from them.

ISBN 978-1-84954-513-6

10 9 8 7 6 5 4 3 2 1

A CIP catalogue record for this book is available from the British Library.

Set in Baskerville

Printed and bound in Great Britain by
CPI Group (UK) Ltd, Croydon CR0 4YY

CONTENTS

ACKNOWLEDGEMENTS

I am grateful to everyone who helped me assemble this biography of John Bingham, 7th Baron Clanmorris of Newbrook. In truth, it was a pleasant task as no one had anything but good to say about him. Above all, the assistance given to me by his children, Simon, the 8th Baron Clanmorris, and the Hon. Charlotte Mary Thérèse Bingham, has been invaluable. Together with Gizella, Lady Clanmorris, and Charlotte Bingham's husband, Terence Brady, they provided me with a framework and were assiduous in spotting errors of emphasis and fact throughout the process.

Of John Bingham's friends and colleagues, I was helped greatly by his goddaughter Rosy Burke (née Denaro), Livia Gollancz, Maureen Johnston and the late Arthur Spencer. Their reminiscences and insights gave me an understanding of a multi-faceted man.

In my researches I must single out Chara Connell of Orion Publishing who rashly offered to commandeer the photocopier to reproduce documents from the Orion archive. At Boston University, Adam Dixon tirelessly wheeled boxes of documents lodged in the Howard Gotlieb Archival Research Center. At Cheltenham College, Jill Barlow was an accomplished sleuth in helping me identify the schoolmaster Ackersley from John Bingham's first novel. And I am delighted that the daily sifting through 1930s and 1940s issues of the *Hull Daily Mail* and the

Sunday Dispatch did not prevent my indefatigable research assistant Tess Harris from earning her first-class degree.

Several people contributed valuable comments after reading the manuscript. Of these I am particularly grateful to Frances Burton, Janey Burton, Captain Seth Johnston (US Army), Chris and Frances Pye and Adam Sisman, biographer of David Cornwell, as well as my son and daughter-in-law James and Dr Elizabeth Jago. The latter helped further in explaining the nature of a specific phobia, an ailment that John Bingham suffered from. Further medical information concerning transient ischaemic attacks was supplied by Juliet Jamieson. Alysoun Sanders at Macmillan opened her archive and facilitated my research. For their help in recreating the young John Bingham through the eyes of their father Jacques de Moncuit de Boiscuillé I am indebted to Hervé and Geoffroy de Moncuit in the village of Tigy in the Sologne. Their mother, 'Mami', also helped with her memories of political discussions in pre-war France.

For constant encouragement I am indebted to my agent Andrew Lownie. At Biteback Publishing, Mick Smith's laconic comments and more expansive advice from my editor Hollie Teague have transformed the writing of my first book from a mere task to an exciting project.

The customary formality is to thank one's wife for her support. My wife Carol has lived with this project for almost two years and has unstintingly contributed her editorial skill and calm wisdom – so this expression of gratitude is greatly more than a formality.

PREFACE

It was mid-afternoon before the agent was able to leave London. There had been a panic about two spies who, the *Abwehr* suspected, had been 'turned' by MI5, the British Security Service. Since the cancellation of Operation SEA LION and, more markedly, since the launching of BARBAROSSA, the invasion of the Soviet Union on 22 June, the infiltration of German spies into Britain had slowed to a trickle. Moreover, the flow of refugees from western Europe had eased after the panic-filled days of July and August 1940, and MI5 was now able to free resources and focus more on weeding out German agents already in Britain. When the invasion scare had been at its height after the fall of France in 1940 and the sheer volume of refugees from France, Belgium and the Netherlands had occupied all the British interrogators at the reception centres, *Abwehr* agents had been able to move about Britain more easily. All that had changed by November 1941.

The agent shivered and pulled his travelling rug around him. This month had brought the worst weather since the winter of 1843 and, as he headed north on the A5, his thoughts turned to the soldiers in the army group centre engaged in the Battle of Moscow, which had started a week before. Over there the temperature was minus 12 centigrade and the 3rd Panzer Group was lurching east towards the Moscow Canal, hampered by a supply crisis that had slowed it down since October. However cold it was in England, it was nothing compared with what the *Wehrmacht* was being subjected to on the Eastern Front.

Finally, he was out of London's northern suburbs with a clear road ahead. As he passed the road to Coventry, he cast his mind back a year almost to the day, to 14 November 1940, the night that 515 bombers of *Luftflotte 3* had carried out Operation MONDSCHEINSONATE and smashed one of the principal manufacturing centres of the British war effort. A new word, *coventriert*, had entered the German language after that raid. *Reichsminister* Goebbels now talked of cities being 'coventried'. That was a night that the British would take a long time to forget.

He was a natural agent, thirty-three years old, unglamorous, stocky, slightly above average height, taciturn, a patient listener. He spoke fluent English as well as German with a compelling, mellifluous voice, and had that ability all the best agents have: to efface himself, to vanish into a crowd. People thought of spies as being exotic, demonstrative, he reflected, while he was the opposite. Mild, almost shy, he took pride in being a forgettable man, someone who could pass unnoticed among his fellows.

He would need to be unnoticed tonight, he thought, if he was to get what he wanted. His appointment outside Stafford was at 7:30 p.m. and he needed to park his car in the outskirts of the town and walk a mile and a half through the early snow, anonymous, unremarkable, to meet Irma Stapleton when she left the factory. He checked his watch. More than halfway to Stafford with two hours before he met her. If the snow didn't get worse, he was in good time.

He thought ahead to the meeting. If Stapleton was telling the truth – which he knew was a rare commodity in his world – she would bring him a 22-millimetre Oerlikon shell, which the factory was manufacturing. He had also sent a secure message to her to bring the details of the location of the Royal Ordnance factory and of the several factories around Stafford owned by Wade's Chain Garages, together with their production figures, if possible. If he succeeded in getting hold of these, he reckoned, the drive from London would have been worthwhile.

He was in Stafford by 6:30 and the streets were quiet in the blackout. The shift changed at the factory at 7:00 that Wednesday night and Stapleton had a ten-minute walk to their rendezvous. Stepping out briskly, he was at the meeting point by 7:25.

When Stapleton arrived, she looked about her cautiously before digging in the bag she carried. She had brought every-thing he had asked for: a map with the location of every Wade plant, their production figures and, as she had promised, an Oerlikon 22-millimetre shell, as well as a two-pound anti-aircraft shell igniter and a 22-millimetre shell base plug.

As Irma Stapleton handed them over to the agent, three burly men appeared from the shadows and handcuffed her. The agent turned to flee but he too was almost effortlessly overpowered and handcuffed. The men identified themselves as officers of the Special Branch of the Metropolitan Police.

Screaming that she was a loyal British subject who had been approached by German Intelligence, Stapleton pointed at the agent and denounced him. She had gone along with the meet-ing, she protested, only in order to hand him over to the police as soon as she had the chance. She was innocent; the agent had come from the *Abwehr*, from the *Gestapo*. She knew her duty and she was going to denounce him as soon as she could, but the Special Branch men had arrived before she could do so.

She demanded to be allowed to make a statement. She would go with the officers to the nearest police station and clear up this ridiculous misunderstanding. The agent was the spy, she shouted, not her. Still screaming, she was bundled into a police car and driven away.

One officer stayed behind to guard the handcuffed but unflustered agent. Turning the key to remove the handcuffs, he looked into the face of his prisoner for the first time and smiled.

'Can I give you a lift to your car, Major Bingham?'

CHAPTER 1

ANCESTRY, 1100-1908, AND EARLY LIFE, 1908-27

For my forwardness in her Majesties servis, for other faulte,
he could not finde in mee, nor ever shall.
Sir Richard Bingham to Sir Francis Walsingham,
12 November 1580

B y the twelfth century the de Bingham family was established
at Sutton Bingham, a few miles south of Yeovil in Somerset.
The first notable Bingham was Robert, brother of Sir Ralph de
Bingham, squire of Sutton in the reign of Edward III. Robert
was born in 1164 and in 1229 was consecrated Bishop of
Salisbury. Succeeding Bishop Poore, who had begun the building of the cathedral in 1220, Bishop de Bingham took charge
of the construction, which was completed in a mere thirty-eight
years. His legacy to Britain is the uniquely homogeneous church,
entirely built in Early English Gothic.

His nephew, second son of Sir Ralph, married into the
Turberville family, they of Thomas Hardy's novel *Tess of the
d'Urbervilles*, and acquired the manor house in the village of
Melcombe, known today as Melcombe Bingham. For three
centuries the family remained obscure country squires between
Dorchester and Blandford Forum until the rise to prominence of
Richard Bingham, an ambitious third son. Leaving Dorset for a

military career, he succeeded in making powerful enemies but also in gaining the favour of Queen Elizabeth I, who commissioned him admiral, knighted him and appointed him Governor of Connacht.

A bloodthirsty man who shot or hanged 1,100 shipwrecked survivors of the Spanish Armada – excepting those who might bring a tidy ransom – he laid the foundations of his family's fortune by the simple expedient of appropriating the land of the Irish rebels he suppressed. At the end of a controversial career, Sir Richard bequeathed at his death in 1599 a substantial legacy to his brother George, the Governor of Sligo. A grateful Queen Elizabeth had a memorial plaque erected in his honour in Westminster Abbey.

Thus was founded an Anglo-Irish dynasty that produced the two most famous branches of the Bingham family. Henry, the elder son of the governor, was created the 1st baronet; his great-great-grandson Charles, the 7th baronet, was created Baron Lucan of Castlebar in the County of Mayo in 1776 and was further promoted to Earl of Lucan in 1795. The younger son, John, fathered the line that, five generations later, produced John Bingham, ennobled as the 1st Baron Clanmorris in 1800.

John Bingham controlled two seats in the Irish Parliament – Newbrook in County Mayo and Fortfield in County Dublin. Delivering these two votes in favour of the Act of Union between England and Ireland, he received from a grateful sovereign a cash sum of £8,000 and a barony, together with a bonus of £20,000 in order to live in the style befitting an English nobleman. Assuming the Scottish-sounding title of Lord Clanmorris of Newbrook (as a Scottish peerage carried more prestige than an Irish one) and adding to his coffers the equivalent of £3,000,000 in today's money, the 1st Baron, with substantial estates in Galway and Mayo, could be well pleased with the Act of Union.

His daughter, the Hon. Maria Letitia Bingham, married Robert ffrench in 1815. The ffrenches, an established Anglo-Irish family, had fallen on hard times, and Robert's estates were encumbered with debt. In 1829 ffrench borrowed £25,000 – £10,000 for his own use and £15,000 for that of his sisters – by mortgaging his estates to the 2nd Lord Clanmorris. The value of that loan in today's money is in excess of £2.5 million – a not insubstantial amount to lend to a brother-in-law.

The source of such wealth was land, enormous tracts of it. The will of Henry Bingham, who died in 1789, reads like a gazetteer of western Ireland as he lists his properties in County Mayo. In 1805, according to a letter from the 1st Baron to Lord Hardwicke, the rent roll produced an annual income of £12,000, the equivalent of £1.2 million today.

Unlike many Anglo-Irish landlords, the Binghams were thought benevolent. During the nineteenth century the down-trodden indigenous Catholic Irish saw their hopes for expansion of the Irish economy consistently dashed; resentment of all English landlords, benevolent or exploitative, absent or present, spread across the west and south-west of the country. Yet the Binghams survived and even flaunted their wealth. Prodigious feats on horseback, possession of 'the best stud of hunters and steeplechasers that Ireland contained', travels to and fro with a stable of racehorses – these diversions occupied the Binghams while their livelihood was threatened by the spectre of renewed Irish uprisings.

In an accidental fire in October 1837 the family seat at Newbrook burned to the ground; buckets of water passed hand-to-hand failed to stop the eight-day blaze. The elegant, spacious square house became another Anglo-Irish ruin, never to be rebuilt.

Eight years later, when blight destroyed the potato crop in the summer of 1845, predictable tragedy followed. The famine, followed by widespread disease, brought mass emigration. A financial crisis in 1847 reduced any wish the English government might have had to provide effective relief for Ireland. Conditions in the west of the country, where the Clanmorris estates lay, were especially dire; the population of Connacht fell by 30 per cent in the 1840s.

In 1847 John Charles Robert Bingham succeeded to the title as the 4th Baron. Two years later he married Sarah Persse, member of a family that periodically intermarried with the Clanmorrises. Their union was blessed and, after two daughters, John George Barry Bingham was born on 27 August 1852. In the same year, Sarah's brother Burton Persse became master of Ireland's most famous hunt, the Galway Blazers, a position he would hold until his death thirty-three years later. Rebellion might be gaining momentum in Ireland, but the Anglo-Irish aristocracy in Galway continued to hunt, to send their children to Eton and to intermarry.

When crops failed in successive years from 1844 to 1847, the value of Irish land plummeted and, once again, the counties to the west – Galway and Mayo above all – were most affected. Even the most compassionate landlord lived in fear of financial ruin and agrarian rebellion. Emigration was the solution for many: suddenly landlords, having evicted their poorer tenants, began to lose their good ones too. With huge swathes of Galway still uncultivated, the fragile landlord–tenant contract simply evaporated.

The famine fuelled the Fenian movement, which demanded Irish freedom from British rule. As the first Fenian uprising was suppressed and its leaders executed in 1867, John George Barry Bingham completed his education at Eton and began his military service. By that time, the rent roll enjoyed by the 1st Baron had shrunk and the family strove to perpetuate its pleasures from the residual income. 'Hard-drinking and hard-riding', they continued the life of opulent squires, maintained their stables, their hounds, their fishing lodges. The future 5th Baron, moreover, had formed a close friendship with Prince Arthur, Duke of Connaught, and such royal friendships rarely come at little cost. By 1878, not to put too fine a point on it, the barony was on the financial rocks.

But it remained a barony, a highly marketable asset. On 27 June 1878, having succeeded to the title two years before, the 5th Baron bestowed on Matilda Catherine Maude Ward the title of Lady Clanmorris. Possessed of a substantial fortune and the impressive Bangor Castle, she lacked only a title. This the 5th Baron, though now bereft of other assets, could provide. The young couple were married in Bangor before 120 family members and friends. Fine presents arrived from England – a gold bracelet, set with pearls and diamonds; antique silver; a richly encrusted Etruscan necklace. The Irish situation, however, dissuaded the English from attending in person.

It was, on the surface, a splendid match for both bride and groom. In simple terms, 'Clan' provided the title and Maude provided the money. Maude came from a hugely wealthy Ulster family with impeccable Protestant credentials. Clan had royal connections, Maude provided a solid base – the Victorian Bangor Castle that her father, razing the original castle to the ground, had completed in 1852.

There was harmony in the arrangement, but beneath the placid surface surged discord, philosophical and physical. Clan was 'the typical hunting-drinking man of his day' and hunting was supplied in the west by the Galway Blazers, of whom he was master from 1890 to 1895. This modest-sounding position was the apogee of the Anglo-Irish aristocracy. The roll of past masters of the hunt reads like a Who's Who of the Protestant ascendancy, and the exploits of members, both on and off horse-back, were exotic. The hunt, originally known as 'The County Galway Hunt', acquired its cognomen 'The Blazers' in the early 1800s after the hunt members set alight Dooley's Hotel in Offaly during after-hunt revelry.

As for the drinking, Maude rapidly realised that Clan was happiest in the company of his hunting friends when 'Clan's end of the long table in the castle dining room was always loud with laughter and the glasses were always full, while Maude's entourage found the going sticky'.

A caricature of the Anglo-Irish ascendancy, Clan enjoyed hunting or fishing. Despite the decline of his estates in the west, he had hung onto some good salmon and trout fishing and a handful of lodges. He took Maude out with the Blazers, but her outings ceased in mid-season when she became pregnant for the first time. On 22 June 1879 she presented Clan with a son and heir, Arthur Maurice Robert, named after Arthur, Duke of Connaught but always called 'Maurice'.

After Maurice's birth, Maude remained almost permanently in a state of pregnancy for nine years. Maurice was followed by John Denis Yelverton (1880), Edward Barry Stewart (1881), Harriette Ierne Maude (1882), Emily Ina Florence (1884), Hugh Terence de Burgh (1885) and Henry Derek Thomas (1887). A brief pause ensued before the births of Eleanor Clare Alice (1892), George Roderick Bentinck (1894) and Richard Gerald Ava (1896).

This would have made for a picture-perfect Victorian family but for certain obstacles. Paramount were Maude's intense dislike of pregnancy and lack of interest in her children; secondly, Clan was by then making substantial inroads on her fortune, inroads impeded only by the Married Women's Property Act of 1882, protecting a woman's rights over her property when she married; thirdly, Clan began to make regular trips to Paris, ostensibly to have his adored brown poodle clipped but really, the family suspected, in order to enjoy the more celebrated attractions of that permissive city.

Maurice followed his father to Eton and was twenty when the Boer crisis erupted in South Africa. War was declared on 11 October 1899; Maurice joined the 5th Royal Irish Lancers on the following day and shipped out to the Cape.

They were soon engaged. Heading north under General Buller to relieve the British garrison of Ladysmith, they fought at the Battle of Colenso on 15 December. This was a bloody affair, fought all day in blistering sunshine. The cavalry, although tactically of little value, were fortunate to be mobile as the relentless slaughter unfolded around them. Maurice wrote to Clan in jovial spirit: 'Dear Father, I have had some pretty good experiences the last few days. I got my baptism of fire last Friday at the battle of Colenso.' Only later did he admit that he was 'nearly done for at Colenso'; in the ethic of his class and era, modesty had forbidden that he mention it at the time.

During the first half of 1900 the war dragged on inconclusively. The Battle of Belfast, the last important set piece of the war, ended on 27 August 1900. When it became clear that no peace could be negotiated without unacceptable concessions from the Boers, General Louis Botha's strategy of conducting guerrilla war was adopted.

To guard against simultaneous revolt at several points in Cape Colony, Maurice's regiment was posted to Cape Town and brought its war to a relaxed end amid Cape society. Despite its Dutch origins, Cape Town was by 1900 a very English town, its social life modelled on British lines, offering, like any colonial capital, an agreeable way of life to visiting army officers.

Rest and relaxation in Cape Town were most welcome to Maurice and his fellow officer Lieutenant George Capron. We can imagine the two handsome, dashing cavalry officers settling easily into the to and fro of society on the Cape, prominent within which were the five vivacious daughters of Gordon Cloete, a justice of the peace and lay preacher.

The Cloete family in South Africa dates back to 1652, when Jacob Cloete sailed to the Cape with Johan Anthoniszoon 'Jan' van Riebeeck, the founder of Cape Town and the first Dutch Commander of the Cape. To have sailed to South Africa with van Riebeeck even today carries the same prestige as having crossed to England with William the Conqueror or having arrived in the American colonies on the *Mayflower*, and by 1701 the family was among the principal farmers on the Cape.

Two hundred years later, Gordon Cloete lived close to the original Cloete farm, in the suburb of Rosebank, in the shadow of Table Mountain. His five daughters were stalwart members of the socially conscious life of the city. Years later, John Bingham would write of the five sisters that 'the Cloete family created such havoc among the English officers sent to fight in the Boer War that I think they occasioned more casualties than the Boers'.

Vera, the eldest daughter, captured the heart of Colonel Ted Noding of the Royal Army Medical Corps; the younger officers, Maurice and fellow Lancer George Capron, were smitten by Leila and Effie. Renée, the youngest, dreamed of marrying an English gentleman but did not meet him on this occasion. Inez alone saw her future in South Africa.

Effie, 'the prettiest and fluffiest' of the five girls, accepted George Capron's proposal and returned to England with him as a married woman. Ted Noding, too, pressed a successful suit and Vera also moved to London. Renée came to England in search of a husband; but not before England had been hurled into another war in 1914.

Which leaves us Leila, vastly attracted by the notion of becoming an English baroness but, at this stage of her life, at least, a thoroughly practical young woman. She viewed her encounter with Maurice as a temporary wartime liaison contracted after the heat of fighting. She was surprised, therefore, when Maurice, posted after the war as ADC to Lord Ranfurly, the Governor of New Zealand, chose to prolong and extend their brief friendship, urging her to marry him immediately. She stalled, saying she would accept once he was promoted to captain. When this occurred in 1906, Maurice cabled her, held her to her promise and sailed to Cape Town. The young couple were married on 5 June 1907.

This was the zenith of Maurice's life. Heir to a substantial inheritance, he had acquitted himself well in a decent regiment, rubbed shoulders with the *nomenklatura* of the British Diplomatic Service, and wooed and won a vivacious member of Cape Town society. He would return to Britain, he doubtless imagined, stay in the army until he attained field rank, then resign his commission to take up a few directorships, possibly run as a Unionist Party candidate for Bangor, and spend his life between Bangor Castle and Westminster. This was his due, what he had been brought up to do.

Now he brought his new wife to the neo-Gothic battlements of Bangor Castle, its vast halls, and its rigid routine laid down by Maude, the last of the Wards, the 5th Baroness, who ran 'her' castle in her way. Possessed of a considerable fortune, married into a recent but respectable barony, a sharp and realistic assessor of the values, moral and financial, of her successor, she – more than Clan – was the critical arbiter of the bride that Maurice carried home from the Cape. A commission in the Cavalry, she would have agreed, is a good thing. If the wages of that commission are an 'entanglement', then it is better to be entangled with breeding or a substantial dowry.

Leila Cloete, for all her singular virtues, brought neither to the fortified walls of Bangor Castle. Her Dutch pedigree, stretching back to 1652, may have cut some ice in Cape Town, but a Boer heritage sat ill with the Anglo-Irish aristocracy. Allowances for foreignness needed to be made, of course, at the beginning of the twentieth century. Many English noblemen – Lord Curzon, the Duke of Roxburghe, Lord Randolph Churchill, the Duke of Marlborough, the Earl of Craven – had been so rash as to marry Americans; collectively, American heiresses brought $25 billion to rejuvenate the British ruling classes and preserve their stately homes, but approval tended to be conceded in direct proportion to the asset value of the bride.

In short, Maurice appeared to have been improvident in his choice, a characteristic that was to play its part throughout his life. Maude's reception of the returning lovebirds was, one can be sure, correct. One can be equally sure that it was also chilling, that, to use a well-worn phrase of her era, she was not amused.

Leila, for her part, was equally unamused by the state in which she found herself. From her early acquaintance with Maude until 1941, when Leila herself finally became chatelaine, she referred to Maude as 'The Mother'. Excited at the prospect of ennoblement, she had to suffer being married to the heir, an heir on a strict allowance doled out by the lawyers of the sitting baroness, in whose eyes, she knew, she was not at all the thing. She was a lively young woman, not without ambition. She had married a man with a future, but that future was vested in assets firmly beyond the young couple's grasp. In the meantime, she would have to live a 'normal' life: she and Maurice would have to create their own income, live on it, keep house. By 1903, Bangor Castle was a relic of a past era, and Belfast society was not at all what Leila had chosen. London beckoned, full of opportunity, full of hazard. Leila saw only the former.

London society, viewed from a distance in Cape Town, was

one thing; the reality of Leila's situation, marooned in the north, was another. Her husband held a commission in the army and his regiment was based not in Belgravia but in Acomb, a village to the west of York. In Cape Town she had belonged to a leading family in a narrow world; in Yorkshire she was a mere captain's wife in an equally narrow, equally stratified world.

Maurice's relations with his colonel deteriorated during his time at Acomb. As he was held to a strict allowance, with the riches of Bangor Castle no more than a distant prospect, Leila can hardly have felt that her dream of taking Mayfair by storm was likely to be realised. There were other concerns, moreover, to limit her horizons. In early 1908 she became pregnant. In a difficult birth on 3 November, John Michael Ward Bingham was born. The entire experience of pregnancy and lying-in had been distasteful to Leila and she took care that the episode should not be repeated.

Maurice resigned his commission in 1909 and the family moved to London. His friend Captain George Capron had become his brother-in-law, having married Leila's sister Effie. The two Lancers renewed their friendship and embarked on the first of Maurice's business ventures, none of which would realise the expectations – or repay the capital – invested in them. Their plan was simple: to buy young cattle in Ireland and import them to their farm in the Home Counties where they would be fattened for market. The slump in Irish agricultural prices and increasing middle-class wealth in England gave the business a very fair chance of success. Indeed, things were progressing reasonably well when Britain was hurled into war in August 1914. The two business partners, officers on the reserve list, were promptly called up, abruptly ending their venture.

John was five years old when the war broke out. To an only child, brought up by a nanny like so many of his class, his parents were distant figures; the one was consumed with making a living outside the army, a need accentuated by the other's obsession with society and conviction that life could not be lived without at least a brace of servants. To such a couple a young child was an encumbrance and, whenever possible, Leila shipped nanny and John off to Bangor to stay with his grandparents.

Here, too, he was left much to himself. Routine was sacrosanct at the castle; Maude applied a rigid schedule to her life, spending much of her time 'visiting' in Bangor, a process that involved being driven in the Daimler at a sedate 20mph to call on families around town. Clan had mellowed but, now sixty-two, had little interest in a boy from London who acquitted himself ill on horseback.

John's memories of those early years consist mainly of the solitude of roaming the grounds of the castle, hunting vermin with his beloved catapult. Neither happy nor unhappy, he learned the discipline of 'getting through' and of 'sticking it out'. Physically unimpressive, possessed of a squint caused by severe shock when his nanny burned him while changing him by the fire, he had learned to be a loner, a close observer, essentially alone.

At the front, meanwhile, Maurice, the dashing young subaltern of 1899, now a 35-year-old reservist captain, was appointed Inspector of Cavalry in 1914, an unglamorous, routine post. As a reservist, he had little status. Moreover, he had resigned his commission, according to his daughter-in-law, because he was on bad terms with his colonel. Now thirty-five, with a wife and young son, he could be forgiven for being no longer eager for death or glory.

Three of Maurice's brothers had 'good' wars. John Denis Yelverton, brevet lieutenant-colonel in the 15th/19th Hussars, was twice mentioned in dispatches, won a DSO in 1918 and was decorated with the *Légion d'honneur*. Edward Barry Stewart joined the Royal Navy at the age of fourteen and won a

Victoria Cross at the Battle of Jutland in 1916. George Roderick Bentinck fought as a captain in the Royal Welsh Fusiliers. Maurice's youngest sibling, Richard Gerald Ava, a second lieutenant in the Royal Air Force, was killed in action on 10 October 1918, a scant month before the Armistice.

Meanwhile Maurice, the heir to the barony, had little opportunity to add to the family's accomplishments. Further humiliation followed: he was bitten by a supposedly rabid dog, sent to Paris for treatment, and shipped back to England. His father died in 1916, so the Armistice found the 6th Lord Clanmorris back in Yorkshire, commanding a prisoner-of-war camp outside Ripon.

On his father's death, Maurice was descended on by lawyers acting for his mother in Northern Ireland. Maude, whether from prescience or the simple knowledge that her eldest son was no financial wizard, had kept his allowance at its modest pre-war level. As Madeleine Bingham puts it succinctly, '[Maude] had managed to save her fortune from her husband, and she was not disposed to let her heir dissipate the rest. Nor was Maurice the only one Maude might have to support: there was his wife who, imprudently, had no money either.'

Accordingly, she was quick off the mark to secure her interests when the 5th Baron died. The Irish lawyers sugar-coated their agreement with Maurice, writing that Maurice, acting 'out of duty and filial affection', chose to forgo his valid claim on his father's estate, allowing Maude to retain everything. Doubtless it was an act of generosity, but the action was, one supposes, made easier for Maurice by the knowledge that, in time, it would revert to him anyway.

Towards the end of the war Renée, the youngest Cloete sister, came to England to seek a good match. It was expected that Leila, now Lady Clanmorris, would use her aristocratic contacts to achieve this.

With the assistance of the casualty lists, Renée did join the landed gentry. William, the second son of Colonel Charles France-Hayhurst, had accepted his lot as a younger son and learned the profession of estate management. When his father died in 1914 and his elder brother was killed in Flanders, he unexpectedly found himself master of Bostock Hall, a minor stately home outside Middlewich in Cheshire.

The new squire set out to find a wife and secure the succession. On meeting Renée he decided to look no further. Renée extricated herself from a liaison that promised her far less, waved a fond goodbye to her former fiancé, accepted William and moved to Bostock Hall in 1918. During the same year, she became pregnant and Leila allowed her to take John's nanny, no longer needed now that he was at prep school, to help during her pregnancy. Tragically, Renée died in childbirth, fulfilling a premonition she had had early in her pregnancy. Her daughter survived and was named after her.

Maurice and Leila, by contrast, had no control of their putative inheritance, an asset that was gradually shrinking. The Clanmorris estates in 1876 had comprised 12,337 acres in County Mayo, 5,295 acres in County Galway and 479 acres in Galway town. By 1906 much of Clan's land was untenanted; in March 1916, the last year of Clan's life, the family sold 3,053 acres of the estate in County Mayo to the Congested Districts' Board for £16,121 – marginally more than £5 an acre.

With few qualifications and no capital, Maurice discussed with Leila the option usually given to a younger son: a new life in some corner of the Empire. If they were to embark on that course, then the obvious option for the couple was to pull such strings as Leila could gather together in South Africa, the country of her birth.

From Madeleine Bingham's enchanting pen portrait of Leila,

her mother-in-law, we gain the impression of a not entirely superficial nor yet profound woman, susceptible to suggestion, ever on the lookout for an original and startlingly profitable idea, equipped with all the optimism but little of the determination required to bring a project to fruition. From her reservoir of such ideas came the notion of farming in Pondoland, where land and labour were still cheap.

Pondoland, a fertile strip on the Indian Ocean stretching from Port Elizabeth in the south to Durban in the north, had been annexed to Cape Colony in 1894. It was still a land of opportunity, open to settlement. Maurice's brother Roderick, fifteen years his junior, had already moved to South Africa, where he owned a flower farm. Maurice and Leila too planned to farm – it was unclear exactly what they would farm, but the options were as vast as the African plains. Whatever they chose would be more exotic and more lucrative than making ends meet on a modest allowance in post-war Britain.

Accordingly Maurice, Leila and John, now aged eleven, sailed south in March 1920. The trip, Maurice and Leila decided, would be valuable for them and also good for their son. John was not happy at his prep school. Short sighted and still debilitated by his squint, he was subjected to merciless teasing and bullying from his arrival at Clifton House in Harrogate. He was stoic about it all, but the memory lingered long. As late as 1953 he was to describe with feeling his experiences at prep school in his second novel, *Five Roundabouts to Heaven*.

Less emphatic are his diary entries during the South African jaunt. Bored by the whole adventure and the only child among a family of Afrikaans-speaking strangers, he spent long periods alone. He was accustomed to this and, as at his grandfather's estate around Bangor Castle, his principal enjoyment lay in hunting birds and squirrels with his catapult and befriending the chickens in the back garden at Rosebank. His diary suggests that his prep school, even with the bullying inflicted by his peers, would have been more interesting. In the event, neither the ostrich farms nor the orange groves tempted his parents to emigrate. They seem scarcely to have taken the project seriously. It was four months before they left Cape Town by train in August in search of farms. By September the family had returned to England – and John to Clifton House – taking back with them one notionally positive benefit: Maurice had tasted the possibility of working for himself and amassing his own capital. Once back in London, he would go into business. Quite what business he would choose and how, without capital, he would get started were problems he would solve when he arrived home.

The second difficulty was solved by a method familiar to many aristocrats in straitened circumstances in the 1920s. Had he not 'done the decent thing' in allowing Maude to retain her wealth for her lifetime? Was he not soon to inherit that fortune, rightly his according to the laws of primogeniture? Could he not borrow against that future capital and put the money to better use? Either the business venture would yield sufficient profit for him to repay the capital borrowed or, at the worst, a mere portion of his inheritance would settle his indebtedness to the bank wise and progressive enough to lend him the money.

Thus reassured, he followed many of his peers to the City of London and, in common with them, found that banks were by no means averse to making loans against future inheritance. It was all too simple: not once but several times did Maurice approach the bankers, 'borrowing insanely' as his granddaughter Charlotte describes it. The first tranche of £15,000 (over £500,000 at today's value) enabled him to invest in a hardware export business; subsequent drawings gave him the wherewithal to buy the lease on a house in Montagu Square, to employ a brace of maids and a cook, and enjoy an income of a couple of thousand a year, a respectable amount at the time.

Maurice enjoyed this new opulence until the hardware business collapsed. Overnight, the family lost a considerable portion of his putative inheritance. The house in Montagu Square was sold, the servants were let go, the couple moved into a flat; according to Madeleine Bingham, even more exotic remedies were discussed: 'It was even mooted that [Leila] should look around for a millionaire to marry. Leila, all her life, had a touching faith in the healing power of millionaires.'

Quite how Leila's marrying a millionaire while she was married to Maurice would have been achieved, or how the arrangement would have helped Maurice, is unclear.

Maurice took a series of jobs where his title was an asset, first on the board of a film company and then selling advertising space for a regimental magazine. Withdrawn, not at all the dashing officer of the turn of the century, he nonetheless became a professional guest, making regular trips to Bangor and visiting relatives who lived in far greater style than he and Leila enjoyed. They took to spending Christmas at Bostock Hall, where Leila's brother-in-law Billy France-Hayhurst lived in grand splendour. Leila, having failed to meet the right millionaire, took a job with Madame Luander, owner of a dress shop in Albemarle Street. Despite her declared dedication to her job, Leila's employment did not solve the pressing need for money. Fast approaching, moreover, was the expense of public school for which fees, then as now, were considerable and, worse, ineluctably payable in advance. At all events, on 31 May 1922, John was registered to attend Cheltenham College from January 1923.

The application was made when John was already thirteen years old. Generally, English boys are 'put down' for their public school much earlier, often at birth. The natural deduction is that he had been put down for Eton, but that the higher fees were, by 1923, beyond his parents' means. John's daughter Charlotte explains how this obstacle was overcome:

> My grandfather, having been ruined by what he used to refer to as 'the city boys', was helped out with my father's education by his brothers and sisters, all of whom forked out for him for everything ... He couldn't go to Eton; they had to settle for Cheltenham, because of the lack of pennies in the coffers.

With the help of the family, John left Clifton House for Cheltenham College in December 1922. The graduation represented no milestone in his life. He later admitted to being 'sad and depressed to leave' his prep school, commenting only that 'it was really just a matter of keeping your temper and sweating it out. In the end you won through.'

John Bingham's first two novels contain a wealth of hints about his prep and public school days. In *Five Roundabouts to Heaven* we see an autobiographical picture of a physically unimpressive boy, his poor eyesight and inadequate physique emphasised by thick glasses, waiting inside the school building until his schoolmates had dispersed and he could emerge without fear of being bullied or chivvied.

John was ragged mercilessly at school, as happens to all boys who have a particular phobia; small boys have a nose for discovering weakness and punishing it relentlessly. John's weakness was a fear of confined spaces. His schoolmates cheerfully exploited that by bundling him into a trunk and closing the lid. The horror of being shut in a tiny space was exacerbated by the presence of several dead moths on the bottom of the trunk. With his face pressed against them he was terrified, and for all his life had a horror of moths.

Success at public schools at that time depended principally on athletic ability and secondly on academic skills. With his poor eyesight he had little chance of achieving distinction as an athlete, and while he did eventually play rugby for his house third XV, this was a modest achievement.

Academically, he performed no better than average. He had not spent his childhood among intellectual parents. By himself he was a voracious reader, but his parents encouraged neither reading nor other intellectual pursuits. In his own eyes he was a poor specimen; in his first novel he refers to himself as 'an influenza germ' in the eyes of a schoolmate. With these deficiencies, perceived and actual, he turned up for his first term at Cheltenham College.

There were three options of study open to him: classical, military and modern. The classical side was the preserve of the better brains, providing, via the university, access to the professions. The military option was a fast track to the Royal Military Academy at Sandhurst, and the modern side contained boys who had not been identified as belonging to the top stream but who might distinguish themselves academically and become candidates for Oxford or Cambridge. If so, they would stay on for the Sixth Form. The young Bingham was enrolled to study the modern curriculum.

Maurice gave his London address on the college application form, but John, a boy who had grown up with space and land around him, was quite unprepared for life at Cheltenham. The college is compact, built around the playing fields, buildings clustered together. It more resembles a modern university campus than an ancient public school like Harrow or Eton, which effectively occupy the entire town that houses them.

John, used to roaming around his grandfather's estate, was appalled by the layout of the college. From the start he felt constrained, trapped, and he yearned for air. The experience of having several hundred boys as close neighbours was also unsettling for an only child.

Initially his academic performance was undistinguished but adequate. In his first term he finished fourteenth in a class of twenty-one, showing ability in English, French, Latin and drawing. English, particularly, seemed his forte, as he finished second in his class.

As he worked his way up in the school his academic performance fluctuated dramatically. It is clear that, when he applied himself, he could outperform his peers but it is equally clear that he rarely applied himself more than was required to steer a middle course.

Teenage boys need role models and it seems unlikely that John was finding them at home. Maurice was achieving little that might impress his son during that period. The year 1925, moreover, had seen another member of his family humbled. Maurice's younger brother Denis was involved in a sensational divorce case. He was cited as co-respondent when a fellow officer sued to divorce his wife for adultery. Divorces of notables were given considerable tabloid space in the 1920s and the mournfully sentimental letters from Denis to the lady in question were splashed across the popular papers. The affair was given added spice by the fact that she was a master of foxhounds, a detail that the press were delighted to stress to maximum effect. John, with the prurience of a sixteen-year-old boy, cut the sordid, explicit clippings from the popular newspapers and pasted them into his scrapbook.

When he reached the Middle Fifth Form in 1925/6, he evidently encountered an encouraging teacher, probably a teacher of English: suddenly his academic performance improved in stellar fashion. From being an undistinguished scholar consistently in the lower half of his class, he leapt to the top, finishing second in a class of twenty-three and first in his class for English, and maintained this throughout that academic year. When he had been considered a mediocre student, he was placed at the front of the class and was able to read everything on the blackboard. Having distinguished himself, he was moved to the back of the room among the better scholars and had trouble reading anything on the board because of his poor eyesight. He began to write short stories and verse, submitting pieces for the school magazine and selling a story to H. G. Wells for a magazine he edited. For this he received the unimaginable sum – for a seventeen-year-old – of five guineas, a reward that impressed his father vastly more than his being published in a magazine edited by a left-winger.

Boys on the classical side were expected to win at least a place, preferably an open scholarship, to Oxford or Cambridge. Boys on the military side needed to achieve decent grades to be accepted to Sandhurst, but for a boy of average ability, stuck in the Fifth Form on the modern side with less incentive to perform, there was a tendency to question the point of it all.

By the academic year of 1926/7 it was clear that John would not make it into the Sixth Form, a prerequisite for applying to university. He merely had to serve one more year before leaving school and heading into the world. With no goal to motivate him, in that year, unsurprisingly, he came in seventeenth, thirteenth and tenth out of twenty-six boys in the three terms.

In his second year at Cheltenham he had joined the Officers' Training Corps, where he was determined to do well. He rose to be a sergeant, passed his Certificate A and was a first-class signaller. This would have been a key to gaining his father's respect; certainly, with his poor eyesight, there was no chance of a conventional military career.

In spite of these modest successes, he still lacked confidence and held a jaundiced view of himself throughout his time at

Cheltenham. To illustrate this we need read just one passage from his first novel, *My Name Is Michael Sibley*. In this piece of fiction, he has Sibley spend part of his annual summer holiday with his Aunt Nell, a splendidly aggressive woman with a grand house and estate. Despite a domineering manner, she is fond of Sibley and takes an interest in his performance at school. Cross-examining him on his progress, she succeeds in making him deeply uncomfortable. When he arrives at her door, she greets him with a gruff welcome, demanding to know if he has won his rugby cap. When Sibley answers that he plays for his house side, she booms, 'Not good enough. Not good enough by a long chalk!' She turns to cricket, and Sibley replies that his eyes aren't good enough for him to play in the first XI. Finally, she demands if he is in the Sixth Form. By now, thoroughly despondent, Sibley, 'blushing crimson', mutters that this distinction, too, is beyond his grasp.

'God bless my soul, Michael!' Aunt Nell thunders. 'What are you good at?' Sibley collapses and replies that he isn't particularly good at anything.

Aunt Nell, who leaps from the pages of *Michael Sibley*, is modelled on his great-aunt, the Hon. Mrs Burton Percy Bingham (1869–1935) of Ivy Mount House, Athenry, Co. Galway; John spent part of each summer in the west of Ireland to keep alive his connection with the region. She is described vividly in the 12 October 1900 issue of *Golf Illustrated*:

> Mrs Bingham, who was both niece and daughter-in-law of the late Lord Clanmorris, is well known as a good all-round sportswoman, and though punting, so far, takes first place in her affections, she is keen on all games and devoted to country life.

At the end of John's third year in the school an event occurred that was to have a lasting impact on him. The assistant housemaster in Cheltondale House was a 43-year-old man named Laurence Shuttleworth. Judging from the account in *Michael Sibley*, Shuttleworth was a retiring man, ineffective as a disciplinarian, one of those teachers who are mercilessly ragged by boys.

Shuttleworth's wife suffered a prolonged illness before dying of cancer on 24 June. On the same day her bereft husband took his service revolver and shot himself in the head. His suicide haunted John. Schoolchildren are callous creatures and the sport of ragging a mild or ineffectual master is common. Suddenly John saw another side to the man's tortured life. When the news reached the boys in their study hall, the chattering and giggling was offensive to John and his friend John Parks. They discussed Shuttleworth's action and the morbid cruelty of the boys for whom the suicide was simply more sport.

John began to understand that schoolmasters have a life outside the classroom, that they suffer from the same desires and needs as the rest of the human race. Shuttleworth had found a refuge with his wife. There he had his private life, his books, the comfort of married life. When his wife died, he was unable to look forward with any pleasure to a life alone, and promptly took his own life.

If we accept the picture of Sibley as a schoolboy as substantially autobiographical, we can envisage the young Bingham as a loner, an only child who had few friends at Cheltenham. Throughout his later written work this theme of loneliness returns. He believed deeply that human beings should be strong enough to deal with events that threatened them; he placed huge emphasis on being able to cope. Yet, when confronted with an example of the blind terror of facing a life alone, he shows a deep compassion. It was an emotion that he personally was able to understand, and the memory of Shuttleworth's solution remained powerful for him.

It was during his time at Cheltenham that he had begun to write. Two examples of his work, cleverly contrived and bristling with the pretentious style of an adolescent writer, were published in *The Cheltonian*, the school magazine, in his third year.

The first of these, drawing from the story of Agamemnon returning from the Trojan War, has a hint of the future mystery writer. The second, an ambitious piece of romantic verse, has more than a touch of the Irish poet William Butler Yeats, who was swiftly making a name for himself in London and Ireland. From 1916 to 1929 Yeats lived at Thoor Ballylee at Gort, near Galway, a short distance from John's great-aunt's house at Athenry, and the poet would have been an iconic figure for a romantic young Anglo-Irishman. The lilting anapaestic rhythm has a distinct, haunting flavour of the Binghams' homeland of western Ireland, as the first two stanzas show:

'The Isle of Enchantment'
Far to the east lies the Isle of Enchantment
Girded by reefs whereon murmur slow waves:
Lazy lagoons with gentle caresses
Creep through the coral and lap in the caves.

Hard by the shore stands a magical palace,
Pearly its walls and jasper its floor;
There as a maiden I dwelt in the forest,
Thence would I go to dream by the shore.

Bingham's time at Cheltenham, which came to an end in July 1927, was, as his son describes it, 'undistinguished'. Like many schoolboys of that era, he neither enjoyed it nor hated it. Public school was a rite of passage to be endured; one made friends, gradually discarded them later, always recognised the kinship of the Old School Tie and occasionally returned for Speech Day and similar occasions. It was a life apart, emotionally far from home, and boys became part of an isolated community that had little or no relationship to the world beyond its walls.

In later years Bingham was reticent about his schooldays. The only mention he made of it to his children was when he recalled a visit of his parents to the school. On one Speech Day Maurice and Leila had appeared, dressed as though they were destined for Royal Ascot or Eton, rather than the rituals of an afternoon at Cheltenham. He was mortified by his father's tailcoat and topper, by his mother's flowing dress, parasol and splendid hat.

Without fanfare, without prospects, he had no easy entrée to a career, yet he appears not to have seen the matter as urgent. One idea, however, had begun to form in his mind. A voracious reader, he had consumed the works of Edgar Wallace, the most popular crime writer in Britain in the 1920s. It was from Wallace's work that he learned of the Colonial Service and decided that it sounded glamorous, vaguely clandestine. In the summer of 1927 he applied and was invited to an interview. Once more, he records events in *Michael Sibley*, painting himself in a poor light. He imagines that the interviewer recorded that he was ordinary in appearance, ill at ease, bereft of any real academic qualification and, that most damning description, a spectacles wearer.

That is how he chose to record the interview in the fiction, principally to enhance the picture that he paints of Sibley as a weak, unimpressive character. The truth is more complex, as he recorded in later life:

> Largely because I had read deeply about Colonial District Commissioners in the works of Edgar Wallace, I, too, wanted to be a Commissioner. But the Colonial Office, as it was then called, only took would-be District Commissioners from the age of 21.

I was 18 or 19. To fill in the intervening years, a job would have been convenient. But with no experience and no special skills, a job eluded me. I was unemployed and apparently unemployable.

The interviewing officer suggested that it would help his application if he could add a couple of languages to his qualifications and reapply when he reached his twenty-first birthday in November 1929. This sound advice posed problems, however. Maurice and Leila were struggling financially and were in no position to fund a jaunt abroad, a jaunt that would stretch two years into the future.

In a short reflective piece of writing from 1985 or 1986 he comments, 'Those were the days when aunts and uncles often had money to spare and if somebody liked you he (or she) paid for a sojourn abroad.' His eccentric Cloete aunts, equally, had no money to spare; indeed, Aunt Effie was perennially involved in litigation and permanently trying to relieve any available relative of funds to promote her 'case', a complicated lawsuit whose outcome, she assured everyone, would make them mountainously rich.

Once again Maurice's brothers and sisters chipped in. They had rallied round to ensure that John went to a decent school and once more they saw the value of an extended trip to France and Germany. But their bounty was wearing thin and this was to be the last time that the family bailed Maurice and Leila out.

An advertisement in *The Times* provided the solution for the first leg of the journey: the owners of Château de la Matholière in the Sologne welcomed a small group of the right people to their estate to learn French language and customs. In an exchange of letters they confirmed that they did have space for a young Englishman to join them in September. As to the next stage, there was ample time to make arrangements as John's stay in France would last until the following July.

In September 1927, with his next two years settled and the prospect of a job on his return, he set off on a trip that would be instructive and pleasurable. It would also fashion his political beliefs and, indirectly, influence his choice of career twelve years later.

CHAPTER 2

POLITICAL AWAKENING, 1927–9

We had no doubts. We worked a little, we played tennis, gardened, and bathed in the lake in front of the château. In winter we went shooting. We fell in love.
John Bingham, *Five Roundabouts to Heaven*

There are periods in all our lives that we look back to with nostalgia, with the sense that for that month, that summer, that year, life was as perfect as it could be. For John Bingham, the nine months he spent at Château de la Matholière in Tigy were his halcyon days. For the rest of his life he would look back at 'the château' as a haven of rustic peace, sanctified by its aura of unreality, by its moat where he fished for frogs and by his first love, whom he refers to in *Five Roundabouts to Heaven* as 'Ingrid'. Everything about Tigy retained a magical significance for him. Much later in his life, when he had difficulty focusing his mind on writing, his memories would drift back to Tigy, to its moat and the frogs, to his year in Arcadia.

He had a purpose when he left England for the European continent in 1927. For his stay in Tigy his packing list was impressive: he would need tennis whites, a dinner jacket, a shooting jacket and most of the accoutrements of a country gentleman planning an extended stay at a stately home. Of his hosts, the family of Baron Frédéric de Moncuit de Boiscuillé, he knew little beyond the fact that they took in paying guests who wished to learn French and acquire a little *chic français*. Familiar with the architecture of Bangor Castle, he expected something similar to be his home for the year.

When he arrived, he was at first disappointed. One meaning of the French word *château* is 'castle' and he hoped for crenellated battlements, towers, archers' arrow loops, a bailey, ramparts and the flag of the de Moncuits flying from the round tower. He did not know that *château* more often denotes a manor house, the 'big house' in the town. Château de la Matholière did have a moat, which gave it a certain cachet, but in every other respect it was simply a manor house set in a heavily wooded estate in the Sologne, a backwater south of Orléans, as different from the grandeur of Chenonceau and Amboise as could be imagined.

Having overcome that minor setback, he settled in quickly, basking in the leisurely life of a French country gentleman, shooting game and vermin on the wooded estate, dressing formally for dinner with *apéritifs* on the terrace beforehand. He formed a friendship with Frédéric de Moncuit's son Jacques, two years older than him who, in later life, became mayor of Tigy. The friendship lasted and Jacques, in due course, was best man at Bingham's wedding and godfather to his son Simon.

Hervé de Moncuit, son of Jacques, remembers his father saying that their guest was at first overwhelmed by the warmth and openness of family life at Tigy. 'His own parents could never get rid of him soon enough,' Hervé recalls, 'and so it was a new experience for him to be welcomed into a family.' It was a boisterous family, five boys with a passion for mopeds, rabbit hunting and outdoor sports. With his weak eyesight, Bingham was a poor shot but, instead of being made to feel inferior, his incompetence with a shotgun became a familiar joke, a source of friendly amusement among a welcoming family. Tennis, too, was a daily fixture during the summer; here, too, he was conspicuously ill qualified to play, but again suffered nothing more than friendly banter – a far cry from the competitive sports of Cheltenham.

La Matholière quickly provided kinship, a sense of belonging that his adolescent life had lacked. An only child, he had sought his own entertainment, roaming the grounds of Bangor Castle with his beloved catapult. School had its own special milieu, part social, largely duty and routine. Now, for the first time in his life, he found himself on close terms with a group – two groups, in fact: the de Moncuit family and their long-term guests – where he was immediately accepted and welcomed for himself. Naturally, he acquired a nickname: at Tigy he is remembered today as 'B' (pronounced *Bé* in French) – B for Bingham and B for baboon. The 'ugliness' that he regretted in himself was no more than an amusing characteristic among his new family. In 1934, when he revisited Tigy with his new wife, she signed herself in the visitors' book as 'La Baboonette'.

Later in life, indeed throughout his life, the château at Tigy reappears. In 1952, when he wrote his second novel, *Five Roundabouts to Heaven*, he set the early chapters there, creating Philip Bartels, a character whose social awkwardness mirrors his own. Bartels has a wide mouth, poor eyesight and is happiest when fishing for frogs in the moat. This is certainly an image of the eighteen-year-old Bingham. The guests at Tigy are all young men and women, taking their first tentative steps into adulthood and, from this picture created twenty-five years later, we can visualise the young Bingham. We can imagine him finding himself, moving into a larger world after four not entirely happy nor entirely unhappy years at public school.

Life at the château was a privileged existence. The de Moncuits, the first family of tiny Tigy, owned the local brick factory but sought other sources of income. Close to the river Loire but sufficiently far from the main line of royal châteaux between

Blois and Chinon to enjoy the peace of a heavily forested back-water, it is easy to imagine a well-born French family, hosting the well-to-do of several countries who came to learn not only the language but also the *style de vie* of the rural French landowner.

According to the description in *Five Roundabouts*, the young people who gathered there came from Norway, from Germany, from the United States, but predominantly from England. The English contingent came for a variety of reasons: one before going into the wine trade, another before joining the family hotel business, one to improve his prospects at the bank where he worked, another, the daughter of a solicitor from Worthing, because it was *de rigueur* for a well-brought-up English girl to speak French. It was as varied a group of privileged youth as can be imagined.

Bingham was able, probably for the first time, to be part of a group that was not, by its nature, inbred and conformist. There will have been strict rules at the château – there usually are anywhere in France – but those rules will have been of decorum rather than the bizarre rules of gradated privilege that English public schoolboys learn to resent and kick against.

Despite being completely accepted for himself, Bingham still lacked confidence. He was still, in his own view, misshapen, toad-like and saddled with that symbol of the physically weak: thick spectacles. By 1952 he had acquired the self-confidence to ignore these real and imagined defects. It is clear, however, that in 1927 they concerned him greatly.

His picture of Tigy in *Five Roundabouts* introduces us to life at the château. There is the gamekeeper who grumbles when the young men put a ferret down after a rabbit and lose it; there is Madame, announcing to the young residents, all in evening dress, that dinner is ready. There are excursions to shoot game, tennis in pressed whites, *apéritifs* on the terrace before dinner – a way of life that built character in a very different manner from the trenches of English boarding schools. To recall it in later life was, in Bingham's words, the 'sweet pain of thinking of times now gone forever'. All it needed was an *affaire* of the heart to complete the deliriously sweet picture. And that was also available at Tigy.

In *Five Roundabouts* there is a delightful representation of the young Bingham, in love with 'Ingrid', rising early and picking a morning bunch of radishes that he would wrap in a handkerchief and toss to the window of her room for her breakfast. The passage – indeed, every sentence in which Ingrid is mentioned – swells with innocent passion. Writing a quarter of a century later, he recalls in enchanting detail his feelings for a young Norwegian girl. Fast forward to thirty years later, more than fifty years after his time in Tigy, and we find Bingham jotting notes in an attempt to insert the château and his Norwegian girlfriend into his last book.

'Ingrid' reappears at different points in Bingham's life, but there is a certain mystery attached to her. His daughter Charlotte recalls that her father spoke to her about 'Ingrid' and that the de Moncuit family, observing the growing friendship between the two, decided that she should return home early. Yet this young romance apparently had no effect on the family's affection for Bingham. There is no suggestion that he behaved improperly; Ingrid was sent home to Oslo while he remained at the château.

When he left Tigy in the summer of 1928, he strove in his recently acquired French, formal and correct yet halting, to express on paper what the nine months in the Sologne had meant to him. In the visitors' book of the château he begins grandiloquently:

Loyalty to God and to the King, true courtesy, cheerfulness – three good qualities that one often encounters separately but, sadly, not

always together in a single family. Yet I have had the good fortune
to find them like that here and I can state without any hesitation
that the nine months I have spent here have been among the
happiest of my entire life (my entire life – so long at 19 years old).[†]

Apart from his ultimately pointless trip to South Africa eight years
before, this had been Bingham's first experience of 'abroad', and
he strove to make sense of it, as he wrote in the visitors' book:

Here in the country there is one thing above all that I have
noticed. That is that you French, you are lucky. There's no doubt
of that. Your France is much larger than England, England that
is dear to me. But England is becoming an industrial country,
so one sees towns and normally in the country many large
estates with many labourers: the good peasants, small farmers
of independent mind, the valiant 'yeomen', as we call them, are
disappearing fast. Alas! Too bad for us! But in France you still
have the space and everyone can have his 'little corner of France',
of which he can say 'It's mine – and mine alone.' It's that, and
not communism, that produces patriotism.[‡]

[†]   *La fidélité au Dieu et au Roi, la vraie courtoisie, la gaieté – trois très bonnes qualités
      qu'on trouve souvent séparément, mais malheuresuement pas toujours unies dans une
      seule famille. J'ai eu pourtant la chance de les trouver comme ça ici, et je peux constater
      sans aucune hésitation que les neuf mois que j'ai passés ici ont eté parmi les plus
      heureux de toute ma vie (toute ma vie – très longue à 19 ans)*

[‡]   *Ici, dans la campagne, il y a une chose surtout que j'ai remarquée. C'est que vous
      Français, vous avez de la chance. Il n'y a pas de doute. Votre France est beaucoup
      plus grande que l'Angleterre, chère a moi. L'Angleterre devient un pays industriel,
      ainsi on voit les villes et, ordinairement dans la campagne les grandes propriétés avec
      beaucoup de laboureurs: les bons paysans, les petits fermiers d'esprit indépendent, les
      braves 'yeomen', comme nous les appellons, disparaissent vite. Hélas! Tant pis pour
      nous! Mais en France vous avez encore la place, et chacun peut avoir son petit 'coin de
      France', dont il peut dire, 'c'est à moi – et à moi seulement'. Ça produit la patriotisme
      – non pas le communisme*

Despite the idyllic picture of life in the Sologne described by Bingham, there were many kinds of storm cloud gathering over Britain and the continent of Europe, all of them hostile to the British aristocracy.

By 1927 the Soviet experiment was ten years old and had attracted many aristocrats, disillusioned with prolonged class struggle and the divisive politics of post-war Britain, ultimately convinced that an aristocracy, if not western capitalism itself, was doomed. In his comprehensive study *The Decline and Fall of the British Aristocracy*, David Cannadine lists the several defections from the upper classes to the Left in the 1920s and 1930s, revealing the impressive array of scions of famous landowning families who became socialists, communists or fellow travellers. Bingham, as his writing in the visitors' book makes clear, was not one of the British upper class who felt that communism was the cure for Britain's ills.

Communism in France was in its infancy in the 1920s. The *Parti Communiste Français* had been formed in 1920 but it remained aloof from the mainstream of the French Left for several years. France then – as now – depended on small farmers to produce quantities of wheat, and wheat in the early 1920s still fetched a reasonable price. The fall in wheat prices and the consequent erosion of farmers' income, the agricultural crises and the rise of the 'Greenshirts' were to beleaguer France in the 1930s. The rustic peace of 1927 was very different from the urbanisation that Bingham decried in England. But that difference was merely chronological: a decade later the plight of the French peasant whose lot he eulogised had become a national political issue.

There was widespread complacency in France. The war was over; the German menace had been overcome, albeit at huge cost; reparations had been imposed on the German aggressor; everything could return to business as usual, whatever the antics of the politicians in Paris. Gaston Doumergue, President of France from 1924 to 1931, was a radical who came to power through the *Cartel des Gauches* and who was committed to curbing a resurgent Germany. His term as President had seen no fewer than four Prime Ministers in three years until Raymond Poincaré of the *Alliance Démocratique* came to power in 1926.

At la Matholière there was much discussion at the dinner table of the future direction of France. Governments came and went at bewildering speed between the wars; the distinctions between the Democratic Alliance, the Radical Socialist Party, the Republican-Socialist Party and the Republican Federation must have been baffling to a young man fresh from Britain where power traditionally shifted between Conservatives and Liberals. Understanding the nuances of French politics was an infinitely harder proposition.

Even if the finer shades of the Left and the Centre Left were lost on him, Bingham took away from his stay in France a firm respect for democracy. Its volatility might render it, in Winston Churchill's words, 'the worst form of government except all the others', but he became convinced of the value of a parliamentary system, even if it created a ministerial revolving door.

According to Hervé de Moncuit, Bingham had arrived with the flimsiest understanding of the political issues of his day. He had inchoate views, principally an instinctive dislike of any totalitarian system, but he was 'waiting to be woken up'. Fundamental political and religious issues were the stuff of conversation at la Matholière; it was a novel experience for him to discuss a wide range of political ideas and to grasp how vital that discussion was to his contemporaries in France. It is hard to imagine a more instructive time to have been in France than in the 1920s; the atmosphere was very different from that of Britain under the staid government of Stanley Baldwin.

By the end of the First World War the great Whig tradition had been brought low by the defection of many of its constituent families; disgust with the Lloyd George coalition was widespread; there existed among disgruntled patricians a frustration with the direction of British politics. This, harnessed to a distaste for the extended franchise and democratic innovation, led to a growing and widespread interest in one or another form of totalitarian rule. To Anthony Blunt (born 1906) and Kim Philby (born 1911), both very much of Bingham's generation, and a host of public figures from John Strachey to Oswald Mosley to Christopher Isherwood, it was the Left that promised to 'get things moving again'.

This enthusiasm for the Left was countered among many of Bingham's fellow patricians by the conviction that only firm government from the traditional ruling class would provide a solution for Britain's ills. Distrust of Stanley Baldwin and anodyne Conservatism tempted many among the British aristocracy to gaze wistfully at Benito Mussolini and the Italian Fascist Party. To forestall the growing power of trades unions and a feared lurch towards communism, they felt that only similar authority would be effective. During that decade there was no home-grown equivalent. Disenchanted Conservatives like Oswald Mosley had joined the Labour Party; it was not until the 1930s that the British Union of Fascists was born.

There was, meanwhile, renewed interest and concern at the renaissance of Germany but no signs that the conflict between Left and Right would be resolved in short order. It would take the theatrics of Adolf Hitler in the 1930s to seduce the British aristocracy. In the 1920s that outcome appeared unlikely. To observers in London as well as in Moscow, it seemed that Germany was ripe for communism.

When he left Tigy for Mecklenburg in June 1928, Bingham

was paying his first trip to Germany at a time when the National Socialist (Nazi) Party was still a marginal group; it had won fewer than a million votes nationwide and held a mere fourteen of the 491 seats in the Reichstag. Unlike the pilgrimages to Germany made by the Prince of Wales, by Oswald Mosley, Diana Mitford and her sister Unity, by a whole pack of fawning aristocrats in the 1930s, Bingham's trip was taken when the future of the Nazis was precarious, when Hitler was still viewed by most Germans as a posturing demagogue. As in England, there was division among noble families concerning Hitler and Germany's future: one family with whom Bingham became friendly in Germany contained two cousins, one a devoted associate of Joseph Goebbels, the other subsequently a member of the von Stauffenberg plot to kill Hitler at the *Wolfsschanze*, his headquarters in East Prussia, on 20 July 1944.

Among Bingham's immediate forebears there were few who were involved in politics. Maurice and Leila had no involvement with any political party and it is hard to imagine profound political conversations at home:

> My mother, born in Cape Town, was only interested in what she called Society, which was at that time an unpaid, and largely unpayable, segment of life whose dying days were between the end of World War One and the outbreak of the Second World War.

Uncle Herbert, later Lord Glentoran, was a politician and he, more than any other close relation, may have been an influence on Bingham's political thinking. Even that, however, is speculation. Later we find a moderate, centrist conservative, keen to preserve what he saw as valuable, morally and politically, in a changing world. In the seventeen years from 1928, when his ideas were unformed, to 1945, when he emerged from the war as a passionate anti-totalitarian, committed to maintaining what he considered to be 'English' values, we can trace growing conviction, matched with a determination to devote his life to preserving those values. It was a shift from being a passive believer to becoming a passionate advocate of common-sense ideals; the journey exposed him to extremists of both Left and Right. It endowed him with a cynical distrust of doctrinaire philosophy of all kinds. His stay in France had been an idyllic basking in the last summer of youth; his stay in Germany was the portal to a vastly more aware adult life.

Mecklenburg in the late 1920s had many similarities with the Loire Valley. The Loire has a host of fine country houses built for the French aristocracy and is, in the age of motor transport, a short drive from Paris. Mecklenburg, stretching from east of Lübeck in the north-west to Prussia and modern Poland in the east, tracing the Baltic coast, is at its southerly point less than 80 miles from Berlin. With over forty listed castles and hunting lodges of interest, it too was an area used for weekend relaxation by Berlin's élite.

Bingham met several such élite families. He told his children stories of cross-country skiing from one castle to another. It is five miles across country from the Jagdschloss Bellin to the von Schmidt-Pauli Schloss at Charlottenthal and, in the bitterly cold winter of 1928–9, this would have been an exhilarating outing on skis. Ten years later, in the 9 March 1938 issue of *Punch*, he wrote 'Uncanny Intuition', a short story about a shooting party at Bellin where, to the horror of an English gentleman, it was permitted, indeed encouraged, to shoot foxes.

Among the neighbours and friends he met at the shooting parties were scions of two of Germany's most distinguished families. Friedrich Graf zu Solms was a friend of the von Schmidt-Pauli family and, in 1952, married Renata, the daughter of the family.

She was two years older than Bingham, and the three young people became close friends.

Another family that he met, who owned a Schloss close by, was a branch of the Herwarth von Bittenfeld family from Berlin: the father Hans-Wilhelm, known as 'Hawi', his wife Elisabeth and their three sons Hans-Wolf, Hans-Jürgen and Hans-Christoph. After the war, when their uncle Hans-Heinrich became the first ambassador to London from the newly created Federal Republic of Germany, Bingham re-established contact with him and was devastated to learn that of the three von Herwarth brothers he had known, Hans-Jürgen had died in 1943 during the Allied invasion of Sicily and Hans-Wolf had died soon after the war. Only Hans-Christoph, who had followed his uncle into the German Diplomatic Corps, had survived the war intact and was, by then, serving in the German consulate in Chicago.

The von Herwarth family owned estates in Prussia but was based in Berlin; another more distant branch of the family were grand landowners in Bavaria. Hans-Heinrich (known as 'Johnnie') worked closely with Count Claus von Stauffenberg in 1943–4 and, like his superior officer, was a passionate patriot who believed that Hitler was doing irreparable damage to Germany. Closely involved in Operation VALKYRIE, the 20 July 1944 plot to kill Hitler, von Herwarth was fortunately absent from Berlin when the plot failed. Miraculously, he was not betrayed, and he survived to become a much-respected and distinguished ambassador in London.

He had, for a long time, believed that Germany was on the wrong track. As early as 1939 he had secretly communicated to Chip Bohlen at the US embassy in Moscow the details of the Ribbentrop–Molotov pact between Germany and the Soviet Union, in the belief that such an alliance was not in the long-term interests of his country. Such an act took considerable courage.

Hans-Wilhelm was a sincere patriot but also an anglophile, and in the years before the war he had become friends with Fitzroy Maclean, later a successful novelist, when the two diplomats were serving in Moscow. In 1944 Maclean was chosen by Churchill to head a mission to Yugoslavia and 'find out who was killing the most Germans and suggest means by which we could help them kill more'. By then a brigadier, Maclean commanded a group of Yugoslav Partisans who overran a German HQ in the autumn of 1944. He was puzzled when one of his officers found a written German order that, if he was captured, Maclean was to be taken to Army HQ, where further instructions would be issued regarding his disposal. For years Maclean wondered what his fate might have been.

After von Herwarth became the first ambassador from the Federal Republic to London, Maclean and he met at the embassy and von Herwarth, pouring a glass of Maclean's favourite whisky, suddenly exclaimed, 'Well, I had that drink waiting for you, but you never came to get it.' He reminded a baffled Maclean that, before the war in Moscow, they had agreed that if either of them were captured, the other would see that he got enough to drink. Von Herwarth had a staff job in Yugoslavia in 1944 and, aware of Maclean's activities, had issued instructions to all German formations that, if he were taken prisoner, he was to be brought to him. 'After that,' he said, 'my friends and I would have done our best to see that you didn't come to any harm.'

Before both the First and Second World Wars the sense of impotence of like-minded people was felt on both sides. Hans-Heinrich von Herwarth perfectly describes the feeling of futility and sorrow that overcame diplomats in the British and German embassies in Moscow as it became clear that friends and colleagues would, in a short time, find themselves in opposing camps in a world war. Fitzroy Maclean's anecdote illustrates how decent men could, in some small way, circumvent the system that had caused such fissures between like-minded colleagues.

John Bingham must have felt something of this as he watched events unroll in 1938 and 1939, as it became clear that the young friends he had made in Mecklenburg would become his enemies if Hitler's ambition could not be checked.

There will have been, moreover, animated discussions as young German disagreed with young German over the rise of the National Socialist Party within Germany. Many German aristocrats were certain that Hitler would be useful in doing the dirty business of suppressing the German Communist Party and, once he overreached himself as he undoubtedly would, he could be removed and replaced by a more acceptable, more traditional Chancellor. It was a terrible miscalculation.

In 1928 and 1929, the shape and scale of the Second World War lay ten years in the future but fear of a repetition of 1914–18 was uppermost in the minds of all those young men. As they ate, drank, went shooting together in Mecklenburg, returning again and again to discuss where Hitler might lead a revivified Reich, the possibility that they might one day be fighting each other recurred.

This was Bingham's first exposure to the politics of a country radically divided. The Herwarth von Bittenfeld family was divided against itself; passionate Nazi supporters were viscerally opposed to their anti-Nazi cousins. At home, fellow Englishmen of his age and class shared a view of what England stood for. Changes were taking place in England – the first Labour government of Ramsay MacDonald was elected in Britain just as Bingham was preparing to return to England – but upheaval on the scale of Germany in the 1920s and 1930s was unthinkable. Despite the solid body of values shared by young Englishmen and young Germans, there were fundamental issues that would divide patriotic German from patriotic Briton.

In many ways those discussions prepared him for the work that dominated his life once the war was over. In common with most thinking Englishmen in the 1930s, he wanted war with Germany to be avoided at almost any cost. The real enemy, in their eyes, was Moscow, not Berlin. Hans-Heinrich and the like-minded of his colleagues watched with mounting dismay as Britain and France made increasing concessions to Hitler. They believed that if only Hitler could be checked, his fall from power would inevitably follow. In London during the Munich crisis, Bingham believed equally fervently that Neville Chamberlain was merely postponing war by granting Hitler's demands on Czechoslovakia. From quite different perspectives and for different reasons, he and his friends had similar convictions that war could be and must be avoided. All would have agreed that an alliance of Germany and Britain was essential as a bulwark against the emerging threat from the east.

But it would be twenty years before that became accepted wisdom in Bonn, London and Washington. In the meantime, the young friends went different ways, fought the same war on different sides, and it would not be until 1953 that they resumed contact. By then Europe was divided. Mecklenburg was in the Soviet zone of Germany; the Solms family had lost 17,300 acres of its estates, first to Himmler as an indemnity for their support of the von Stauffenberg plot, then to the Democratic Republic of Germany; Charlottenthal and Jagdschloss Bellin had ceased to be private residences. The world that the young aristocrats knew a quarter of a century before had vanished.

In the summer of 1929, then, Bingham returned to England. His parents were setting out on a trip to Paris, Fontainebleau and Le Touquet. He persuaded them to include Tigy on their itinerary and hitched a lift with them. They spent the last week of August at la Matholière before he parted from his natural family, allowing them to head off to Le Touquet. He was more at home with the de Moncuits, particularly with the five boys, the brothers he never had.

Maurice and Leila left la Matholière on 31 August, writing rather woodenly in the visitors' book that 'we think anybody who comes here to learn French is very lucky to be able to do so in such ideal surroundings', and hoping that 'it will only be "au revoir" to M. le Baron and family and our charming hostess Madame la Baronne'. Signing their inscription somewhat formally as 'Lord and Lady Clanmorris', they left the Sologne for the fashionable pleasures of Le Touquet.

Their son preferred to stay and help the de Moncuits pull up the reeds in the moat, to fish for frogs, to play some tennis and simply be part of the family's everyday life. There was, however, a crisis during his stay: the Baron, Jacques's father, was diagnosed with Parkinson's disease that month and went to hospital for treatment. He was still absent when Bingham left after a five-week stay, leaving his best wishes for 'that very gallant gentleman'.

His days in Arcadia were fast coming to an end. In September 1929 it was, all too early, time for him to return to England and the tiresome but increasingly urgent business of finding a job. The halcyon days of his last youthful summer were over.

CHAPTER 3

JOURNALISM AND MARRIAGE, 1929–39

Although I am a southerner, I must confess that I never encountered in the south such warmheartedness among townspeople or such comradeship among newspapermen as I met with on the Palesby Gazette.
John Bingham, *My Name Is Michael Sibley*

When Bingham returned to England in 1929 he had added a command of French and German to his armoury but was still below the minimum age for admission to the Colonial Service. His mother, reluctant to see him unemployed for several months, involved herself in his affairs.

Leila had an abiding optimism. Whenever things looked bleak, she placed her faith in the healing power of a millionaire to relieve the gloom. Her son described the sequence of events of September 1929 in his autobiographical notes:

It was then, in the darkest hour, so to speak, that my mother, totally unexpectedly, changed the course of my life ... She thought she might always 'meet somebody useful'. And this, though she did not know it, was precisely what she did.

Leila had heard of a millionaire who was looking for a private secretary. Bingham duly went for an interview and felt he was doing well until the question of shorthand and typing was mentioned. No problem, he responded; he would go to Pitman's forthwith and learn those skills. The millionaire accepted that there would be a short delay and hired Bingham to begin work after completing the secretarial course.

He enrolled at Pitman's College in London in September, confident that there was a job waiting for him at the end of it. A month later, however, on 24 October, the New York stock market crashed. Leila's millionaire promptly vanished, leaving Bingham at Pitman's acquiring a skill that he would not otherwise have chosen.

There were compensations, however, that kept him on task. At an adjoining desk sat an attractive dark-haired young lady who made as many typing errors as Bingham. Against all regulations, he had a rubber eraser and they surreptitiously corrected their typing before the hawk-eyed instructor could catch them. In this conspiratorial mode they exchanged a few personal details, the lady mentioning that she had come to Pitman's having first attended a Catholic school in Surrey and then spent a year learning French at a convent in Brussels.

The young lady, Madeleine Ebel of Massetts, a Tudor house in Sussex, was pleased to find a letter on her desk one morning addressed to '*Mademoiselle du Couvent*', enclosing the visiting card of 'The Hon. John Bingham' and a letter inviting her to lunch and a theatre matinée during the break between the winter and spring terms. The first date was kept and was a success; then they went their separate ways for the short vacation.

Returning to Pitman's in January, they began to see each other outside their shorthand and typing courses. When these came to an end in March 1930, however, their ways parted again as Bingham promptly headed for la Matholière for the month of April.

From comments made to the de Moncuit family during his stay, it seemed that his enthusiasm for the Colonial Service had waned during two years away from England. When he originally applied, he had left Cheltenham only a month before, he had not travelled as an adult and he saw his destiny through the prism of a conventional British public school. Now, having spent time outside Britain and seen that there were perfectly acceptable ways of life very different from the traditional British model, he was less enthusiastic about the job.

A month-long stay at la Matholière soon became a three-month sabbatical. Jacques de Moncuit also had time on his hands and he and Bingham decided to take off to the south of France on a motorcycle trip. Once again, the contrast between the staid life of Bingham's parents' flat in London and the carefree existence of his adopted French family is stark; it is easy to imagine the attraction of spending the spring away from London.

Returning to Tigy, the boys joined the rest of the family in building a golf course in the grounds of the château. Sheep grazed on the fairways and the boys dug the bunkers; May came and went; the strawberries ripened and Bingham had the responsibility of keeping the birds away. May passed into June and still he was at Tigy.

Having succeeded in postponing the evil moment when he would actually begin work, he was compelled to 'trade the tranquillity of Tigy for the noise and the smells of London' at the end of June.

'The visit was as happy and glorious as ever,' he wrote to the de Moncuits, 'I cannot express my thanks for all the wonderful hospitality that ... all the family showed me. And, as I have never done anything to deserve such generosity, your kindness is the more inexplicable.' His obligation to perform his *'devoir publique'*, he tells them, is the only reason for his departure.

'Otherwise I would outstay my welcome – if I haven't already done so.'

When he turned up for his second interview for his *'devoir publique'*, he hit a brick wall. During the two years since his first visit to the Colonial Office, regulations had changed. Entrants were now required to have a university degree. Although his interest in the Colonial Office had diminished, he became concerned that the one job he had been reasonably certain of landing was denied him. In the three years since he had left Cheltenham he had acquired some skills but, in honesty, had come no nearer to finding anything that could be called a job.

When he wrote to Madeleine Ebel to let her know that he was back in England, she responded by asking him to Sunday lunch. He willingly accepted and took the train to Sussex to meet her family.

Madeleine Mary Ebel was born in February 1912 to Clement and Charlotte ('Lottie') Ebel, the one from a family with roots in Alsace, the other from an Irish background. The oldest of four children in a close-knit family, Madeleine showed, from an early age, a multi-faceted personality. On the one hand a strong-minded advocate of her own interests, something of a rebel, on the other hand staunchly conventional, she inherited characteristics of both her parents.

Clement, her father, to whom she was very close and on whom she was more emotionally dependent than she cared to admit, was a self-made man who saw the world as full of dangerous incompetents. He was the dominant person in Madeleine's life, an emotional and practical anchor before and during her marriage. His presence, foibles and all – perhaps especially his foibles – provided the continuity she needed. Irascible yet frequently gentle, passionate in his hobbies, with a tendency to roar when thwarted, demanding and generous, intolerant of fools and 'mugwumps' but devoted to his family, he was the backdrop to Madeleine's early life.

Lottie, her mother, was a more conventional character, a caricature of the strong, sensible woman that every colourful man needs to clear up after him. Shopping with Clement was an experience: nothing but the best – and lots of it – would do, for he maintained that the best was always the cheapest in the end. Shopping with Lottie was to watch her tend a housekeeping budget that could be cut by circumstance at any moment. When Clement would return with a box of peaches, ripe and fresh, ready to be eaten that day, he would explode on finding out that Lottie had put them away for later consumption. 'But they're ready today,' he would roar. 'Not on Monday. Today.'

Clement enjoyed moving houses, seeking out new furniture, hiring gardeners to tend each new and more elaborate garden. Lottie would bemoan each extravagance, each successive grand gesture, ultimately bearing it with fortitude, always with one eye on the cost. They were a remarkable team: Clement needed Lottie's parsimony; Lottie enjoyed Clement's rollicking, though ultimately serious, approach to the business of life.

Clement's exotic style never quite masked his solid and practical substance. He had made his way by sheer hard work, by assiduous attention to detail, by learning about things, mastering them and putting them into practice. His only notable failure was in learning to play the violin for, despite his determination to succeed, he lacked the musical sensibility of Lottie's family, all of whom were highly musical; several were professional musicians.

Clement was managing director of Trollope & Sons, 'Artists in Decoration Since 1778'. The business had catered to monarchs as different as George IV and Victoria; it boasted an impressive and varied client list that included sundry dukes, the Dorchester Hotel and various London clubs, Mrs P. G. Wodehouse and the

Queen Mary passenger liner. The 'darker side' of the job was that Clement developed 'a great contempt for the really wealthy', which derived from their complaints and contemptuous attitude to 'trade'.

Madeleine's memoir, *Peers and Plebs*, contrasts the origins and progress of the Bingham family (the Peers) and the Ebels (the Plebs). The Plebs were in the process of overtaking the Peers – until October 1929, when the Wall Street crash on 'Black Thursday' caused panic worldwide. The financial health of Trollope & Sons depended on confidence and a willingness to spend money on luxuries. The crash threatened the company's stability, but, in the event, it survived and continued to prosper, though not without causing considerable worry in the Ebel household.

From this respectable Catholic, middle-class, reasonably prosperous family, Madeleine had come to Pitman's College. Bookish and a little remote, a beautiful, serious, certainly virtuous young woman, she had a limited experience of life. She had no experience of young men with titles; it was not the milieu in which she grew up. But she enjoyed talking to Bingham, finding him amusing and a good listener. Their dates had been pleasant and they stayed in touch, writing to each other when he was in Tigy.

Madeleine admits that Bingham seemed to belong to a world very different from her own. Imagining that his title automatically made him wealthy, she had no idea that their first date was financed by money given to him by his grandmother for his twenty-first birthday, nor that he would routinely pawn his watch and gold cufflinks to take her on future dates.

When Bingham went to Sunday lunch at Massetts, he was concerned about his lack of employment and Madeleine thought that Clement might be able to help him with advice. The day was a success. One can picture Clement, proud paterfamilias, poised to carve the Sunday joint, his precious, sharpened carving knife at the ready. Around the table the boisterous Ebel family traded jokes, gently mocked their father, welcomed Madeleine's friend into their midst. If Madeleine considered his world remote, this lively gathering was very different from the genteel poverty of Maurice and Leila's flat or the rigid formality of Bangor Castle. He revelled in the lively banter of the day, not least because it must have been reminiscent of his other adoptive family in Tigy.

For the noble but indigent suitor, Clement had a warm regard. John was the first of Madeleine's boyfriends that he had tolerated and Clement was generous in the help he offered. Not financial help – for Clement believed that everyone should make his own way – but generous with his time and advice. This larger-than-life figure became a strong influence: resourceful, determined, unshakeable – possessed, in short, of the characteristics that Maurice lacked. As the Binghams drifted downwards into genteel penury, Clement soared, battling the dolts and mugwumps who stood in his way, cursing 'some damn fool' who had done something that offended him, casting a jaundiced eye at the many hazards – blunt carving knives, faulty self-starters, incompetent people – that conspired to thwart him. Unimpressed by Bingham's pedigree – for he knew enough of the failings of the aristocracy from his work – Clement, to Madeleine's delighted surprise, took to him and gave him sound advice on his career.

In an article entitled 'My Handicap Is My Title' in the *Sunday Dispatch* of 20 May 1934, Bingham recounted the advice he received from Clement. All his friends and relations, he wrote, assured him that with French and German, shorthand and typing, with a title and a good public school education, he would quickly find a job. Yet he was unable to do so. Clement, on the other hand, had warned him that the opposite was the case. His title might win him an interview but would never secure him a job. The world was changing, he advised Bingham. Commerce and industry were in new hands. There were no longer 'nicely lined niches available for every public schoolboy when he leaves school'. Clement counselled him that his 'coronet [was] a danger signal' now that commerce was run by self-made men. This down-to-earth advice contrasted starkly with the woolly reassurances that he undoubtedly received from his own father. While Bingham acknowledged the truth of Clement's words and the equity of these changes, employment continued to be elusive. Summer yielded to autumn 1930 and no solution was found. Worse, perhaps, he still had no clear choice of career to pursue.

Returning Madeleine's hospitality, he asked her to dinner at his parents' flat in De Vere Gardens. Madeleine remembers the evening as sombre: food appeared from an unseen cook, served by a maid; the atmosphere in the flat too was sombre, restrained, very different from the family home with the jolly meals she was used to. While Bingham and his father had formally affectionate relations, she was confident that his life would be different from that of Maurice and Leila. She decided that their friendship should be allowed to develop and they began to see more of each other – not on any exclusive basis, but with growing mutual warmth.

The search for a job continued in the autumn of 1930 until Leila, once again through 'someone useful', came up with a lead. Years later, in his jottings on his life, he recalled his introduction to journalism:

I do not recall the lady's name, though I should. But the lady had a friend, who in turn had another friend, who knew Lord Rothermere, who owned a powerful string of newspapers.

Yes, Lord Rothermere would help and provide a job somewhere in the provinces, on the distinct understanding that there was no room in Fleet Street until the protégé had learned something about newspaper work.

Somebody, somewhere in London, had told W. S. Robinson, *Hull Daily Mail* editor, that I had to be found a job at the express wish of 'him who must be obeyed'. It was the end of the beginning.

The editor of the *Hull Daily Mail* – an evening paper, incidentally, not a morning paper – was a gentle soft-spoken man, who took me along to the reporters' room and introduced me to the Chief Reporter, Don Giles. Giles said little or nothing until we were alone. Then he said, 'How did you get this job? Influence, I suppose.'

'Just applied for it,' I said. I was telling a lie, and he knew I was telling a lie, and I knew he knew, but honour was more or less satisfied. I suppose it was my first brush with Yorkshire directness, and how to skirmish round it.

Thus was John Bingham hired at a salary of £2 per week to learn the trade of journalism. It would be twenty years before he finally left Fleet Street for his preferred career.

In the meantime there was his new life in Hull to arrange. Don Giles asked him where he was going to live, to which he muttered that he was looking for digs. Giles sent for a Miss Gwen Brigham, whose mother rented out rooms at her house in Springbank. Bingham recalls that 'Mrs Brigham and I soon came to terms with no beating about the bush. (I was soon to discover that in Yorkshire bushes were rarely beaten about).' For 'twenty-five bob a week' he had accommodation, breakfast and one main meal a day, which left him 'fifteen shillings to spend on beer or cigarettes, or save up for an occasional trip to London'.

During his time in Hull he made monthly trips to stay overnight with the Ebels. Madeleine was a popular girl with many suitors but Bingham was the one most approved of by Lottie;

his impeccable manners ensured that he wrote her a thank-you letter after each visit. The young couple were close, good friends who shied from any permanent commitment. Madeleine later recorded that neither of them regarded their relationship as exclusive, and Bingham had not forgotten his first infatuation. Between 1930 and 1934 he made two trips to Norway, ostensibly for trout fishing, but he had kept alive his friendship with 'Ingrid' from the château while allowing his relationship with Madeleine to deepen.

On his second day in Hull he met the *Hull Daily Mail* team and was rapidly taken on board by his new colleagues. Alerted by Clement Ebel to the dangers of a title, he was nervous about how he would be received in Hull, a down-to-earth, unpretentious port town.

His colleagues were as unfamiliar with the life of a baron's son as he was with theirs but they immediately accepted him as one of them. For the rest of his life he would recall with warmth the time he spent in Hull, the *esprit de corps* of the journalists, the way they covered for him and helped him with his erratic shorthand notes, how they would spend time in the pub after work, walking home to Ma Brigham's together, eating fish and chips from newspaper. Such things may seem commonplace, but for Bingham they were rare novelties.

As we have seen, much of his early life – Cheltenham and the 1930s – is related in *Michael Sibley*. In the fiction it is his Aunt Nell who finds Sibley the job in Hull and she makes the terse comment that 'it will make a man of you'. Both in the fiction and in real life he admitted the truth of that remark. It was his first job; it made a man of him and he never forgot it.

Bingham rapidly settled into the routine of the office, despite fears that his typing and shorthand skills were below par. Early days on the job were spent very much as a dogsbody, the low man on the totem pole who handled duller stories eschewed by more senior colleagues. Much of this was routine work: telephoning contacts at municipal offices for official releases; attending social events such as dances or the opening of public buildings and hospitals by the mayor; occasionally, if no other reporter was available, handling crime stories.

In *My Name Is Michael Sibley* Bingham describes his first assignment to a crime story. When all other reporters are busy, Sibley is dispatched to cover a murder. Imagining himself on the verge of becoming Sherlock Holmes and discovering clues that the police had overlooked, he rushes – by bus rather than in a high-powered car – to the scene of the crime, only to discover that the murderer has already turned himself in and that his skills at detection will not, after all, be needed. Bingham describes the events dispassionately but a strand emerges, a strand central to all Bingham's writing: one of empathy, understanding and compassion.

The suicide of Lawrence Shuttleworth, the master at his public school, had shocked him, and the impact of it, particularly the perceived futility of life lived alone, had continued to disturb him. In the aftermath of the murder case, Bingham has Sibley recall the memory of Shuttleworth ('Ackersley' in the fictional account) and the forces that cause human beings to break.

In the fiction, the murder victim, Mary O'Brien, is a prostitute. Sibley scans the room where she was killed, the tawdriness of the surroundings, imagines her descent from a respectable Irish Catholic family to prostitution, and considers her killer's motive. He learns from police that she has been killed by a 'Lascar seaman', a seaman named Geoffries from the Indian subcontinent who loved her but who, hearing that in his absence she had returned to her trade as a prostitute, despaired at the thought of losing or sharing her, killed her by stabbing and promptly walked to the police station to confess. It is a sad and shabby drama, enacted on a sad and shabby stage. But it drove Sibley – and, presumably, Bingham – to reflect on the horror of such loneliness, such desolation in human relations that can drive a man to murder, as Shuttleworth's loneliness drove him to suicide.

In the fiction, both in *Michael Sibley* specifically and as a theme running through his work as a whole, he returns to the need for companionship, to the fear of growing old alone, to the incompleteness of a solitary existence in a bedsitting room – and, curiously woven into these themes, the need to retain an objective view of circumstances, the necessity of avoiding the corrupting emotion of pity. Bingham could tell the difference between compassion, which he saw as an essential element of human decency, and pity, which he considered distorting and debasing. In Hull he acquired the objectivity of a good reporter and yet retained the sensitivity to understand human need and the frustration of failure. He developed the ability to weigh pressures and circumstances while applying a precise gauge of his own reactions. Compassion always reigns; but retaining that objectivity he never debases compassion with pity. It is powerful self-analysis, demonstrating how clearly Hull did indeed make a man of him.

It is an oversimplification to say that *Michael Sibley* is purely autobiographical; moreover, every novelist, particularly in a first novel, tends to write from personal experience. In the case of *Michael Sibley* the autobiographical impulse is vastly more far-reaching: not only does Bingham bring much of his life to the book, but the entire work is an apologia, to himself as well as his readers, about early periods of his life that later, more mature and self-confident, he is able to regard with dispassion, almost as if someone else had lived them.

He paints himself in the worst possible light in *Michael Sibley*.

He is able to do so because by the time he wrote it he was, like Michael Sibley in the last chapter of the book, 'emancipated'. He was the finished product that became George Smiley for John le Carré. He recognised how removed from reality his childhood had been; by 1952, when the book was published, he had restored the balance with experiences that the callow cub reporter of 1930 could never have imagined.

For those reasons the reader should treat his first novel as an expression, at least partial, of the development of John Bingham the person, and use the book as a framework for much of his early life, viewed from the vantage point of 1952, when he was nearly forty-three. There will be anomalies in detail; not everything is – or should be – completely congruent. But in the words of John le Carré, we should try on the clothes and see if they fit.

To an almost eerie extent, we will find that they do. But we must be on our guard against making too many identifications between the novel and the life. Written some twenty years after the period that it describes, it adduces many observations made through the prism of a later era, judgements made by a more mature man.

After a few months, he began writing a humorous column for the *Hull Daily Mail* with the byline of 'Motley'. It was his first attempt at amusing a reading public and had an adolescent quality that smacked more of public school humour than of a tough northern town: clipped one-liners commenting on news items garnered from the press and the radio. Published under a column headed 'As I Was Saying', it was a worthy attempt by a 22-year-old to attract readers to a regular feature of the newspaper.

An early column, on 1 September 1931, foreshadows what would become one of his pet peeves – City financiers. Under the sub-heading 'Schoolboy howlers', he quips, 'Contango ... a slow dance popular among stockbrokers.' The column, his first attempt at social comment, is dense with similar one-liners. It had none of the incisive, often mischievous and satirical wit that he later developed at the *Sunday Dispatch*, but it was a popular feature that reflected his irreverence.

The element of his writing that brought him early fame – in 1952 with *Michael Sibley* and in 1954 with *The Third Skin* – was his understanding of police methods. This stems from his period in Hull, where he spent many hours in the police courts covering a variety of cases. He became interested in police procedure, both personally and in the professional mechanics of investigation – the cornerstone of his two later careers.

In *Michael Sibley* and in every subsequent crime story, the most gripping, tensely realistic passages involve the systematic building of a case by the police. Progress from respectful treatment of a member of the public to incisive, tough questioning in which the suspect is wrong-footed and humiliated is a trope frequently returned to and one which is never disappointing.

As the books were written after the Second World War, after he had acquired a reputation as a talented and effective interrogator, the structure of the interviews also draws on his later experience. The groundwork, however, was done during his observation of the police in Hull. There are subtle shades between the inspector who ruthlessly builds his case, frankly indifferent to any consideration of justice, and the considerate, albeit relentless officer who shows compassion alongside dogged determination in an investigation. We meet those extremes – and many shades in between – in Bingham's books.

In the spring of 1933 he was summoned to the editor's office. His initial thought was that he had unwittingly libelled some local dignitary – the abiding fear of reporters on a local paper. As he later wrote,

If the alleged victim of libel demands, say, £100 to soothe his supposed ruffled feelings and compensates him for some supposed loss, he is likely to get it. It is the easy way out. Even if the newspaper to be sued defends itself and wins, there is no guarantee that the other side has the necessary ready cash to pay the costs and the newspaper may be left to pay the costs of its own successful defence. Somebody will pay, and it is well known that newspapers are made of money.

Concerned that he was about to pay for a libel with his job, he was astounded when the editor ('The Great Man' as Bingham referred to him) announced that he had been offered a job at the *Sunday Dispatch* with an incredible salary of £6, three times his current wage, rising almost immediately to £10 per week. The *Dispatch* was a popular paper that mixed serious news on the front page with gossip, trivia and women's serials inside. The offer came as a total surprise and he hesitated for a moment as, despite the welcome raise in salary, he felt comfortable in Hull.

London, however, was his home town, despite the kinship that he felt for his colleagues in Hull. An immediate answer was required and it was positive. The *Mail* reporters clubbed together for a small silver cigarette case – which, to his immoderate fury, was stolen from him in Germany fifteen years later – and with mixed feelings he shook the dust of Hull from his chariot wheels. Hull had established him, given him confidence, but now he was headed home.

The move to London precipitated a decision. He had visited 'Ingrid' in Norway at least once between 1930 and 1933, but now back in London he gravitated towards Madeleine. 'There were women in the picture,' he confesses in *Michael Sibley*, 'but now they were women of a more erotic and sophisticated kind; I record this with some shame.' Madeleine ('Kate' in the fiction), he believes, 'had in her bones a sense of history, a feeling for the past, a love of old things and ways, of traditions and customs. It is a curious yardstick by which to measure them, but I should say that [she] was the more patriotic.'

This remarkable statement encapsulates his own patriotism. Love of Britain entails a love of tradition, of the values that made Britain great. To bow to modern fashion is to undermine that tradition, to trade substance for style. Madeleine, with her love of old things and ways, represented substance. She later wrote several plays, one of which was a modest success, and a number of biographies. Two of these – of the playwright Richard Sheridan and of the playwright and architect Sir John Vanbrugh – dealt with her beloved eighteenth century. In the summer of 1933 he and Madeleine took the decision to become engaged.

During the late 1920s and early 1930s, Bingham's father Maurice held several inconsequential positions, principally ones in which his title was an asset. One such position was on the board of directors of a film company, and there was consternation among the family lawyers when the company was involved in apparently shady financial dealings. In 1931, at Maude's urging, the lawyers drew up a family trust to control all the family's assets. Maurice and his son would receive an income from the trust, but capital and tangible assets would remain entailed for two generations.

John Bingham's income from the trust, which later rose to £1,500 annually, was probably a few hundred pounds a year in 1931. Not a fortune, but enough to allow him to marry. The engagement was announced and was taken very differently by the two families involved.

To the Binghams, the liaison was not to be rejoiced over. From Bangor, Maude sent a cautionary note: 'You're doing well,' she wrote, 'but don't go and lose your head.' Maurice and Leila were distinctly cool, Maurice writing to Clement Ebel that he could not provide any allowance but hinting that Clement might step in. The idea of a dowry would never have occurred to the latter.

The Ebels, by contrast, welcomed the engagement. Madeleine wanted a quiet wedding, but Clement would have none of it; it was to be a grand affair. Massetts was let go and a new house acquired; Clement was confident that he would have it in good shape in time for the wedding. Maurice and Leila were invited to Sunday lunch. The meeting went well but Maurice failed to understand why Clement, apparently prosperous, made no allowance to his daughter, particularly as Madeleine was, as she wrote later, of 'dubious foreign origin, impecunious, and, for a Northern Ireland family – the worst strike against me – a Catholic'.

The difference in religion was the principal reason why Bingham and Madeleine felt that a quiet wedding would be in order. That difference was rectified by his admission to the Catholic Church. There were other concerns, skeletons in the Bingham closet, and, once the engagement was announced, one of them was not slow in appearing. Everyone carries some burdens through life – in Bingham's case, the impedimenta of eccentric aunts – the Cloete sisters.

Of Leila's four sisters, Inez had stayed in South Africa while Renée, Vera and Effie had all come to England. Renée had died during childbirth and Vera's husband Ted Noding had died during the 1920s. Vera and Effie remained to breeze in and out of Bingham's life for several years. Amusing from a distance, ultimately embarrassing to him, they were a comical pair.

Vera was simply eccentric, a harmless widow with a penchant for spiritualism, prey to any medium who might exploit her – as many did. Effie, married to George Capron, remained an enigma throughout Bingham's life. On one occasion she and George tried to borrow £100 from him, then dropped to £50 and were 'eventually seen off with a fiver'. For all his experience with human deception and interrogation, he could never decide whether his mother's sister was merely a dotty, scatty eccentric or whether she was an accomplished small-time fraudster. By and large, he inclined to take a tolerant view.

As Aunt Effie ran up bills with tradesmen, relieved relatives of small amounts of money, claimed that she was the true inventor of the tank as she had seen one in a dream (a claim that she took all the way to the House of Lords), she retained one valuable weapon which was going to repay all creditors and bring enormous wealth to the family. The weapon was known in the family as 'Effie's case'. It involved a claim against her husband George's brother, who had inherited massive legacies that, she insisted, rightfully belonged to George. These were not small amounts – indeed, great swathes of the city of Paris were involved – and it was merely a matter of time and of finding the right lawyer before these claims would be satisfied in full. Everyone would be mountainously rich once justice was done, but to oil the wheels of justice, naturally, some small investment would be needed. Later, Bingham looked back at the extraordinary life of Effie and George Capron, and the skill with which Effie identified possible 'marks', among whom was her sister, his Aunt Vera:

If really driven into a corner, my aunt would have resort to her final unbeatable defence – a séance. When the Spirits made a statement from the Other Side nobody was in a position to gainsay it. The fact that money changed hands – changed aunts would be more accurate – made little difference to the stern course of justice: one aunt ended up with less money than the other.

These séances always started in the same way. My aunt Effie, who needed the cash to pay the butcher, not to mention various other people who had been stolidly awaiting the breaking of the wonderful new financial dawn, would have us all holding hands round some convenient table.

The séance would begin by my aunt Effie asking clearly and distinctly, 'Who is there?' Having posed the question herself, she found no difficulty in answering it. 'Father!' she would cry triumphantly. My heart would sink, but not so rapidly as that of my aunt Vera, who knew from bitter experience that somehow she would end the séance a poorer if not a wiser woman, while my other aunt, smiling happily, doubtless told herself that once more she had evaded a fictional debtors' prison.

Once the engagement was announced, the inevitable occurred: Effie, scenting an affluent mark in Clement, brought George with her to visit the Ebels in their new house, Copyhold Place in Lindfield. Madeleine recalled that they arrived 'wearing extraordinary, out-of-date clothes, and attempted to touch Clement to help with some project she had in mind'. The 'touch' was not successful but it increased Madeleine's and John's worries about how their very different families would blend together at the wedding.

Bingham was now established at the *Sunday Dispatch* and had taken the model of his 'As I Was Saying' column from Hull, fashioning it into a more mature, more incisive column. Entitled 'All Things Considered by J.M.W.B.', it culled news items from a variety of sources and added a brisk, usually dismissive comment. One new element was added to the column – lightly self-mocking comments on his own life.

Creating a character called Wilhelmina to represent Madeleine, he reported his and Madeleine's slant on current events. As the date for their wedding approached and they bought their flat off Beaufort Street in Chelsea, moving in and having the place made habitable became material for the column.

The style of writing was inspired. He concealed his name, continuing to write as 'J.M.W.B.', but it was clear that he moved in or on the fringes of high society; he gave Madeleine an aristocratic name; he resonated well-born poverty; he integrated elements of his life with social and political commentary, winning the reader's respect for his character and, subtly, for his political views. When he made serious social or political points, his position as a friendly, chatty columnist must have greatly influenced the reader's reaction to his more deeply held beliefs.

He created a cast of characters who moved in and out of his columns. When he moved towards social commentary, he invented caricatures of a rabid socialist and an imprisoned victim of the class war to flesh out the dialogue; he gently mocked Lord Donegall, who wrote the *Sunday Dispatch* social column, and Viola Tree, who dispensed advice to the lovelorn. He brought the reader inside the offices of the newspaper in a welcoming manner. He caricatured his editor, frequently referring to imagined differences between them, at the end of which the editor would put his foot down and J.M.W.B. would slink back to his office to write the required 2,000 words. In a spirit of gentle – and shared – mockery, he developed what the *Sunday Dispatch* was pleased, on 16 December 1934, to call 'one of the most popular newspaper features in Britain'. At that point his identity was revealed as 'John Bingham' with a photograph captioned 'ex-J.M.W.B.'.

Interspersing the prose with light verse, for which he displayed a growing talent, he commented on news items in the manner used by the satirical magazine *Private Eye* thirty years later, essentially taking an idea, however absurd, and flogging it to death. Sometimes this was to make a valid social or political commentary, sometimes for the sheer joy of it.

There are delightful portraits of 'Wilhelmina', and the dog Huxley is introduced; frothy article follows frothy article. On 7 January 1934, after the Foreign Secretary, Sir John Simon, had equivocated at the League of Nations in Geneva, appearing unconcerned by the imperial ambitions of Germany, Italy and, particularly, Japan, Bingham satirised Simon's indecisiveness in a piece of comic verse, pillorying the Foreign Secretary and the League itself.

Discord at Geneva was an early hint that 'The War to End All Wars' might not have achieved its purpose, that 'the German problem' had not, after all, been neatly solved by punitive reparations at Versailles and the creation of the League of Nations. Mussolini had been treated either as a joke for his foolish choice of being Italian or as the strongman needed to sort out inefficient Latins. As for the 'Manchurian incident', there was little cause for concern at a large-scale violation of China's territorial integrity. Generalissimo Chiang Kai-shek was a military genius, after all. Britain, secure in its alliances with France – supposedly the greatest military power in the world – and in its cultural ties with the United States, need not fret about comical figures like Mussolini or Hitler, the 'Austrian corporal'.

Bingham was less certain. From 1934 onwards he aired his concerns – albeit not too brazenly, as he was a humorous columnist rather than a foreign correspondent. His role was to amuse rather than alarm the readers of the *Sunday Dispatch*. Rather than ask disturbing questions about French military strength or the value of the Maginot Line, a humorous columnist's role was to mock them gently for their Gallic ways, which Bingham mercilessly continued to do. Another favourite target was the United States, a traditional butt for humorous writers. No fan of popular culture, particularly of Hollywood films, he singled out the tinsel of Hollywood glamour for periodic attack.

As the day of the wedding approached, Bingham undertook

the preparation of the Chelsea flat. At the top of four flights of stairs, populated by various rodents with whom 'J.M.W.B.' developed close relations, the flat was badly in need of renovation. It was a daunting task for someone with no skills as a handyman and little understanding of what the work involved. 'Matrimony', he wrote two weeks before the wedding, 'is a time when the average Englishman's inherited genius for finding money in the most remote and unlikely places is seen at its best. It needs to be.'

Despite Clement's determination to see his daughter married in considerable style, Lottie was horrified at the idea of a clan of hunting Binghams descending on her house. In the event, only one uncle, Admiral Barry Bingham VC, made the journey from Bangor to Haywards Heath on 28 July 1934. Overcoming his concerns about the venue, St Paul's Catholic church, the indomitable sailor held his peace until the papal blessing was read, at which point he was heard groaning and repeating, 'Oh my God! Oh my God!' At the reception, however, lubricated by Clement's hospitality, he felt able to clap his nephew on the shoulders and assure him that it was important, nay vital, to follow one's heart in such matters.

To record in his *Dispatch* column the events of the happy day, Bingham adopted his best self-mocking tone: should he wear spats or not? He puts them on, takes them off, puts them on again. Jacques de Moncuit, his best man, tells him he looks absurd in spats. Takes them off again. He referred once more to the expense of it all: '2:15 pm, short chat with parson. Unbelted largesse and handed over same to parson. Careless gesture implying plenty more where that came from. Parson unimpressed. Said marriage very expensive business, haw haw haw.'

Spats or no spats, with hidden wealth or not, John Michael Ward Bingham and Madeleine Mary Bingham, duly man and wife, departed for a fortnight's honeymoon at San Sebastian. On their return they made their mandatory pilgrimage for a ten-day stay at Bangor Castle.

Uncle Barry's approval may have been important, but there was a far greater obstacle to be cleared: obtaining the blessing of the redoubtable Maude, now aged seventy-six, implacable chatelaine of Bangor. Maude had discovered that Madeleine was a Catholic, not through Barry Bingham but from reading the *Morning Post*. When the newlyweds visited Bangor, Madeleine had no notion of the gulf between Catholic and Protestant in Northern Ireland. Met at the dock by a Daimler emblazoned with the coronet of a baron, they were driven to the castle. Madeleine and Maude met for the first time at breakfast, served punctually at nine o'clock. The castle, Madeleine recalled, was grey against grey skies; imposing and solid, it had one cosy room: the library. The dining room was pure Victoriana – yellow oak panelling, intricately carved chairs and huge windows overlooking the grey town and the grey sea beyond.

Maude was an impressive woman with elegant clothes and fine jewellery, but with a wig that made her look older. She greeted them distantly and sat down to breakfast. Barry Bingham joined them, as did a cousin who happened to be staying. Both were two minutes late and received a reproving glance from Maude.

The Victorian atmosphere overwhelmed Madeleine: silver chafing dishes, a silver coffee pot kept warm over a methylated spirits heater. There were small bowls of fruit – small because, according to Madeleine, the head gardener was selling the harvest for his own profit, which, Madeleine asserted, he spent on drink. Leila once found him insensible on the potting shed floor and mentioned it to Maude. 'I don't want to *hear* of it,' she replied. She lived in a remote and a more elegant past when everything ran smoothly as everything in a grand house should.

Bored by the remote snobbery of life at the castle, the young Binghams would slink away to play tennis in the public park or swim in the icy sea. To Madeleine, the castle was stuck in a time capsule. Nothing was changed or remarked upon; the reserve was intimidating, formal and boring. Both at Bangor and at Bostock Hall, she had the impression that everything was run to cater to people who, already old, wanted no change of procedure: the same marmalade, the same biscuits, the same everything as had always been ordered.

Writing years later, Madeleine admitted to the intolerance of youth:

As I had no understanding of what it must have meant for Maude to watch her world slowly slipping away, I also had no understanding of what it must have been for Maurice to have been born to the grandeur of a castle and to have been forced into a four-guinea a week hotel.

In 1934, however, a Catholic in a Protestant world, with a husband regarded with mild distaste by the grand Binghams as 'some sort of journalist', bored by the decaying society of Bangor, Madeleine yearned to escape. 'We had no intention of becoming hangers-on or catchers of the crumbs which fell from the Bingham tables,' she wrote later. 'We had our way to make in the world and we were not going to hang around waiting for dead men's shoes.'

Bingham and his new wife returned from Bangor to London, where Oswald Mosley's blackshirts, encouraged by the mass rally at Olympia in June 1934, were becoming more vocal and violent. Their antics aroused, as they had done at Olympia, counter-demonstrations and – to the glee of the blackshirts – increasing levels of mayhem. Bingham, equally repulsed by extremism from the Left and the Right, attended a rally at Hyde Park on

9 September and ridiculed both extremes of the political spectrum in the following week's *Dispatch*.

Bingham's life had changed dramatically in five years. He had returned from Germany in 1929 with no job and no prospects, few marketable talents, no money and no plans for acquiring any, and a romantic and probably unrealistic passion for a Norwegian girl. By July 1934 he had a job, a decent wage and four years of experience as a provincial and London journalist with several witty and well-crafted articles to his credit. He had an income from the trust, a pretty and talented wife and a flat in Chelsea. It is not in the nature of the young to pause and wonder why, but on occasion he may have been baffled by his own good fortune.

At the end of the year, by a twist of editorial capriciousness that he never quite understood, and having survived rounds of sackings and replacements as new editors came and went, he became the newspaper's caption writer and was rapidly promoted to hold the poisoned chalice of Picture Editor. His column 'All Things Considered' was discontinued with his promotion; instead, it morphed into the column 'In Good Humour'. His wit was still inventive, satirical, cynical; several topics were covered, as before, in one column, but instead of inserting swathes of undergraduate humour, he began to concentrate on more serious subjects, even if he treated them with apparent levity.

He had become increasingly politically conscious – inevitable if one is working at a major newspaper chain – and his choice of subject reflected current events much more than it had done before. Stock characters made regular appearances: the communist Mr William Flummock, committed enemy of the Boss Class; 'the Duke', a depraved British landowner ruthlessly oppressing and exploiting his tenants; and, of course, corrupt stockbrokers. Whenever possible, Bingham would also give a gentle dig at the film industry and 'box-office appeal'. Increasingly, however, events in Germany provided material that induced anything but good humour.

Sixteen years later, during which a World War and the collapse of the social order of the 1930s had intervened, he would look at his role as a journalist and consider it peripheral, frivolous, on the fringes of social reform – able to criticise but unable to influence events. This malaise was beginning to take form in 1936. Wherever he looked, he saw either selfish perpetuation of the status quo or selfish determination to destroy it. He took refuge in mockery, occasionally singling out individuals for special treatment, more generally bemoaning in a satirical manner the lunatics bent on destroying the British way of life.

On 25 October 1937, his life was dramatically altered. In the *Dispatch* on 31 October he expressed his astonishment that nobody had noticed. Voicing the feelings that every new father experiences at the birth of his first child, he marvelled that the rest of the world somehow didn't notice that he had become 'what is generally known as A Father'. Instead, life carried on much as before this momentous event; the new father received no congratulations from the tobacconist or the bus conductor. 'To all outward appearances it was quite a normal sort of day.'

All the standard information was dispensed: that mother and son were doing well, that the infant weighed 8¾ pounds, that the baby's complexion was 'lobsterish', adding in newspaper parlance that he measured 'three columns wide, by about, I suppose, two thirds of a column deep'. The baby, Bingham recorded, 'has a very fierce face' and in that one adjective he conjured up the character that would from then on feature prominently in his newspaper columns – the infant journalist who became known across Britain as 'Fierce Baby'.

Thus was announced to the world – or at least to the readership of the *Sunday Dispatch* – the arrival of Simon John Ward

Bingham. The unwitting newborn made his debut as a journalist with his father's readers on 17 April 1938. By then he had already survived a brush with death.

Madeleine recalls the event and her sheer relief when Simon recovered:

> Simon was four months old and staying with Jack's cousin Cecile in Kent. Cecile had some sixth sense that Simon was very ill and he was rushed to London. In the days before penicillin, lobar pneumonia was serious. He survived.
>
> We should have been worrying ourselves sick about Hitler but ... we were grateful for the sunshine, the sight of Simon, the baby, bronzed and healthy, recovered from his illness, the equal recovery of my father's antique business, and Jack's survival of seven editors in Fleet Street.

The visits to doctors and the treatment was an expensive process and Bingham approached his parents for a loan to help with the costs. Leila, perhaps smarting from the perceived indignity that she and Maurice suffered under, with an allowance but no control of the family's money, grudgingly chipped in but told him that 'this is the last of any money you'll see from us'.

Leila's frustration in 1937 was intense. She had married a dashing subaltern, the heir to a barony, in 1907. She had been Lady Clanmorris in name alone since 1916; since 1921 she had seen the wealth that she had assumed would be hers evaporate – first in huge tranches borrowed from banks, later in interest payments gradually gnawing away at what was left. Through prescience or simple parsimony, Maude Ward had retained her position at Bangor Castle and arranged her income to support her way of life – and that way of life was steadily eating away at residual capital. Meanwhile, Leila and Maurice, unable to afford those simple essentials of life – two maids and a decent cook – were compelled to live in straitened circumstances.

Now, not only did her son have a job, a commodity that had proved elusive for Maurice, but he also had a wife, an heir, a flat in Chelsea and the wherewithal to maintain his household. Now he proposed to chip away still further at their dwindling assets. Leaving aside the acerbity of her response to the request for help, one can understand her dissatisfaction at the hand she had been dealt.

Simon survived pneumonia and became the prism through which Bingham projected a disintegrating world to his readers. In sporadic articles for the *Dispatch* he had previously created a world as seen by his dog Huxley, attributing human ambitions to Huxley and his peers, creating a canine community that, under an ordered surface, seethed with the emotions and petty vexations of adult human life. These had been delightful *vignettes*, inserted among the miscellany of other news.

Now, however, the thoughts and emotions of Fierce Baby would be more than sporadic: they would be the stuff of the column. As a humorist, Bingham was supposed to make people laugh; as a human being, he watched Europe tilt towards war while he made frivolous comments about 'The Duke' and Rich Relations. His job was not to comment on worsening diplomatic relations between Germany and Czechoslovakia. Very well then! Fierce Baby would comment on his view of the darkening situation.

For the first three months of 1938 'In Good Humour' contained the usual miscellany of light verse, parodies of Chaucer, thrusts at the Inland Revenue, tirades against rich relations, grumbles about decay in the British way of life, together with radical solutions for improving the world, discussed, naturally, with Fierce Baby. Soon, though, 'In Good Humour' was replaced by a column headed 'Out of Turn' in which Fierce Baby's Journal appeared regularly. Fierce Baby displayed mature feelings and opinions, especially with regard to his 'Good Looking Day Nurse'. His manner of expressing himself acquired a clear style, dispensing with definite and indefinite articles, cutting straight to the heart of the matter. By 22 May 1938, Fierce Baby had displaced 'Out of Turn', and for almost two years, until 14 April 1940 – three weeks before Hitler's Panzer divisions swept across France – 'Fierce Baby's Journal' delighted *Sunday Dispatch* readers.

The appeal of Fierce Baby to his audience derived, in large measure, from the freedom accorded to a baby to think and say things forbidden to adults. He was able to introduce taboo subjects such as class, race and sex into his journal. Fierce Baby simply said things that would not be accepted from mature journalists, opinions that resonated with readers who were muzzled by their adulthood. Fierce Baby achieved congruence with the attitudes and prejudices of his readers. Neville Chamberlain, in abandoning the Czechs to their fate at Hitler's hands, described the Sudeten crisis as 'a quarrel in a faraway country between people of whom we know nothing'. Fierce Baby expressed the same popular belief for his audience.

Even as Hitler's demands for the Sudetenland became ever shriller, British custom provided an interlude of pageantry. In July 1938 the young Binghams were presented at Court. *The Times* described the occasion:

> The Lady Clanmorris wearing a gown in cactus blue satin richly embroidered with crystal beads, a train of silver sequins lined with rose tinted chiffon to tone with her shaded ostrich feather fan, presented her daughter-in-law, the Hon. Mrs John Bingham.

To the Hon. Mrs John Bingham it was a delightfully unreal episode inserted into the depressing series of world events. Her mother, as ever, had spared nothing in outfitting Madeleine for the occasion. Resplendent and youthful, she was enchanted by the experience, reporting later to her sisters that 'the whole scene was like something out of Tolstoy'. Nonetheless, she wrote, her fine clothes would be set aside after the presentation, and 'Jack would be back in the half-tone department of *The Sunday Dispatch*'.

The Munich Conference took place; Fierce Baby made no comment. Bingham interrupted Fierce Baby's Journal to voice his concerns in more serious vein. He was increasingly pessimistic about the eventual outcome of the widening crisis. Certain that war with Germany must be avoided, and equally certain that the democracies must stand up to Hitler, he found himself less able to treat serious issues light-heartedly and Fierce Baby now avoided commenting on world events.

For Bingham, the months after Munich were disheartening. He felt powerless to influence events and sickened by the concessions to Germany that men of his class were urging. He had kept in touch with the friends he had made during his time abroad twelve years before. Jacques de Moncuit had been a regular visitor to London, acting as best man at Bingham's wedding and godfather to his son. That friendship would last throughout his life, continuing with the next generation of de Moncuits. As to his German friends, they had not been greatly different from him in their world view, but he was certain that they would be ranged against him and his countrymen before the year was out.

He was right. By August 1939, Lieutenant Egbert von Schmidt-Pauli, Lieutenant Friedrich Graf zu Solms and Lieutenant 'Johnnie' Herwarth von Bittenfeld were platoon leaders in the 3rd Cavalry Regiment. They and Bingham could now merely begin the countdown to the inevitable war that the Führer had set his heart upon.

CHAPTER 4

FIGHTING FASCISM: MI5, 1940-45

When the war broke out, each officer 'tore around' to rope in likely people;
when they knew of none themselves, they asked their acquaintances.
Report by Sir David Petrie, Director General of MI5

As the Weimar government proved incompetent in the late 1920s and Germany seemed increasingly vulnerable to a *putsch* from either the Right or the Left, it was fear of communism that most exercised the majority of Britons. The more distasteful aspects of fascism were accepted as necessary, temporary expedients. Ranged against the communist threat, the Security Service (MI5) operated on the principle that the Nazi Party, not inherently dangerous, would be useful in dealing with the perceived threat from the Left. Such wishful thinking evaporated after 1933. Within nineteen months of coming to power, Hitler had outwitted the complacent German aristocracy and established for himself an almost invulnerable position as head of state.

Over the next five years, the Führer consolidated and expanded any legal forms of power he could, including bringing the army under his control. In 1938 he replaced the *Kriegsministerium* (Ministry of War) with the *Oberkommando der Wehrmacht* (Supreme Commander of the Armed Forces) under General Keitel, whose loyalty he could command. Blind to Hitler's repeated violations of the Treaty of Versailles, which limited the German army to 100,000 men, Britons placed their faith in the French army and the Maginot Line, rationalising that Hitler was merely restoring Germany to its rightful place in Europe and that, by disposing of communism, he would remove the greater threat to European security.

Only in 1938 did the majority of Britons become concerned at Hitler's territorial ambitions. After the *Anschluss* annexing Austria to Germany in March and continuing 'incidents' in the Sudetenland, there followed the Munich Conference. Meeting with Hitler, Neville Chamberlain, French Prime Minister Édouard Daladier and Benito Mussolini agreed to allow him to occupy the Sudeten region of Czechoslovakia.

It is difficult, in the light of subsequent events, when the word 'Munich' has become synonymous with 'appeasement', to imagine the relief that Britons – and the world – felt at the partition of Czechoslovakia. The protagonists of the Munich Conference were lauded as great statesmen; *Time* magazine chose Hitler as Man of the Year for 1938.

This shabby brokered peace convinced Hitler of the weakness of the western democracies and strengthened his resolve to proceed with the full invasion of Czechoslovakia. Prime Minister Neville Chamberlain returned to London proclaiming 'peace for our time', but it took a remarkable optimism – or ignorance – to be unaware of the German Führer's aims.

The Binghams had watched with horror in 1936 as Sir Oswald Mosley and his blackshirts marched past their Chelsea flat, swaggering up the King's Road. Madeleine recalled forty years later that 'they looked invincible'. After the Munich Conference, realising that the avoidance of war entailed tolerating Hitler's regime in Germany and, very possibly, a lurch to the Right in Britain, they took stock of the political battlefield.

The choice between communism and any form of fascism was simplistic and false. There were fundamental differences between Germany and Britain, where, despite the upheavals of the 1920s, democracy remained in place. Bingham saw no significant ethical differences between the extreme Right and the extreme Left; as one of his articles in the *Dispatch* demonstrated, he was a member of that rational centrist group that believed, above all, in preserving the 'British way of life'. Chamberlain, he and Madeleine felt, had betrayed those principles at Munich.

Not an 'intellectual' – he would assume an air of faint amusement at the term – he was a man of practical action. His responsibility, as he saw it, was twofold: to hope for the best and prepare for the worst. He and Madeleine did both. Along with several of his Fleet Street colleagues, he applied to join the Territorial Army; Madeleine's brother Mark joined the Royal Naval Volunteer Reserve. If war was to come, they would be among the first to see action.

To his chagrin, his eyesight proved to be a serious obstacle as he failed the vision test several times. By memorising the positions of letters on the testing card he managed eventually to pass the test and was accepted into the Royal Engineers.

In a spirit of greater optimism, he and Madeleine were members of a small group that founded a new political party, the British Democratic Party,[†] whose simple manifesto was opposition to the Munich agreements and determination to check Nazi Germany. Recalling the views of his German contemporaries ten years before, he believed that peace with Germany was essential, but not at the cost of accepting Nazism.

The British Democratic Party was a source of some amuse-

---

† The British Democratic Party of the 1930s should not be confused with the extreme right-wing party of the same name, a splinter group from the National Front that emerged in Britain during the 1980s.

ment to Madeleine's father, who pointed out to his idealistic daughter that it took more than anti-Munich commitment to launch a political party. Bingham's uncle Herbert Dixon, Member of Parliament for Belfast East, took a more serious view. Summoning his nephew to the House of Commons, he pulled a British Democratic Party leaflet from his pocket and reproved him severely, saying that it was inappropriate for a serving officer to dash about hither and thither organising political meetings. The army was the army, and politics was quite a different thing. Bingham replied, reasonably enough, that he was not a serving officer but a lowly driver in the Royal Engineers Reserve. Uncle Herbert harrumphed a little, said no more, but was far from appeased.

In spite of its small membership and ultimate ineffectiveness as a political force, the British Democratic Party set in motion a sequence of events that changed Bingham's life. Some months after being 'carpeted' by his uncle, he contacted him again. At their previous meeting Dixon had suggested that the Security Service might well become interested in the formation of a new political party and this had convinced Bingham that his uncle had some contact within MI5. On the second occasion that they met, in early 1939, he asked his uncle to arrange a meeting with an MI5 officer – not with the Metropolitan Police or Special Branch but specifically with an MI5 officer – as he had information of interest to them.

There are two very different accounts of the nature of the information he intended to impart. The first version, the 'authorised' version, is that he had overheard a German couple on a train commenting on the location of military bases and installations in the countryside. Concealing the fact that he spoke German and had understood every word, he bided his time and, later in the journey, chatted casually with the couple in English, ascertaining where they were staying and making a vague promise to visit them.

This account, attractive though it is, was certainly put out as a cover story. In fact, the story derives from MI5 folklore surrounding the early days of the Security Service in 1911, and is related by Stella Rimington in her autobiography, *Open Secret*. According to the story, an agent working for Sir Vernon Kell, the founding director of MI5, had heard two men speaking German, a language that he understood, on a train in Scotland. One of the men mentioned a letter that he had received from Potsdam and which asked questions about British preparations for war. In the event, it emerged that the speaker was one Mr Holstein, the German-born landlord of a Scottish hotel, and that he had already turned the letter over to the authorities. The story was well enough known and Bingham had undoubtedly heard it.

A less flattering account comes from Bingham himself. In about 1985 he wrote a short autobiographical piece headed 'Ambition', a confession long after the event:

> It was my secret ambition to be a full-time MI5 officer. I knew therefore that I must make contact with MI5 on a firm continuing basis. Being just a casual 'contact' was not good enough. I had to be a career officer, fully employed by MI5 and paid monthly on a regular basis.
>
> I therefore searched around and in due course came across a man who could, by a stretch of the imagination, be a German spy. I know now, as I think I knew then, that I was probably wrong. I was libelling a perfectly good man, of German birth, who had settled down in England, eyeglass and all.

Bingham makes light of his desire to join MI5 but he also makes clear that he had a more than casual interest to become involved in intelligence work. At no stage does he reveal his motives in writing, but we can certainly reconstruct them from the scraps of evidence available.

His interest in clandestine work stemmed from his reading of Edgar Wallace's novels and the stirring works of John Buchan in his teens. As a staunch patriot, he imagined himself fulfilling secret work in the Colonial Service until that avenue was closed to him. That interest probably lay fallow during the early 1930s, when he recognised Germany's growing power as a threat to Britain, not only to her Empire but to the entire British way of life. As a journalist, he was able to report but not to have any decisive effect on events – and that was a role he longed for. Not for glory or for public recognition, but because he could not bear to stand idly by and merely write about momentous events.

So he enlisted, though not with the commission that a man of his education and class might have expected, for his poor eyesight disqualified him from active service. Acting from his heart rather than with his head, he quickly realised that as a driver in the Royal Engineers he was as unlikely to affect events as he was in Fleet Street. After Munich he had become desperate to influence events, to do all he could to preserve the British way of life and, after careful analysis, he decided on the Security Service as the organisation in which he could do most good. To what extent he discussed this with anyone – with Madeleine, or perhaps with his Uncle Herbert – is unclear, but certainly such baring of the soul would have been quite out of character for Bingham.

In due course, Bingham was asked to present himself at one of the department's 'safe' offices. He found himself in a bare office with a desk and some chairs. Behind the desk sat an officer who introduced himself as Captain King of the War Office. In fact, he was in the presence of Maxwell Knight, known in the Service as 'M', head of Section B5b, the counter-subversion section of

MI5. Good-looking in a hawk-like way, with a large beaky nose and iron grey hair, a ruddy complexion and a pleasant, charming manner, he immediately struck Bingham as a model for one of Buchan's heroes:

> He was dressed in grey tweeds to match his hair. His age was forty-odd and he had been a midshipman in World War One. He had been recruited into MI5 when quite young and belonged to that small dedicated band of ex-officers whose job in life was quite simple – to catch spies. Anything they could do to catch spies they did. There was little electronic gear in those days; they had eyes and ears; their agents had eyes and ears; and that was that.

Knight was a direct man, able to speak without restraint. This appealed greatly to Bingham, who, from the first meeting, felt that he had found his home. Knight asked some questions about the British Democratic Party, established to his satisfaction that it was not subversive, then asked some questions about various fascist-inclined journalists, some of which Bingham could answer, some he could not. After a brisk, business-like interview, Knight stood up, thanked him for coming and bade him good afternoon.

There had been several U-turns in MI5's approach to the far Right during the 1930s. Sir Robert Vansittart, the Permanent Under-Secretary at the Foreign Office since 1930, had predicted that 'the present regime in Germany will, on past and present form, loose off another European war just as soon as it feels strong enough ... We are considering a very crude people, who have few ideas in their noodles but brute force and militarism.' The Director, General Sir Vernon Kell, who had held his role since MI5's foundation in 1909, agreed with Vansittart, and the focus of MI5, until then directed principally against the Communist

Party of Great Britain (CPGB), was turned on the British Union of Fascists (BUF) and similar organisations.

Knight took the view that there was no threat of a fascist coup in Britain. The high point for the BUF was the Olympia rally of June 1934. In the following two years, the BUF became generally irrelevant to the mainstream of British politics; it saw its subsidy from Mussolini cut from £3,000 to £1,000 monthly and went into a decline, enjoying a brief resurgence after the Battle of Cable Street in October 1936. But while MI5 did not regard the BUF as a serious peacetime threat, they recognised its potential danger if war were to break out.

That war seemed increasingly likely and Knight kept Bingham's name in his mind. There would soon be a need for able officers and the method of selection was somewhat arcane; Kell placed more importance on recruits being 'our sort of chap' than on objective qualifications. In his report after the war, Sir David Petrie, who succeeded Kell, alluded to Kell's frantic methods of selecting officers, which concentrated more on their sporting ability than their suitability as intelligence officers in wartime. It was not a scientific process.

Knight, along with Guy Liddell, was considered one of the star recruits of the inter-war years. In 1930, five years after join-ing MI5, he had become a case officer and been put in charge of placing agents inside the CPGB. His stock had fallen sharply, however, in 1935 when his first wife Gwladys was found dead in circumstances that suggested suicide. Such an event was not at all the kind of thing that happened to 'our sort of chap'.

Three years later, however, he had regained the confidence of Liddell and Kell through his handling of the case of the Woolwich Arsenal spy ring in which Percy Glading, a Soviet agent, and three co-conspirators were exposed and convicted of espionage in March 1938. Riding high after that success, he tended to get his way within the department. His section was his personal fiefdom, run from a flat in Dolphin Square that he had purchased in his second wife's name. When Anthony Blunt was recruited to MI5 in 1940, Liddell suggested that he be shown around Knight's office. Knight's response was immediate and succinct: 'I'm not having that bugger looking around my section.'

When war was declared on 3 September 1939, the Security Service addressed the internment of aliens, particularly resident Germans, but it was not until May 1940, following the German invasion of France and the collapse of the French army in a mere six weeks, that wholesale internment under Regulation 18B was introduced. The speed and success of the German advance, the British public believed, must have been due to fifth column activities. When the evacuation of the British Expeditionary Force from Dunkirk was completed in early June 1940, fears of a German invasion, supported by a fifth column within Britain, were widespread.

Liddell had argued since the previous December that additional agents would be needed within the Security Service to handle the increasing flow of refugees. By March 1940 he was certain that his branch would need 'at least another dozen officers and a great deal of equipment'. When, in the following month, seventy MPs threatened to raise the question of enemy aliens in the House of Commons, Liddell admitted that 'owing to ... government policy we are singularly ill-informed in a variety of directions. Of the 74,000 aliens at large in this country we know practically nothing.'

Calls for mass internment of aliens were blocked by Home Office concerns for democratic process. Liddell commented that, during a meeting at the Home Office on 21 May 1940, he was strongly tempted to point out that 'if somebody didn't get a move on there would be no democracy, no England and

no Empire' and that delay of even a few days could have cata-
strophic consequences.

On 5 June a Home Intelligence report to the Ministry of
Information noted that 'fifth column hysteria is reaching dangerous proportions'. This hysteria found many outlets among the
public: markings on telegraph poles were assumed to be directions for enemy paratroopers once they landed; in fact, they
were identification plates used by the Post Office. The Security
Service had failed to learn the lessons offered by the First World
War and Sir David Petrie, appointed Director General in 1941,
commented that alarmist rumours tended to 'clog the wheels of
the real counter-intelligence machinery'.

The fall of France brought about Chamberlain's resignation
and Winston Churchill's long-hoped-for arrival in 10 Downing
Street. The new Prime Minister was determined to shake up
Britain's security system and, according to Jack Curry's in-house
history of the department, by the time France fell, MI5 was
in 'a state which can only be described as chaotic'. Churchill
summarily sacked Kell on 10 June; Kell's deputy Sir Eric Holt-
Wilson promptly resigned once Kell told him of his dismissal.
Liddell was promoted to run B Division and, according to Hugh
Trevor-Roper, was 'a remarkable and very charming man who
gave the B Division its special character: open, genial, informal,
but highly professional'.

Liddell authorised Knight to hire five new officers on 18 June.
Knight had already decided that Bingham was 'our sort of
chap', and he immediately contacted his commanding officer to
have him transferred from the Royal Engineers to his section. As
Knight reported after the war:

Mr. Bingham had come to my notice before the outbreak of war,
curiously enough through his offering some information to the

Department. At the time when I first met him, Mr. Bingham was the Art Editor of the SUNDAY DISPATCH, and although a young man, he had worked his way up into this position through all the various grades of newspaper journalism.

Mr. Bingham had volunteered for the Army before the outbreak of war, and had seen Military Service, but owing to bad defects of eyesight, he would never have been able to serve in the field; and it was therefore clear that he would be of more use to us as an officer than as a private in the Army.

The team that he joined was eager to prove its efficiency in the face of the threatened German invasion. The transformation was immediate and rapid. As a result of the able work of Sir David Petrie, supported by Guy Liddell, Dick White and Tar Robertson, MI5 became a powerful force that achieved dominance over German intelligence and retained that superiority throughout the war. *Esprit de corps* was excellent; Sir John Masterman later wrote that it was 'a team of congenial people who worked together harmoniously and unselfishly, and among whom rank counted for little and character for much'.

With the collapse of France and the influx of French refugees, the Security Service was under pressure to expose and arrest the alleged, often non-existent, fifth columnists. 'This office is being absolutely inundated with ridiculous enquiries from every possible quarter,' Liddell recorded. 'The worst come from the highest circles.' At meetings of the Security Executive Liddell tried without success to calm the mounting hysteria, commenting that the authorities were suffering from 'fifth-column neurosis'.

Every kind of unusual behaviour was reported to the police and thence to MI5. As a result, Bingham travelled the length and breadth of Britain investigating reports of supposed enemy agents. Some leads reflected genuine security concerns, others were baseless. A lorry driver who gave his name as 'Leafland' crashed his lorry in a protected area and claimed to the police that he had come to Britain as a refugee without papers, having worked for an international intelligence organisation. Liddell and Knight assigned the investigation to Bingham, who two weeks later revealed that 'Leafland' was a British deserter named Wood with no intelligence connections whatsoever. A fortnight had been wasted in a fruitless investigation.

Three weeks later he was dispatched to Crewe to check for German 'plants' and Quislings among 200–300 Norwegians and several German prisoners who had been captured in a raid on the Lofoten Islands. No enemy agents were identified and, in due course, the Norwegians were released and the Germans treated as prisoners of war.

In August 1940 Lord Beaverbrook, Minister of Aircraft Production and proprietor of the *Daily Express*, became concerned that the Security Service was exceeding its authority in a manner that jeopardised the democratic process, and threatened to use his newspaper to present his views to the public.

Liddell promptly instructed Bingham to set up a Press section in B Division. This was the first occasion on which he had instructed him directly as, nominally, Bingham reported to Knight. Within a month the Press section was operational and Derek Tangye, formerly press officer at the Savoy Hotel, who had joined MI5 in 1940, was appointed to run the section and circulate a weekly bulletin with information from regional officers.

The speed and efficiency of the creation of the Press section impressed Liddell and he began to see Bingham as an officer who could be used in a variety of ways. Family events, however, intervened before his next assignment.

On 14 February 1941, Maude Ward, the Dowager 5th Baroness, died, aged eighty-two. Maurice and Leila had incurred

Madeleine's contempt when, long before war broke out, they 'packed up their acres of suitcases' and moved back from London to the relative safety of Bangor. They had kept Maude company in her last years but, when war broke out, she had become depressed and remote, 'worrying about her sugar ration'.

Thus, when John and Madeleine obtained permits to travel to Bangor for the funeral – no easy matter in wartime – Maurice and Leila were already in residence. Their son and daughter-in-law were astonished to learn that Maurice had already taken steps to sell Bangor Castle as his need for ready cash was so urgent.

As soon as Maude died, Maurice's creditors reappeared to demand repayment of the money lent to him twenty years before. Perhaps unaware of how much their inheritance had diminished in recent years, Maurice and Leila may have seen the sale as a quick fix to end their penury, the means, at last, to advance to a more fitting style of life.

Bingham was horrified at the alacrity with which his father proposed to dispose of the family seat and contacted his solicitor to seek advice. The latter urged him to persuade Maurice to hold on at least until the end of the war before selling. The castle stood on valuable land in a developing seaside town; surely Maurice could temporise until the property market improved, as the resultant increase in the property's value would far outstrip the interest accruing on his debts.

John and Madeleine held off for a day or two before broaching the matter. According to Madeleine, when they passed on this legal advice Leila treated Madeleine with haughty disdain, as though she were a 'usurper'. They were unable to persuade Maurice and Leila to stay their hand.

According to Madeleine's account, negotiations began with indecent haste to sell the castle for a ludicrously low price to the City of Bangor. Furniture was sold for a song. Relatives descended to divide the china, silver and other spoils. The castle was soon stripped of valuables.

Madeleine attempted to save some things from Bangor Castle for posterity but without success. She paints Leila as being single-minded in her desire to slough off books and items of sentimental and family historical value. When the sale was finalised some years later, the contents of the library were sold 'by the yard' to a local trader; precious mementos were simply thrown away. In 1941, after a brief stay in Bangor, as relations with his parents became increasingly brittle, John and Madeleine returned to England.

Since the autumn of 1939, Liddell had argued for versatility in MI5 within its essentially military structure. The volume of refugees flooding into Britain from France, Belgium, the Netherlands and Poland had necessitated an immediate increase in the number of officers to interrogate suspected enemy agents, but Liddell wanted more from officers in B Branch. At a January 1940 board meeting he identified a need for officers with initiative suitable for special missions. By this he meant *agents provocateurs*, specifically officers who could play a part in the deception operation that became DOUBLE CROSS ('XX').

Both Liddell and Knight were impressed by Bingham's attentiveness and discretion as a listener; Liddell was also pleased by the tactful efficiency with which Bingham had organised the Press section. Now, as the DOUBLE CROSS operation took shape, he increasingly involved his new recruit in identifying and 'turning' agents. Once identified, agents would be interrogated and 'turned' to feed false information to the German intelligence services, the *Sicherheitsdienst* and the *Abwehr*. This involved painstaking interrogation and cat-and-mouse patience on the part of the interrogator. Having worked as a journalist, Bingham had developed a natural scepticism alongside his ability to listen. He also enjoyed, as his later writings show, a shrewd eye and a remarkable memory for detail. As he honed these talents, he developed the ability to penetrate human motive with precision, making him an astute and effective interlocutor. In common with the true craftsmen of espionage, he abhorred violent methods, relying on patient persistence to produce results. Much later, asked by his daughter Charlotte if he had tortured Germans during the war, he joked that, in an interrogation, if you showed your target a naked woman and a bottle of whisky, then withheld them until you had the answers you wanted, you could soon break him.

During late 1940 the operation became highly efficient and, according to John Masterman, who oversaw the xx committee, by early 1941 MI5 'actively ran and controlled the German espionage system'. Crucial to its success were the identification and turning of agents and the treatment of information given to the agents to communicate to Berlin.

Liddell involved Bingham in both of these functions. Appointing him to take charge of interrogation of suspects at the Royal Patriotic Schools, the centre used to process aliens entering Britain, was the first step to identifying potential agents. From this step followed the process of turning them. One example illustrates that stage of the operation.

On 7 April 1941 two German agents, codenamed GLAD and MOE, were arrested near Aberdeen. They were sent to Camp 020, the MI5 interrogation and detention centre in Ham. The camp commandant, Colonel 'Tin Eye' Stephens, determined that they were willing to cooperate and recommended that they be given a lavish dinner and turned to act as double agents. This job fell to Bingham, who took them to dinner and accommodated them in his flat as part of the 'softening-up' process.

The second phase of the operation, the collecting or manufacturing of 'intelligence' to be fed back to Germany, was equally crucial. In March 1941 MI5 received a report that security at naval ports was lax. Bingham was dispatched to check on the efficiency of guards and gatekeepers and to develop a feeling for general security among servicemen stationed in the area.

His first destination was the port area of south Wales. He spent 3, 4, 5 and 6 March posing as a journalist and checking on 'loose talk' in Newport, Cardiff and Swansea. His first check was on gate security at the docks themselves. He would take a taxi to the docks and chat casually with the taxi driver along the way, drawing him out on what he knew about port traffic, comings and goings, general security. At the gate he would fumble to find his identification and see if the guard was punctilious in making him show his pass. On most occasions he was waved through and on one occasion the taxi driver commented, 'You could take the German army in and out again without trouble.'

The bulk of his time on these missions was spent in pubs near the docks. He made the rounds of the pubs, propping up the bar between opening and closing time, grabbing a quick lunch, recording his impressions and returning to his pub crawl for the evening drinking session. In a short time he assembled an enormous number of impressions, encouraging servicemen to talk about their jobs, listening sympathetically – but very closely – to all they had to say, sifting truth from the braggadocio that emerged after they had enjoyed a few drinks. In general, he found that security was good and that people became more guarded when he asked general or specific questions about port traffic. Clearly, huge amounts of alcohol were consumed in the course of this as on 6 March he records that he was invited for a drink by an army captain and that it was the last thing on earth that he wanted.

Following his tour of south Wales, he spent four days in the Liverpool area performing the same task. He established himself as a close listener, able to put people at their ease and assemble a mass of information by asking the most casual questions. By coincidence, Madeleine's brother Mark, then a midshipman about to board his ship in Liverpool, saw his brother-in-law questioning people at the docks but, as he wrote to Madeleine, assumed that he was operating under cover and thought it would be unwise to greet him.

This assignment served two purposes. At one level it was valuable to check the efficiency of the security surrounding British shipping. On another level his role was to collect information in pubs and hotel bars, much as a foreign agent would, in order to feed this back to Germany, ostensibly as information collected by *Abwehr* agents.

At first, Bingham was unaware of the importance of the role he was playing, as the ultimate purpose of DOUBLE CROSS lay three years in the future. The strategic goal was to mislead the German High Command as to the chosen targets on D-Day. For this to succeed, the *Abwehr* needed to believe implicitly in the authenticity of the reports fed to them. Only after D-Day did MI5 realise how effective their feeding of disinformation had been. It was vital to the success of the Normandy landings that the *Abwehr* should believe that the invasion would be spearheaded by General Patton's (non-existent) army based in East Anglia and that the landings would take place in the Pas de Calais. This deception succeeded and Hitler retained three Panzer divisions in the Channel ports during the Battle of Normandy, deceived into believing that the main assault was yet to come and that the Normandy landings were a feint.

Parallel with the apprehension and turning of aliens was the identification of British nationals with German sympathies. In this more conventional area of counter-subversion Bingham had two principal roles to play.

Adopting the alias 'John Bentley', he played the role of a thirty-something man about town, a regular at nightclubs and restaurants in the West End. As ever, his talent as a listener was his principal asset and, after a day of interrogation of suspect aliens in Wandsworth, he would don his evening clothes to play the role of *bon vivant*.

More demanding and certainly more exotic was the role he played with British nationals whose German sympathies, through some indiscretion, had come to the attention of enemy agents. In such cases he assumed the persona of an *Abwehr* officer on the lookout for agents in Britain. Several Britons of doubtful loyalty were arrested as a result.

One case of this kind was that of Irma Stapleton. Stapleton was German by origin and a British subject by marriage. Her name had come to MI5's attention through Special Branch, who learned that she worked in an ordnance factory in Staffordshire and had expressed pro-German opinions. When Bingham, posing as an *Abwehr* officer, met her on 19 November 1941, he tape-recorded their meeting and Stapleton was promptly arrested. Three months later, in February 1942, she was convicted of espionage and sentenced to ten years in prison.

Between visits to Glasgow, Aberdeen, Crewe, Stafford, the Welsh ports, Liverpool and the 'safe house' that the Service had established in Wales for DOUBLE CROSS agents, in addition to his evenings as a listener-about-town and being arrested, there was little time for a private life, and Madeleine rarely saw him. She had joined the Service as a secretary and in 1940 had been posted to Blenheim Palace, which the Duke of Marlborough put at the department's disposal during the war. Along with most of the women working at MI5, she was accommodated in Keble College, Oxford, having arranged for Simon to stay with her sister Suzanne in Kent. She recalls interminable evenings when she had arranged to meet her husband at the Mitre Hotel in Oxford, waiting for him to appear, which he only sometimes did; more often he would be detained by work. On the occasions that they could meet, however briefly, she was impressed by his dedication to the job. Clearly he had found his *métier*. In a somewhat purple passage in her memoir *Smiley's Wife*, directly referring to her husband as 'Smiley', she recalled that year:

> Smiley, older and perhaps less sentimental than he was in 1940, has changed very little ... I sometimes thought that Smiley looked at my dashing good-looking brother with nostalgic admiration. There he was, tall, elegant and fighting in a destroyer. A figure of romance. Smiley's job was more humdrum, but if Mark was the prototype of the gallant naval officer, Smiley was the prototype of the hard-working, dedicated Intelligence officer learning his job. Learning how to judge people, learning about treachery and trying to forestall it ... Out in the darkness, in the black-out in his second-hand car, with the searchlights sweeping the sky, he went about doing his best with his small piece of the war.

Soon after the trip to Bangor, Madeleine was transferred from Blenheim to the St James's Street office, which enabled her to have more time with her husband. Bingham was living in a one-bedroomed flat in Knightsbridge but in April, in order to economise, he moved to Harrington Gardens in South Kensington. Barely two weeks later, on 10 May 1941, the Knightsbridge house was bombed, leaving a surgical-looking hole in the ground.

For the first time the reality of war was brought home to Madeleine. Working at Blenheim she had seen bombers in the sky, but they had seemed distant, somehow removed from the effects of the destruction they caused. Their proximity to that night of bombs, one of the last heavy assaults of the Blitz, disturbed her profoundly. But Hitler's sights were by now trained on Operation BARBAROSSA, the invasion of the Soviet Union. As a result, the greater part of the *Luftwaffe* was transferred to the east and after mid-May 1941 the Blitz effectively came to an end.

The flow of aliens through the Royal Patriotic Schools continued unabated through 1941. In one week in September, Bingham reported to Liddell that he had dealt with 195 suspects and that his staff had examined 750 Norwegians and 180 French in Glasgow. 'He is very anxious to get more staff,' commented Liddell.

In September 1941 it was decided that the RPS should come under the control of Section B1(d) of MI5. This decision put Ronnie Haylor of B1 (d) in command of the interrogation centre and, not unnaturally, was a blow to the newly commissioned Major Bingham, who 'asked to be allowed to consider his position'. In the event, Dick White explained the move as an organisational necessity and was able to talk him round. The episode highlighted the position of wartime recruits: he handled an enormous workload and was performing an excellent job in Wandsworth, but the very importance of the centre demanded that it should be overseen by a permanent officer of MI5, and his position as a temporary recruit was painfully underscored.

Soon after the United States entered the war in December 1941, President Roosevelt and General de Gaulle became embroiled in a dispute over the Saint Pierre and Miquelon islands off the coast of Newfoundland. Despite American objections, de Gaulle, who, after the fall of France, had taken command of the Free French Forces that gathered in England, occupied the islands on Christmas Day, incurring the rage of the American President. De Gaulle pressured Churchill to intervene with the President on his behalf, hinting none too subtly that, if he was to be treated as *persona non grata* by the Anglo-American alliance, he would decamp to north Africa. This sat ill with Churchill, who felt that de Gaulle could be contained for as long as he stayed in London but that he would be a very loose cannon if he established his headquarters in Algeria.

Relations between Churchill and the leader of the Free French had deteriorated. ('The heaviest cross I have to bear', groaned the Prime Minister, 'is the Cross of Lorraine.') Cooperation between Churchill and his Chiefs of Staff on the one hand and the Free French on the other became increasingly strained throughout de Gaulle's stay in London, with the Chiefs concerned that any strategic intelligence given to de Gaulle was immediately leaked. All top secret plans, including those for TORCH (the invasion of north Africa) and even OVERLORD (the D-Day landings), were concealed from the French. This was a source of fierce resentment for de Gaulle.

During 1942, as preparations for TORCH were in motion, MI5 officers were concerned that de Gaulle might reject further cooperation with Britain and make good his threat to move to north Africa. The brief of Bingham and his MI5 colleague Bill Younger was to keep a close eye on the French party and notify 'The Office' immediately if there were signs of imminent departure such as suitcases being moved out to waiting staff cars. They quickly checked into the Connaught Hotel, which de Gaulle and his staff were using as their headquarters.

It was a source of amusement and concern to Bingham that when he and Younger checked in there was only one room available, a double-bedded room on the top floor, and, for security reasons, they were forced to pay their bill with used £1 notes. He was convinced that the staff imagined them to be civilians, black-marketeers and homosexuals to boot. Bill Younger was a good-looking man, ten years younger than him, which, he believed, added fuel to the receptionist's suspicions. His principal concern was that the hotel staff might report the two suspicious agents to MI5 as individuals meriting investigation – an outcome that would not have amused his superiors.

But the hotel had its perks. Inviting his wife to dinner, Bingham enjoyed a surprisingly good meal, far above the typical wartime standard; because de Gaulle and his staff were using the hotel as their headquarters, the food circumvented the restrictions in force in London during the war.

De Gaulle was not the only VIP whom Bingham investigated. Another sensitive assignment came his way in late September. Lady Diana Cooper, daughter of the Duke of Rutland and wife of Duff Cooper, the Minister of Information, was suspected of security breaches in her correspondence with an American friend. Bingham assumed the thankless task of investigating whether or not she was a security risk – a delicate job, as Cooper would have been furious if he discovered that his wife's letters were being opened. He was able to find 'nothing against' her beyond certain indiscretions concerning Averell Harriman, President Roosevelt's special envoy, and Randolph Churchill's wife.

More seriously, however, there was concern about security surrounding the plans for Operation TORCH, the invasion of north Africa planned for the end of October. Reports reached MI5 of careless talk and of apparent German knowledge of the plans.

Additionally, a Catalina flying boat carrying detailed plans for TORCH crashed off Cadiz on 24 September, causing further concern. Bingham spent late September running all suspected leaks to earth and establishing that the plans had not been compromised.

During the summer and autumn of 1942, Bingham worked day and night on security for TORCH. Full work days were supplemented by regular evening outings, when he assumed the name of John Bentley and frequented London's nightclubs in the company of a Portuguese diplomat, Rogeiro Menezes. In July 1942, Signals Intelligence revealed that Menezes, working in London at the Portuguese legation, was passing information to the *Sicherheitsdienst (SD)*, the Nazi intelligence division, in Lisbon. MI5 already had an agent inside the Portuguese embassy and the agent's efforts were now supplemented by a 'sting' operation.

Between 22 July and 3 August, mail censorship intercepted Menezes's correspondence and established that he was using invisible ink in letters to his sister in Lisbon. Despite extensive efforts and tests, the ink on the letters could not be developed ('brought up', in espionage parlance) in its entirety, but there were indications that he was reporting on anti-aircraft defences. Bingham was able to get alongside Menezes with relative ease, as the diplomat lived the life of a playboy and was involved in an affair with the wife of an officer serving in north Africa. Bingham contrived to meet him through an agent, codenamed VIOLET, a friend of the officer's wife.

The initial concern of MI5 was that Menezes was passing details of TORCH to Lisbon, whence, they feared, it was being relayed to Berlin. Throughout the Second World War, Lisbon was a hotbed of espionage. Portugal maintained neutrality throughout the war as the Prime Minister, Dr António Salazar, scrupulously and skilfully juggled his country's relations with the Allied and Axis powers. Determined that Portugal would emerge from the war unscathed and in control of its colonies, and that it should exploit to the maximum its most valuable resource – wolfram, or tungsten, a critical ingredient for weaponry – he strove to balance his favours to the warring countries whose spies infested the capital. This required considerable dexterity and not a little deception.

There was, therefore, a potential bonus for the Security Service if they could unmask Menezes. If they could demonstrate to

Salazar that the neutrality of Portugal was being violated by the *SD*, they would be able to apply diplomatic pressure on him to suppress German espionage activities. By the end of October, as final preparations for TORCH were being made, Bingham was no closer to acquiring definite proof of Menezes's activities.

To compound these problems, there was a mood of anticipation in Fleet Street as the day of the first American involvement in the European theatre of operations approached. Bingham and Tangye were instructed to lead reporters off the scent with disinformation about the intended target. They succeeded in this, and when the landings took place in Algeria and Morocco on 8 November they came as a total surprise.

During November Bingham returned to his pursuit of Menezes, who continued to be 'extremely cautious and suspicious'. The investigation dragged on through December and January, during which period Liddell and Bingham were convinced of Menezes's guilt but were unable to produce evidence that would lead to a conviction. On 22 January 1943, Liddell forced the issue and Bingham fed Menezes a 'barium meal' (the process of feeding false intelligence to a suspect in order to see where it ultimately emerged) detailing anti-aircraft defences and a proposed build-up of British troops in the eastern Mediterranean. This produced the desired result: the incorrect information found its way to the *SD* in Lisbon. On 19 February, Sir Alexander Cadogan approached the Portuguese ambassador and produced proof of Menezes's involvement in a spy ring, even developing a letter written in secret ink in front of the envoy. Finally, after seemingly endless nights carousing with Menezes, his mistress and VIOLET, Bingham was able to close the case.

When the Portuguese government agreed to suspend Menezes's diplomatic status on 23 February they effectively handed him to the British authorities, and he was promptly arrested. Two days later it was established that he had been passing information to both Germany and Italy. In his defence he claimed that he had been blackmailed by the *SD*, and that his actions had been dictated by his fear for the fate of relations in Germany. MI5 remained unmoved by this claim.

During his interrogation Menezes was cooperative and, as a result of information obtained, twenty-three arrests were made in Lisbon, including the head of the *SD*. This was an important propaganda coup in the war of intelligence being waged in the neutral Portuguese capital and it set in train a sequence of events that involved the British and German intelligence services, the Portuguese secret police, the British ambassador to Portugal and Salazar himself.

On 2 April 1943 Menezes was convicted of espionage and condemned to death at the Old Bailey. Over the next two months, Ronald Campbell, the British ambassador to Portugal, used the evidence gained from Menezes to bring increasing pressure to bear on his host government to investigate the activities of the *Abwehr* and *SD* in Lisbon, culminating in a meeting on 29 May at which Salazar gave Campbell the results of police investigations into German espionage in the capital. This brought about the expulsion from Portugal of several German agents. On 31 May, almost certainly as a *quid pro quo*, Menezes was reprieved in London.

After much British consideration of the precedent that execution might set, and after the intervention of Prime Minister Salazar himself, the sentence was commuted to life imprisonment. Even this was relaxed in due course and after the war Menezes was returned to Portugal.

The conclusion of the case was a triumph for MI5. Espionage in the Portuguese capital had long been a severe annoyance to the Security Service; for the rest of the war the threat posed by

German intelligence in Portugal was largely defused. On the day after the commutation of Menezes's sentence, however, an event occurred that may have been a sequel to the story: an act of retaliation by German intelligence.

On 1 June 1943, a DC-3 airliner operated by BOAC, flying Flight 777-A from Lisbon to Bristol, was shot down by a squadron of eight Junkers aircraft above the Bay of Biscay. The plane was carrying seventeen passengers and four crew members. None survived. Among the passengers was the actor Leslie Howard, best known for his performance in *Gone with the Wind*. A passionate anti-Nazi who had come to the attention of Joseph Goebbels, Howard had been persuaded by Foreign Minister Anthony Eden to undertake a propaganda tour of the Iberian peninsula. He was returning to England at the end of that tour, accompanied by his accountant, Alfred Chenhalls.

Many theories have been proposed to explain the attack: that Howard was the principal target; that Chenhalls, a portly cigar-smoking man, had been misidentified as Winston Churchill; that Wilfred Israel, a Jewish businessman who arranged escape networks for refugees, a passenger on the flight, was the target. Equally likely is that the order for the attack was given in retaliation for the British intelligence triumph in Lisbon. The coincidence of the timing of the attack – on the day following Menezes's commutation of sentence – is too great to ignore. In common with every other theory about the attack, however, it is impossible to prove.

While the Director of Public Prosecutions was preparing the case against Menezes, Bingham was once again assigned to keep an eye on the perennially recalcitrant de Gaulle. He had been relieved of that responsibility once it was clear that leaky French security had not compromised TORCH, but now there was further cause for concern. There had been friction at SYMBOL, the Casablanca Conference in January 1943, and Roosevelt was openly taunting Churchill over the position in which the Free French leader had placed him. FDR was wickedly amused that Churchill, waging a life-and-death war against Hitler, was unable to control his ally, the mercurial Free French leader in London. Now it had become clear that de Gaulle would not be happy until he could establish himself in Algiers; on the other hand, while recognising that the Free French should not appear to be a subsidiary arm of Great Britain, Churchill insisted on knowing of de Gaulle's plans well in advance of his departure.

In March 1943, Madeleine received shattering news. Her brother Mark had been standing by in Scotland awaiting the launch of HMS *Vandal*, the Class U coastal submarine that was completed on 20 February 1943. The submarine sailed for Holy Loch, the point of departure for the Russian convoys. Conventional test manoeuvres in the Kilbrannan Sound were scheduled for 22 and 23 February, with deep diving tests planned for the following day, provided that the commanding officer was satisfied with the condition of the boat and the competence of the crew.

Test manoeuvres were completed satisfactorily and *Vandal* left Lochranza on the Isle of Arran on the morning of 24 February. Commanded by Lieutenant John Stirling Bridger, with thirty-seven officers and men aboard including Temporary Lieutenant Mark Ebel GM, *Vandal* sailed and was never sighted again. Although the submerged submarine was located in 1994 and inspected where she lay, no satisfactory explanation of her sinking has been given.

At first the Admiralty, uncertain of the fate of *Vandal*, wrote a formal letter advising Clement and his family to regard Mark as 'missing'. While Clement clung to hope, refusing to believe that his son was dead, Madeleine and her sisters accepted the worst. It was a crippling blow.

In later years Madeleine's writing would return again and again to Mark and to the news of his death. Her play *Submariner* is a tribute to her beloved brother; characters with a likeness to Mark appear in several of her other plays. Most movingly, in *Cheapest in the End*, a collection of family memories, she writes a poignant description of herself, her sisters and their mother eyeing the official letter addressed to Clement as it lay on the hall table.

The summer of 1943 saw a decided change in MI5 operations. With the invasion of Sicily and the first Allied toehold on the European continent, followed by the surrender of Italy, there was a strategic shift towards using double agents to report disinformation concerning the invasion of France. Liddell maintained his position that DOUBLE CROSS was 'primarily for an insurance against penetration, and secondly as a means of deception' but, in truth, this was no longer the case. Without underestimating the pitfalls ahead, MI5 chiefs were looking beyond OVERLORD towards the occupation of Germany and the post-war period.

One troublesome issue facing the MI5 board was the position of Maxwell Knight ('M') and the future of his section. Knight saw the Soviet Union as the ineluctable primary target and was not afraid to voice his beliefs. This created a delicate situation as the USSR was nominally an ally in the war against Germany and it was vital to maintain that alliance. In his own behaviour, moreover, Knight was increasingly autocratic. He was conducting an open affair with Joan Miller, whom he had hired into B5(b) and who had infiltrated the secret right-wing group The Right Club in Knight's triumphant handling of the Tyler Kent-Anna Wolkoff case. Kent, a cipher clerk at the American Embassy, stole secret documents in an attempt to embarrass President Roosevelt in May 1940 and unwittingly asked Miller to deliver a message for Mussolini to the Italian Embassy. The affair caused ill feeling within his section; Bingham commented that 'she completely dominated Max and she quickly became a person of considerable influence. We were all slightly afraid of her for we only needed to get on her wrong side and she would put the boot in for us with Max.'

During the early years of the war, the officers of M's section had been perpetually busy as successive waves of suspected German sympathisers and agents were interrogated. By 1943, when fear of invasion had permanently receded and the end of the war was in sight, discontent within M's section was increasingly voiced. Roger Hollis brought to Liddell's attention a case where four men had been assigned to surveillance of a stateless Russian who claimed to work for OGPU. It emerged that the suspect was already 'thoroughly well known to the police' and posed no security risk. Both Liddell and Hollis felt strongly that Knight was operating 'in the void' and that he was becoming 'somewhat of a danger'. A week later two of M's officers complained to Liddell about him, claiming that too much money was being spent for too little return. Both officers requested transfers out of B5(b).

Planning for OVERLORD was now Liddell's main concern. Knight, increasingly marginalised, had fewer cases to investigate and Liddell assigned Bingham and Norman Himsworth, another of 'Knight's Black Agents', to check on the security of preparations for OVERLORD. Once the outline of the plans was agreed at the Quebec Conference of August 1943, it was vital not only that the landing sites of the Normandy beaches be concealed from the *Abwehr* but also that the impression be conveyed to Berlin that the Pas de Calais was the target area.

At the Tehran Conference in December 1943, Roosevelt, Churchill and Stalin agreed that OVERLORD would be launched in May 1944; General Eisenhower was appointed Supreme Commander and General Montgomery, commander of the land forces, returned to England to develop the invasion plan. Since October, when there had been reports of leaks of aircraft production figures, Bingham had been heavily involved in OVER-LORD security as well as DOUBLE CROSS operations. Now, as preparations for the invasion sped up, he and Himsworth travelled up and down the country inspecting security at the ports and the several factories involved in production.

By the end of 1943 the Combined Chiefs of Staff had decided on the plan for landings on the Cotentin peninsula between Caen and Cherbourg. British and Commonwealth forces would land on Gold, Sword and Juno beaches close to Caen, while the Americans would storm Omaha and Utah beaches further up the peninsula. The plan called for early capture of Cherbourg as a port of supply, and plans were well advanced for a pipeline – PLUTO or Pipeline Under The Ocean – to supply vital petrol to fuel the breakout. It was critical that the maximum possible security surround the companies printing invasion maps as well as those manufacturing the materials for PLUTO.

Bingham and Himsworth chose to visit the PLUTO factory first. To their horror, they found that they were able to scale a wall and enter the factory without being challenged. They walked around a little, then left cigarette packets on the ground to simulate the placement of explosives. When the shift changed in the early morning, they simply walked out with the night shift. Later that morning, Knight paid a visit to the factory, pointed out the markers that his agents had left and security was tightened.

Across London, on the top floor of a building in Clerkenwell, was the printing company engaged in preparing the detailed maps that would be issued to all officers before D-Day. Since the main thrust of DOUBLE CROSS disinformation was now to mislead the German High Command and the *Abwehr* as to the location of the landing beaches, it was vital that no unauthorised person have any idea that Normandy had been selected. Bingham and Himsworth entered the building dressed as Air Raid Precaution wardens and subjected the entire top floor to an elaborate 'inspection'. Probing every corner, desk, table and printing press, they established that security was adequate as they were unable to see any evidence of any map printing.

On 29 June 1942 Charlotte Mary Thérèse Bingham was born, and Madeleine retired from secret work to look after the two children, schooling Simon at home. London was a safer place after the suspension of the Blitz in 1941, but from mid-1943 the Security Service knew that Hitler's references to the secret weapons that would win the war were not idle boasting. Bingham had no illusions as to the risk that the new weapons posed; now the father of two children, he urged Madeleine to take Simon and Charlotte to safety outside London. Madeleine retorted that the bombing was by then no more than an inconvenience and that they would stay in London.

Bingham explained that he was not talking about conventional bombs but about flying bombs and rockets. The Germans had constructed several launch sites in northern France for the V-1 flying bomb, a pilotless plane with a range of 200 miles, and intelligence indicated that construction of launch sites was in progress in Peenemünde on the Baltic coast for the longer-range V-2 rocket. The second bombardment of London, he warned Madeleine, would be more devastating than the Blitz.

With some reluctance, but persuaded that this was the safest course for Simon and Charlotte, Madeleine took a house at Craigwell, near Bognor Regis. While the war entered its critical phase before D-Day, Madeleine and the children spent their time on the south coast. To pass the time, Madeleine, a devoted theatregoer, began to write, finishing seven plays between 1943 and 1946. Her enforced leisure launched her on what was to be her post-war career.

After the successful landings on D-Day, as the western Allies rolled across France, liberated Paris, drove to the Rhine and advanced deep into Germany, the pressure on Knight's section eased. The centre of the action was elsewhere, but Knight watched with mounting concern as the pace of the western advance slowed both in the British sector and in the American sector, where General Omar Bradley's army group was neatly bisected by the German counter-attack in the Ardennes Forest. A month was lost while the 'Bulge' was repaired and in that month the Red Army continued to advance on Berlin from the east. Knight was not alone; the Prime Minister argued vehemently but unsuccessfully with President Roosevelt that Montgomery should be allowed to drive full tilt to capture Berlin before the arrival of Marshal Zhukov and the Red Army.

The last months of the war saw not only Knight but the entire Security Service unclear about the future. Once the centre of activity shifted from defence of the realm to the continent, MI6 claimed the right to handle security. Indeed, during 1945 there were moves to merge the two departments, with MI6 playing an 'offensive' and MI5 a 'defensive' role. It was clear to Liddell and Hollis that MI5 would be the junior partner in such a merger. The uncertainty about the Service's future, together with its ungenerous salary scale, discouraged potential recruits. As for Knight's section, Liddell believed that his officers knew more than he did, that Knight was badly out of touch and an 'unsuit-able head' of the section. Bingham, he confided in his diary, was 'probably able and generally all right'. When cuts were made, however, they would be made on the basis of 'last in, first out' and, overall, it would be Knight's section that suffered the deep-est cuts. Since Bingham could return to Fleet Street at a salary more than twice what the Service could offer, Liddell was not unduly concerned for his future.

In his role as a notional *Abwehr* officer, John Bingham had maintained contact with several Right-leaning groups. In the summer of 1944, when the defeat of Germany was assured, there was discussion in MI5 about how Bingham should define his and their roles. Guy Liddell ordered that he should continue his association with such groups, now largely cut off from their German contacts. In order to neutralise them, he should put out the 'party line' that German defeat was possible, attributing blame to the generals who, in the main, were less pro-party than the diehard Nazi fanatics. The groups, therefore, should accept temporary defeat and await orders to prepare for the next war. This called for subtlety and considerable acting skills. 'The sentiments of these people', Liddell commented, 'are really astonishing.'

On 6 September Liddell noted in his diary that B Division work had virtually come to an end and, by the beginning of 1945, Max Knight's section was a remote outpost. When Jimmy Dickson, whom Liddell had appointed a section head within B Division, came to him in March to discuss the staffing of his section, Liddell told him that he did not feel that anyone from Knight's section would be 'suitable' as his deputy. To his diary he confided that 'Dickson would of course like to have Bingham but he is already too much occupied with other things'. Overtly loyal to Knight, Bingham recognised that his time with MI5 was limited, probably as a result of that association. It was a sad last act.

At this point he wrote to Charles Eade, the editor of the *Sunday Dispatch*, to ask for his old job back. Eade responded positively but admitted that he was uncertain exactly what position he could find.

Liddell recognised Bingham's ability and, as the infighting between MI5 and MI6 intensified, he became convinced that the Security Service should be well represented in the Allied Control Council, the military governing body in occupied Germany. He suggested to Bingham that he take a long leave and be ready to be seconded to the Control Commission at the end of the summer. He predicted that the German apologia for the recent years would be that everything was the fault of the Nazis, who had precipitated and then lost the war. The Allies, he accurately foresaw, would soon be pressured into rebuilding Germany as a bulwark against the real enemy, the Soviet Union.

Thus the thinking of the mainstream in MI5 turned full circle and once again became congruent with Knight's repeated warnings that communist subversion was ubiquitous, a belief that he had preached for a decade. Bingham accepted Liddell's advice, took the leave owed to him and duly set out for northern Germany believing that his association with the mainstream of MI5 was over.

CHAPTER 5

ALLIED CONTROL COUNCIL, 1946-8

*From Stettin in the Baltic to Trieste in the Adriatic an iron curtain has
descended across the continent. Behind that line lie all the capitals of the
ancient states of central and eastern Europe.*
Sir Winston Churchill, speech at Fulton College, Missouri,
5 March 1946

*Here you met it again, hitting you in the face, the German smell, the stink
of defeat and misery.*
John Bingham, *Five Roundabouts to Heaven*

The memories of Germany from 1928-9, steeped in aristocratic tradition, before the excesses of Nazism had
humbled and emasculated the established order, were in
Bingham's mind as he travelled to the country whose defeat
he had laboured to achieve. Between 1940 and 1945 he had
been devoted to tracking, finding and exposing German
agents and sympathisers in Britain. Having given five unre-
lenting years to the defeat of a country he had enjoyed and
admired, he returned to Germany alone, leaving Madeleine
and the children in England. For two years he worked in
Gehrden, a suburb of Hanover, as an officer in the Allied
Control Council, the body that would administer the
conquered nation. It was an unforgettable experience that

shaped his notions of punishment and compassion, revenge and clemency.

The destruction dealt to Hanover shocked him. Accustomed to seeing ruined English cities, he was nonetheless surprised by the scale of the damage in Germany. Greatly more moving, however, was the sense of hopelessness he encountered among homeless Germans and the refugees that flooded into the city. Later he recalled his first impressions:

> A grey picture of desolation. The once great buildings and the wide streets of large houses are piled high on each side with rubble, or half-wrecked houses. All is grey ... The iron girders in the dome of the great Stadthalle are half-exposed. The clothes of the inhabitants are colourless. So are their faces; so are, in many cases, the faces of the children. Or, if not colourless, then an unearthly yellow.
>
> Many buildings do, of course, remain – without paint, with windows without glass, with walls pitted with bomb splinters. Such houses as remain sometimes have a makeshift chimney sticking out of the side of the wall as evidence of human occupation.

The Allied Control Council had been planned by the European Advisory Commission (EAC) since late 1944, as the Red Army rolled across eastern Europe and the western Allies closed on the Rhine. The principal concern of the EAC was that the country should be completely 'de-Nazified'; total occupation would, therefore, be necessary to avoid dependence on former Nazis in the country's administration. The Armistice of 1918, whose legality was dependent on the surrender of the civilian government, had ignited the doctrine that the German army had suffered a 'stab in the back' and the Allies were determined that this myth should not be resuscitated in 1945.

Accordingly, the Allies denied the legality of the Dönitz government, appointed as the legitimate heirs in Adolf Hitler's political testament. Instead, on 5 June, they issued the Berlin Declaration, whereby the USSR, the United States, Britain and France assumed 'supreme authority with respect to Germany, including all the powers possessed by the German government, the High Command and any state, municipal, or local government or authority'.

The country was divided into four zones of occupation: the territory between the eastern border and the Elbe, to include Brandenburg, Mecklenburg, Saxony, Saxony-Anhalt and Thuringia, constituted the Soviet zone; the western Allies controlled the western German provinces. Great Britain under Field Marshal Montgomery handled the area comprising Schleswig-Holstein, Hamburg, Lower Saxony and North Rhine-Westphalia; to the south lay the American zone, incorporating Bavaria and all territory between the Rhine and the Czech and Austrian borders; to the west of the Rhine and as far south as the Swiss border formed the French zone under General de Lattre de Tassigny.

Berlin itself was divided into four zones, of which the Soviet zone was the largest, occupying 40 per cent of the total area. The partition was a recipe for anarchy, administrative chaos and – as became increasingly clear as refugees flooded to the west to escape from the Soviet zone – an opportunity for espionage on a grand scale.

According to the agreement between the Allies, the British and American forces withdrew from their easternmost front lines to the western boundary of the Soviet zone. This created panic among refugees in the vacated areas and renewed attempts by displaced persons (DPs) to find asylum in the British or American zones. Camps were established to house the multinational westward flow of refugees.

With his wartime experience of counter-subversion and inter-rogation, Bingham was ideally qualified to interview DPs and establish which were genuine refugees and who might be Soviet agents being infiltrated to the west. From his arrival at Gehrden he spent his waking hours among a horde of refugees, sifting their stories and their claims to asylum. The plight of the men and women in Hanover shocked him:

> Great queues form up for the trams, several deep, and the people wait patiently in the rain. The people stare at you blankly. There is neither hate nor curiosity, nor anything else in their gaze. But all over Germany when you speak to them and ask the way, they are polite and usually go to some trouble to help you. As one is in most cases a mere stranger from whom they have nothing to gain, this is a pleasant surprise.
>
> Many men still wear their old Wehrmacht uniform, now shabby and the worse for wear. The women are inclined to wear knee-length socks. Material being nearly impossible to find, many wear red skirts, made from torn-up Nazi flags ... Matches are rationed to one box a month. Coats, when obtainable, are made out of old Army blankets, dyed. It takes six months to get lenses for spectacles. There is no issue of coal and the accumulation of wood for the winter has been mismanaged. The general attitude towards the Military Government wavers between bitterness and a feeling that they mean well but are inefficient.

This shifting lake of defeated humanity, augmented by an increasing number of refugees, flowed around the city, with no purpose beyond survival. The centre of the shifting mass was to be found at the railway station, for it was there that they arrived, there that people returned to the city from the country, that place of bounty where one might find eggs, a chicken, unimaginable luxuries that could aid survival, either as food or as barter in a world where official currencies were worthless. Bingham spent many hours at the station, seeking out suspect individuals, interviewing, interrogating, as often as not merely observing:

Out of the sleet and the biting cold into Hannover station, bomb-battered, dingy, dirty from day and night use, come thousands of men and women – refugees from the East. Business men in shabby, shiny suits, clutching attaché cases, women with mysterious bulging cloth carrier bags returning to Hannover after bartering clothes, jewellery or blankets, or anything they possess for food. For the farmers don't want money.

Deep shadows, a few weak electric lights, draughts, the strange musty smell formed by a mixture of German ration soap, German tobacco, and German perspiration ... Down in the bunkers there are two or three thousand people, some there because it is warm, and they must wait somewhere. Some because they have no other roof in all Hannover. Some to do black market deals ... Three men and an accordion are singing, surrounded by a crowd who join in now and then. As you come in, you meet it again, hitting you in the face like a solid warm wall – 'the German smell'. Men and women sit sprawled, head on arms, asleep. You must shoulder your way through the human jungle, stepping over trunks, avoiding handbags, legs, feet and bodies sitting and lying, some conscious, some half-asleep. Here a woman, perhaps seventy years old, grey, streaky hair lankly hanging, squats on a suitcase, head on arms, knees up, eyes closed. And there is a child, one of many, lying across the end of a trunk, her yellow hair touching the ground, ungainly, grotesque as though a giant had used her as a doll and then tossed her down. In the middle, the air is so thick and foul it threatens to choke you like cotton wool. You pick your way gingerly past the woman with the crying baby, past the filthy ragged man mumbling to himself. And with greater care past the groups of long-haired grubby youths who hang about and plot and trade in cigarettes and other unobtainable things. They look at you curiously with their long grey faces and grey eyes; they would dearly love to provoke 'an incident' and beat you up, and rob you. And be gone before the Bahnhofpolizei can arrive. They would boast of it later.

Why do people go to the bunker? Because it's warm. For no other reason.

He had left England, relieved that the war was over and, in common with every patriot, satisfied that the Allies had triumphed, that Nazism was overthrown. He had left a country where talk of revenge on Germany was rife. The Morgenthau Plan had proposed reducing Germany to an agricultural nation after victory was won, dismantling its industry, outlawing manufacturing and imposing an agrarian economy that would punish an entire nation for the excesses of Nazism.

Winston Churchill and Franklin Roosevelt had accepted the plan before wiser counsel prevailed. There were many in England who would have imposed even harsher penalties on the defeated nation. Bingham had, to some degree, felt the same way. It was only when he saw the extent of the destruction, the depth of human suffering, that his philosophy changed. It was easy to sit in London, ravaged but not levelled, and talk grandiloquently of exacting reparations on the defeated enemy. Only after arrival in that country could one conceive of the effect of such reparations on an already prostrate people.

Hanover was but one city – an important city, to be sure, a frequent target for American and British bombers. Just up the road had stood Hamburg, almost totally devastated by firebombing in the last week of July 1943. The toll had been 42,600 civilians killed and 37,000 wounded. Across in the Soviet zone was Dresden, one of the loveliest cities in Europe, against which the British and American air forces had sent 3,600 planes in successive waves of destruction between 13 and 15 February 1945. Was this justice, he asked himself. Was it for revenge beyond such systematic destruction that his compatriots back in England now called?

Nor were the exponents of revenge to be found only in England. Admiral Hans-Georg von Friedeburg had surrendered to Field Marshal Montgomery at Lüneburg Heath, but for many Tommies the war was far from over. There was penance to be exacted and the remaining possessions of civilian families were systematically 'liberated' by the licentious soldiery. There are stories of Tommies taking whatever could be transported to Britain, often with considerable ingenuity: numerous Mercedes cars passed to Allied hands; one group of Tommies liberated a grand piano, shipping it to England, reassembling and selling it by auction on the platform as soon as it arrived at Victoria station. The army, in collaboration with the Allied Control Council, was charged with preventing such abuses.

There was a darker side, too: an enforced separation between victors and vanquished in the form of orders forbidding fraternisation. The Control Commission officers lived in a separate sanitised compound, among, yet profoundly separate from, the community whose lives they administered. In 1947, after the West End run of her play *The Man from the Ministry*, Madeleine left Charlotte with Lottie, her mother, and Simon at his prep school, and went to Hanover to spend some time with her husband. She had read in newspapers that the English officers lived 'in fantastic luxury' and at first she was 'agreeably surprised' by the

bright modern villa ... spacious and well finished inside, and equipped with modern furniture of a utility pattern ... by the china and the chintz curtains, until I discovered the next day that all my husband's friends and acquaintances had exactly the same furniture, curtains and china. Not only that but all the clubs and leave centres in all the towns in the British Zone were similarly furnished, so that wherever you go you always sit on the same chairs and eat off the same plates or use the same cruets. This, although excessively monotonous, gives you the impression that you have never left home.

More surprising to her was when, after meeting her at Hanover station and driving her to the compound, John removed the spare wheel from the car and locked it in the kitchen; he then took his typewriter and radio upstairs to the bedroom. Elementary precautions, he explained. They had a house full of good barter material. Flustered but only slightly alarmed, Madeleine adjusted to the routine.

Despite these precautions, they were burgled three times and eventually acquired a dog to guard the house. In one of the burglaries, the thieves bagged the silver cigarette case that Bingham's colleagues had given him when he left the *Hull Daily Mail*. This was of particular annoyance, and nearly forty years later he wrote, 'I was, and am, very bitter about this, and wish the burglar no good will at all.' Living as apparently plutocratic outliers on the edge of a community that had lost almost everything, British officers' houses suffered regular burglaries. Other wives would routinely ask her, 'Have you been burgled yet?' and at dinner parties there was a jack-in-the-box quality as guests would leap up at intervals to look out of the window and check that their cars were still there.

Living in a suburban British colony did not appeal to Madeleine. She stayed eight months in Gehrden before the insular Englishness and the sheer boredom of having nothing to do beyond visiting the English club and the English shop wore her down. Among the wives the principal topics of conversation were 'what do they have in the shop this week?' and 'how the German nannies spoil one's children'. She felt frustrated at not being able to join the German community beyond superficial encounters and desperately bored by the vacuity of life centred on 'the Club', that essential institution of the British overseas.

Her husband, setting a pattern for their lives, was absent for long hours – all day and well into most evenings. After eight months of such solitary confinement, Madeleine was happy to return to her beloved Kensington.

The straightforward side of the Control Commission's work was the maintenance of civil order and pursuit of black-marketeers. German currency was valueless; British pounds and American dollars were acceptable. Nothing, however, held its value like solid, tangible items that could be bartered for food. Preferred currency was a carton of Camel or Player's cigarettes, objects handled with the reverence more commonly accorded to gold bricks. In an unpublished short story written soon after his return to England, Bingham recorded his memory of his first winter in Hanover:

Nobody who experienced it will forget the cold winter of 1946–7. In England a victorious nation shivered in misery, railway lines and roads were blocked by snow drifts, food was monotonous, power cuts darkened the streets. On the continent, a defeated nation, with neither fuel for their grates nor food to heat their stomachs, struggled merely to remain alive; valuable rings were traded for a load of logs, jewels were exchanged for a few eggs and vegetables, a cigarette was a reasonable tip, and a bottle of gin cost the equivalent of £6 or £7.

Pre-eminent among the Hanover black-marketeers was a gang of petty thieves who had elevated themselves by adopting the

title 'The Edelweiss Pirates'. This group, originally anti-Nazi
when it was formed in the 1930s, had become a loose association of gangsters and thugs who handled a brisk trade in larceny
and violence, justifying their actions as patriotic acts of resist-
ance against foreign occupation. Such grandiose talk cut little ice
with Bingham, who for some time had one of their number in
his cells:

> The Edelweiss Pirate, that's what he calls himself – this cheap
> little petty gangster, bully and thief. Sullen expression. Black
> trousers, broad leather belt, dirty jacket, tie-less, dirty shirt. Aged
> about twenty, perhaps less. He goes about in a gang, never alone
> – the Edelweiss Piraten. They allege that they 'carry on the fight
> against the Occupation'. How? They steal luggage, they steal
> spare wheels, they steal cars, they steal anything they can lay their
> hands on. For the Glory of the Fatherland? No, to sell on the
> black market.

A more complex problem was the growing number of refugees
straggling into north-west Germany. The routine work of sifting genuinely displaced persons and identifying Soviet 'plants'
dragged on, apparently without end. Close to the site of the
Bergen-Belsen concentration camp, which horrified John and
Madeleine, were the former SS barracks. Nearly 3,000 refugees
were shoehorned into the barracks and a makeshift camp nearby.
Conditions were appalling, disease was rife; an air of resignation
overcame the inmates. Survival was a daily challenge. The black
market flourished.

Periodic raids were conducted on the camps, ostensibly to net
black-marketeers and Soviet sleepers; realistically, as a show of
strength and a deterrent. Relationships had changed: the Soviet
ally was fast becoming the Soviet threat. Despite the official

refusal to recognise Soviet intentions, Bingham remained ever alert to the looming schism between east and west.

The Control Commission officers had to tread a delicate but precise line in cases where the bona fides of refugees from *drüben* – from over there – was in doubt. The true cause of a refugee's displacement might be hidden or magnified by the refugee himself. Was this refugee as passionate an anti-communist as he claimed? Was he really from Poland or was he a minor East Prussian war criminal? Or simply a Soviet plant? What would happen to him if he were returned to the Soviet zone?

The last question assumed increasing importance as the Russians demanded – and their British allies accordingly decreed – that all Russian prisoners of war be returned to the Red Army. On the surface such a demand was not unreasonable; in fact, the returned soldiers were treated brutally at the hands of the Red Army and, in most cases, were shipped to labour camps or summarily shot. Soviet officials were concerned that such returning soldiers might have seen something of life in the west and contradict the official propaganda that pictured westerners as living as slaves in an exploitative, plutocratic world. How could the occupying officers reconcile the general order with the knowledge that they were shipping loyal Russians home to probable execution? Many officers felt obliged to exercise a certain discretion in discharging the order. On one occasion Bingham found himself interrogating a Russian named Florentski.

Florentski sat in the cell and smiled. A typical simple high-cheekboned Russian with light brown hair and grey eyes, Florentski was captured by the Germans and put to work with other prisoners. When the Germans fell back through Czechoslovakia he had escaped. He was happy because the Czechs had said that Russian ex-prisoners of war would not be forced to return to Russia and he did not want to go back. He was an officer, he said; the war had interrupted his law studies, so he had registered with the Czech police. But one day a new rule was published: Russian POWs would be returned to Russia. Florentski fled to the US zone, then to the British zone. In Hannover he simply went to the town hall and told the truth, asking with childlike simplicity for papers and ration cards. He would like to live and work here, he said naively to the authorities.

So the authorities arrested him. And there he was in my cells.

And there was I opposite him. And at the back of my mind ran a zonal directive:

All Russian subjects who were members of the Russian Armed Forces on or after June 22, 1941 and who have not been officially discharged, will be handed to the appropriate authorities for repatriation.

'What happens to prisoners of war who are repatriated?'

'Very bad treatment,' smiled Florentski in his atrocious German. 'Not good. Russian who surrenders is traitor. Sent away for many years. Also his family very badly treated. Not good.'

'Those are ordinary prisoners who have returned voluntarily in the ordinary way. But what about you?'

'Not good.' Florentski almost laughed. 'I get shot. Russians know about me from papers I filed in Czechoslovakia. They know I not want to return. Maybe sister and brother get bad punishment too.'

'What do you want to do? What are your plans?'

Florentski gave another of his great smiles and shrugged his shoulders.

'You know you should be returned to Russia?'

The light faded from his eyes. His smile died. He leaned forward. 'You shoot me, yes? You shoot me! Not send me back. My brother and sister, they suffer bad. Not good.'

Bingham exercised discretion and in this, as in many other cases, calmly took it on himself to disobey the order. Florentski was released and allowed to disappear into the greyness of the devastated streets.

Beneath the office in Gehrden were the holding pens in which individuals earmarked for special interrogation were held. These cells were far from comfortable but they were the height of luxury compared with conditions in the DP camps. One such individual, summarily arrested as a possible subversive, was the Ukrainian Nowosilski.

A great figure dressed in black and wearing a round black beret on a great moonlike, bald head rose from the bed in the cell. Nowosilski wanted to speak to an officer. He spoke. The words poured from him in a torrent. His hand was laid on his heart, his eyes rolled heavenwards. On and on he went, pouring out his heart; nothing could stop him.

'Tell me, just tell me, what is against me! What could I do against the English, the English who freed me? In Hamburg already I have been three weeks in prison, and why? Because I went to the DP camp to buy an accordion. I am a musician. I knew a man who had an accordion to sell. I wished to buy it, to earn food for my wife and child in the DP camp at Meerbeck. I go to Hamburg and other DPs say I have visited them with the Russian Repatriation Officer! I work for the Russians! I, whose father was a Kulak and was imprisoned by the NKVD. I who have a wife and little one in Meerbeck now! Surely my poor wife is being driven mad by all her hardships without me. But you English who freed me from the Germans, you will know that I could do nothing against you. You are my liberators.

I just went to Hamburg to buy an accordion for my poor wife

and child who must have food ... and I was arrested. Why was I arrested? Tell me of what I am guilty and I will say "Punish me. Shoot me." But you who freed me; you are my liberators ...'

Again, faced with the reality that to send Nowosilski back to Russia was to condemn him to death or imprisonment, his family to shame and obloquy, Bingham averted his eyes while the Ukrainian and his family quietly vanished into the flotsam of post-war displacement. Allied solidarity, the pretence that the peacetime aims of the western allies and the Soviet Union were congruent, was wearing thin. It was increasingly clear that the naive vision of Franklin Roosevelt for eastern Europe had not survived the surrender.

Bingham was soon convinced that Knight had spoken no less than the truth when he predicted a rapid breakdown in relations with the Soviet Union and argued for retention of experienced officers by MI5 to counter the threat from Soviet communism. But Knight had been a voice in the wilderness against the suspicions of the new Labour government in 1945. Clement Attlee saw the Security Service as a bastion of Rightist prejudice and, like FDR before him, was convinced that a working relationship could be established with Stalin.

The moral balancing act that officers had to perform was, on the face of it, simple, but in reality more complex. Fundamental human decency required that a life be saved where possible; yet even in the waning glow of the east–west alliance, apparently reasonable requests from Moscow could not simply be ignored. The primary task was to establish order in Germany in collaboration with the United States, the Soviet Union and France. But as stories reached the western zones of factories being dismantled in the Russian zone, of vast quantities of machinery being hauled eastwards into the Soviet Union, it was becoming clear that the Russian plans for Germany differed fundamentally from those of her allies.

There are many encounters recorded in Bingham's writings and jottings of those two years in northern Germany. They were defining years for him; he had operated a network of agents to counter Nazi influence in Britain. But now he was among the shattered remains of the Reich he had laboured to dismantle. Instead of triumph he felt sorrow; instead of gratification at the plight of German civilians he felt nothing save compassion. He became more philosophical about human suffering. His godson Geoffroy de Moncuit recalls that Bingham was deeply moved and impressed by the sight of destitute German families calmly stacking the bricks from their levelled houses by the side of the road, confident that they would soon rebuild them. The ability to be objective yet human, to feel empathy without demeaning that emotion with pity, stayed with him all his life. Only occasionally was he jolted back to the reality of the evil that he had fought to extirpate. One such experience came when he was confronted by 'The Girl':

She came to the Mess several times before we suspected anything. She was friendly with one of our officers, and seemed a pleasant good-mannered girl. Her husband, she said, was 'missing', and told us with becoming diffidence that he had been quite an important official in the Hitler Youth. On the Sunday night she had a few drinks – not too many, but enough to make her bold enough to speak her mind. Suddenly she said that she hoped the German people would suffer for years to come. Why? Because they had enjoyed the good times under Hitler and now they complained and betrayed those who had given them the good times. She herself, she blazed, had been a Nazi – she was not ashamed of that – and she would never, never run down the Nazi

system. She was German. She would remain what she was, and
the German people, she hoped, would go on suffering and suffering. She spoke with heat and venom. The concentration camps?
She replied, 'What about the Boer War?'

Hostages? The Americans had shot thirty men, an acquaintance had told her. Germany could not be reproached for
concentration camps or hostages. The Jewish persecution? Yes,
that had been a mistake. But for the Jewish persecution there
would have been no war.

Execution of listeners to the 'black' radio?

It served them right. It was a duty to execute anybody who
listened to or spread rumours. You could not reproach Germany
for that.

Back again to the Jews. The extermination camps?

'The Jewish question – I've already admitted it was a mistake.
It is an entirely different question.' You couldn't reproach
Germany; Germany had done no wrong. 'I am German and I
must defend my Fatherland.'

We argued a bit. One officer went to bed in disgust. We made
no impression. She continued to speak hysterically. All that we
said was lies; nobody was forced to join the Nazi party; every-
body had a good time; everything else was a lie. Lies! Lies! The
German people had to be held firmly by the ears. By a form
of militarism or strong government of some sort. There was no
room for a free democracy in Germany.

We still made no impression. The Hitler Jugend had done its
work too well in the adolescent years. She was past redemption.
A rubber stamp marked 'Nazi', through and through, like a piece
of Brighton rock.

An increasingly dark notion began to prey on Bingham. Prepared
to accept that the power of German indoctrination was a fact,

albeit temporary, that might endure a generation, he foresaw greater problems arising from a different kind of indoctrination. The Nazi Party had been in power since 1933. The Communist Party, by contrast, had been influencing young minds since 1917 and Roosevelt's romantic realism had envisaged a sharing of post-war power with the Soviet Union. Ostensibly, this vision was now an accomplished fact – but while Bingham and his colleagues attempted to change the forms of government, to install democracy in north-west Germany, in the eastern zone the Russians pursued the arguably simpler goal of substituting one totalitarian doctrine for another. It was no less than hypocrisy or sheer simple-mindedness, he believed, to pretend that the aims of the western and eastern allies were congruent. Even if one subscribed wholeheartedly to such a notion, events were vindicating the more cynical view. With increasing frequency there were 'incidents' that indicated that the Soviet Union would proceed unilaterally in its sphere of influence.

Moreover, during 1947, evidence accumulated that the Soviet Union fully realised the value of its trump card, the location of Berlin, and it seemed daily more likely that the USSR would never relinquish any part of eastern Germany conquered by the Red Army. Berlin, though divided into four Allied sectors, lay squarely in the Russian zone. It required little imagination to see that Stalin would be strongly attracted by the prospect of annexing all the capital to the Russian zone without a shot being fired.

During 1946, Moscow had protested at the arrangements for distribution of coal and fuel in Germany, denouncing with mounting acrimony the British and the Americans for collaborating to the detriment of Soviet interests. On 1 January 1947 Britain and the United States combined their areas of control to create the 'Bizone', once more in the teeth of furious Russian objections. The schism between east and west was potentially permanent;

Germany would almost certainly be formally divided into two countries and the western allies began to prepare accordingly.

Preparation took place at two levels: political and tactical. While plans were formed to create a separate state of West Germany, at a tactical level it was important to ensure that Russian agents be denied access to the 'Bizone'. The frequency and intensity of raids on DP camps, ostensibly to catch black-marketeers, in truth to net as many Soviet sympathisers as possible, were stepped up. The west, too, was showing some muscle.

Towards the end of Bingham's assignment in Germany he conducted one such raid, and later wrote a moving account of the squalor of the camp and the misery of its inhabitants. In his unpublished writing, however, there is a resigned recognition that it was an essentially pointless exercise that produced no tangible result beyond further humiliation of the inmates. He clearly expected no arrests from the raid – and none was obtained. The interned DPs were harassed solely to demonstrate to the Soviet Union the determination of the western allies to secure the borders of 'western' Germany. The cynical inhumanity of such *Realpolitik* revolted Bingham.

By the end of 1947, few British intelligence officers had any illusions about the imminent breakdown of harmony between east and west. In many ways, the tacit acceptance of two Germanys was a welcome compromise. Strategic planning in the nuclear age now began to recognise the need for a rearmed Germany as a bulwark against Soviet expansion and thus the creation of the Federal Republic of Germany was central to western security. Events now moved rapidly in that direction.

The Soviet Union, distrustful and deeply suspicious of American aims, especially since Harry Truman had succeeded Roosevelt and declared the Truman Doctrine of containment on 12 March 1947, actively sought an 'incident' that could be invoked to justify the ending of Allied cooperation. Once Moscow was satisfied that the United States and Great Britain were planning to create the Federal Republic, the Russian representative on the Control Commission, Marshal Vasily Sokolovsky, protested vigorously. At a meeting of the four-power Council on 20 March 1948, he proclaimed the Soviet line that, if the western allies intended to act unilaterally – in defiance of the 1945 agreement to establish the Council – it was clear that they had no intention of cooperating with the Soviet Union. In that case, there was no purpose in maintaining the Council, as its very existence was being undermined by the actions of the war-mongering western allies. The peace-loving Soviet Union had no option but to withdraw. So saying, he walked out of the meeting and never returned.

That sealed the official fate of the Commission. While it continued to function in a limited fashion, further positive cooperation between the wartime allies was ruled out, and the schism between east and west was revealed. Future cooperation was restricted to administration of the jail at Spandau. Bingham recognised that his time in Gehrden was fast coming to an end as the British operation was systematically dismantled.

There remained one final act to the drama and the stage was, of course, Berlin. In March 1948 Stalin ordered that western traffic along the 100-mile corridors between the western zones and Berlin be 'regulated'. This 'regulation' led to a stepping-up of harassment for all road and rail transport between Berlin and the western zones, as Stalin was confident that it would be impossible for the allies to replace road and rail transport by air. By barring access to Berlin through the Soviet zone, Stalin aimed to control all essential deliveries to the city and achieve effective control over the lives of all the inhabitants in the four zones. This *démarche*, coming on the heels of the Czech coup of February

1948, was a clear indication of the Soviet aim to control all Europe east of the Elbe and to install communist governments under the spurious claim of the need for 'security' in eastern Europe. Molotov's dictum that 'he who controls Berlin controls Germany; he who controls Germany controls Europe' seemed lamentably apposite.

The British and Americans were confident that the western powers, through the establishment of the Federal Republic of Germany and the introduction of a strong currency to replace the discredited Reichsmark, would increase their control of the capital, and on 18 June they announced the introduction of the new Deutschmark. In response, the Soviet Union on 24 June blockaded all traffic by road and rail to the divided city. Additional harassment in the form of cuts in electricity supply and inter-zone transit in Berlin increased the insularity of the three zones in Berlin controlled by the western powers. At the same time Stalin announced his intention to introduce a new currency, the Ostmark, to the Soviet zone.

After preliminary skirmishes, each raising the level of threat to residents of the western zones of the city, the Soviet Union had at a stroke isolated Berlin, now accessible only by the three agreed air corridors to the city. Confident of the Red Army's massive numerical superiority in conventional forces, Stalin gambled that the two options open to the United States were capitulation and evacuation of the capital or the use of nuclear force to pressure the Soviet Union to back down. While he was confident that President Truman would shrink from the latter option, the world was less certain. The first crisis of the Cold War seemed likely to be the last.

General Lucius Clay, the military governor of the American zone, was adamant that the United States should not back down and remained convinced that Stalin was bluffing. He investigated the possibility of supplying all the city's needs by air. Since the maintenance of a western presence was a matter of huge prestige for the United States, it was, he argued to Eisenhower, essential that pressure should be answered with pressure. A nuclear first strike was indefensible; the only option was a massive airlift of food and essential supplies into West Berlin. Residents in the western zones of the city had adequate supplies for approximately six weeks. There was no time for delay; daily delivery of approximately 5,000 tons of supplies was needed, and the USA and Great Britain between them had, in the early days, enough aircraft to deliver fewer than 1,000 tons a day. Immediate action was required both to increase reserves in the city and to bring a vast fleet of transport aircraft to European airfields.

In the last week of June the airlift began. Neither Clay nor Ernst Reuter, the mayor of West Berlin, were confident it would succeed. Clay demanded that Reuter frankly inform Berliners of the risk and request them to make sacrifices, to tolerate a measure of inconvenience. The alternative, he stressed, was an unacceptable option; the airlift simply had to work.

After initial difficulties – the crash of three aircraft at Tempelhof airfield, the 'buzzing' of transport aircraft by Soviet fighters, slow turnaround of planes and crews – the airlift developed into a miracle of logistics. For just over a year the supply line operated, supplying all the city's needs in an unprecedented and brilliantly executed operation. The Soviet Union lost enormous face; American prestige was boosted; above all, nuclear war was averted. For the future, however, the likelihood of constructive cooperation was remote.

Between the Tehran Conference involving Roosevelt, Churchill and Stalin in December 1943 and the foundation of the German Democratic Republic in 1949, the balance of power had shifted dramatically, and with it had evaporated the prospect of collaboration, of Roosevelt's idealistic notion of the 'Four Policemen' that would safeguard world peace. The Soviet Union had manifestly replaced Germany as Great Britain's principal adversary.

From a different perspective, in the three years since VE Day the United States had reduced its military presence in Berlin to a scant 9,000 men, a token force inadequate to enforce the Truman Doctrine of containment. Great Britain had been reduced to near-bankruptcy by 1945 and was dependent to an unprecedented degree on an American military presence. As for the rest of western Europe, there was grave uncertainty for the future. Unknown to British and American intelligence, Klaus Fuchs had for five years been supplying the Soviet Union with details of the Manhattan Project, and the testing of the first Soviet nuclear bomb was a year away.

The final twists in the story lay months after Bingham's return to London in June 1948. He had spent five years in counter-subversion while the enemy was clear and present; he had spent a further two years as an active observer while a different, vastly broader and more insidious threat developed. By the time of his departure from Germany he had few illusions about the fragile nature of the security of western Europe. Nor did many of his former colleagues in the Security Service.

Yet the country he returned to had studiously ignored the reality of the widening schism between east and west. A Labour government, bent on creating a more egalitarian post-war Britain, deeply suspicious of the motives of MI5, contemptuous of the nostrums of Churchill and his generation, had at first adopted a policy of collaboration with the Soviet Union and the continued suppression of German industry. Only in 1947 did Clement Attlee and Foreign Secretary Ernest Bevin accept the need to endorse the European Recovery Plan (the Marshall Plan) and rebuild Germany's production.

By the time of the NATO agreement in April 1949, Anglo-Soviet relations were more guarded, but anti-German feeling remained strong. General Hastings 'Pug' Ismay, the first Secretary General of NATO, put the situation pithily when he declared NATO's aim was 'to keep the Russians out, the Americans in, and the Germans down'. Bingham had spent two years in post-war Germany and had reached the conclusion that a rebuilt, de-Nazified Germany was crucial to the security of western Europe. Lord Ismay's proclamation must have reeked of the vengeful resentment that he had compelled himself to avoid as he surveyed the destruction of Hanover.

Powerless to affect the direction of the Security Service, feeling himself to be a pre-war relic in a changing post-war world, cynical about the motives of the two 'Superpowers', he returned to a war-damaged Britain. His last civilian job – as picture editor of the *Sunday Dispatch* – had bored him; his previous position – writing frivolous and superficial stories for a readership bent on ignoring reality – was no more palatable. His son Simon was almost eleven, now away at prep school; his daughter Charlotte reached her sixth birthday as he returned. There were four mouths to feed and only the vague offer of a job in Fleet Street; it seemed very possible that a destructive war in Europe would break out at any moment and that he would be unable to contribute anything towards the outcome.

He had subscribed to great ideals and had manoeuvred skilfully to join the Security Service at the outbreak of war. He had served with distinction only to be discarded when the war was won. He had dedicated himself for two years to ensuring that his country's former enemy join the west European family of democracies. Now those efforts seemed destined to be undone. It would not be surprising if, with candid objectivity, he equated his contribution to that of his father. Maurice's military career had begun with dash and brio at Colenso, only to taper to an undistinguished close. And the stakes in 1948 were infinitely greater than those of thirty years before.

It was with the gravest apprehension, then, that John Bingham, infinitely sadder and wiser than the idealistic young man of 1940, returned to Fleet Street.

CHAPTER 6

JOURNALIST, 1948–50

The first vivid memory writer Charlotte Bingham has of her father John, the 7th Baron Clanmorris, was when she was six years old. He walked into the nursery and stood there looking down at her. 'I thought: "Who is this man?",' she recalls. 'I didn't really have any recollection of my father until then. He asked me: "Can you read, can you write?" and I said "Yes" to both questions, and then he said: "Well, I'll see you later." And that was it.'
Interview with Charlotte Bingham, *Daily Mail*, 13 March 2001

It was ten years since John Bingham had lived as a civilian in a country at peace and, now returning to civilian life, he found that much had changed. The advent of a Labour government with a full agenda for socialising Britain had altered the role of his family within society; those changes had brought about its share of upheaval for the Binghams.

When Bangor Castle was sold – a transaction completed under the worst conditions, at the worst possible time, and with the least lucrative result – his parents had decamped to a small hotel in Hove, 'while they looked around'. Living in genteel decay on the south coast, they belonged to a long-discarded generation. Maurice was approaching seventy; he and Leila, *nouveaux pauvres*, were unable to consider living in their own home without the help of a brace of servants. As guests came and went in the hotel, successively bemoaning the cost of domestic help since the war, the prospects of acquiring those servants became increasingly faint. In a piece written soon after his return from Germany, John Bingham traced the changing fortunes of the castle and its extended family, the role reversal of his father and the odd-job man:

Castle and Haven

Punctiliously every three months old Tom the handyman, who has never heard of class warfare, sends a letter off somewhat as follows

'My Lord,

Thank you very much for the money, received safe and sound. I am in good health, and I trust you and her ladyship are, too.

The Council has not made up their minds yet what to do with the Castle. Mr McMahon and others send their kind regards, to which I add my own.

Yours respectfully / Thomas Beecham'

He writes in his room in the basement of the castle, surrounded by such things as an illuminated scroll from the local Orange Lodge, a coloured picture of the King, cut from some magazine, and two or three old photographs now going rather yellow. Sometimes he smiles slightly when he begins the letter. So does the 6th Baron when he receives it in England. Both are mildly amused for the same reason.

Before the First World War, there was always a massive joint of meat for the midday dinner in the servants' hall, and a barrel of beer, and a fair amount of larking and junketing one way and another among the staff, but except for Tom there is nobody left in the whole place now. The stable yard has small weeds between the cobblestones, but the grounds are kept in fairly good condition by the Council, since the place has recently been made into a public park. The lovely lawns and the flowerbeds around the building itself are especially well tended, for they are more or less within the personal province of old Tom.

There were nine children in the house when Queen Victoria's reign was drawing to a close. Tom used to trundle the boys' luggage down to the station at the beginning of the school terms, and back again at the beginning of the holidays. At that period, there was a little private pack of beagles in the kennels, which provided good sport, though they were never known to catch a hare.

Tom trundled their luggage down when two of the oldest boys left to fight the Boers, and also, fifteen years later, when the Kaiser let loose the war which closed an era; the kennels were by then being used for pig-keeping. He made other journeys in 1939, but that was rather an unlucky war for the family, and there was only one lot of luggage to be fetched from the station when it was over.

By then the kennels were being used to house firewood and logs. Now they are empty, as the rest of the castle is empty. Since the day, a year ago, when he trundled the last trunk of the 6th Baron down to the station for the last time.

The Council, having bought the castle, cannot make their minds up whether to turn it into a hospital, a town hall, or a technical college, but they have taken over the services of old Tom.

So one way and another, he is not doing too badly. He has his wages from the Council, his old-age pension, and a small pension from the family.

And his rent-free room in the basement.

No wonder old Tom, who carried coals and water for the Victorian hip baths, and cleaned the boots, and mowed the lawns, and did a hundred and one other humble jobs – no wonder he sometimes smiles slightly when he begins his quarterly letter, and no wonder the 6th Baron also smiles. For the old handyman rightly gives the castle as his private address in letters – he is the only one from all that cavalcade of past splendour who is entitled to do so – whereas the 6th Baron, living modestly on the South Coast, must head his letters 'The Haven' when writing to, say, old Tom.

Both men are philosophers, and though they smile, there is no malice in their hearts.

This engaging nostalgic writing embraced, perhaps, more than the 6th Baron's changed fortunes. Bingham had written in 1934 that 'my handicap is my title'. Now, as the time for him to inherit that title seemed less distant, he re-entered Northcliffe House, the headquarters of Lord Rothermere's newspapers, to rejoin the editorial staff of the *Sunday Dispatch*. It was not something he would have chosen.

Charles Eade, the editor of the *Dispatch*, had served as public relations adviser to Admiral Lord Louis Mountbatten and edited Winston Churchill's speeches for publication. When the war ended he continued to edit the *Dispatch* for a further eleven years. John Bingham rejoined the team as a roving writer and aide-de-camp to Eade. 'He had no specific job,' recorded Madeleine. 'He wrote leading articles and feature articles. He was known to have the ear of the editor. He even occasionally acted as theatre critic.' In that capacity he was predictably down-to-earth when he wrote for the benefit of his readers: 'During the weeks I shall be visiting the films and theatres (on your behalf) I shall view them from the standpoint of the normal cinema- and theatre-goer, and pander but little to the intellectual fuzzy-wuzzies and super-sensitive aesthetes.'

The dismissal of 'fuzzy-wuzzies and super-sensitive aesthetes' was classic Bingham writing, reminding the reader of 'The New Snobbery', a piece of verse that he had written for *Punch* on 9 February 1938:

If someone says 'Come to the pictures,'
I've learned to reply with a sneer:
'American movies or English
Are really too vulgar, my dear.

Your gangsters and lovers and beauties
Are senseless – you see that, I trust?
One must see Intelligent pictures;
One must be recherché, one must.

So come to a decent film, darling,
In Russian or Polish or Erse,
Expressing some Meaning profound, dear,
In dialogue throaty and terse –

A film which is fearfully subtle,
Exuding an aura of Doom,
Maintaining from first shot to last shot
An excellent standard of gloom.

We'll feel that there is a plot somewhere,
Appealing to brain and to heart,
And if we can't really perceive it,
At least we'll be sure it is Art,

And worthy of mention at parties
As a show that was 'perfectly grand' –
For if we feel Leftish and Kultured,
Who cares if we don't understand?

Soon after his return, the remarkable production of *Hamlet*, in
which Laurence Olivier directed his own performance in the

title role, was released. It was a controversial film, as Olivier had severely shortened the original, cutting, for example, the characters Rosencrantz and Guildenstern. Purists were shocked; other critics applauded Olivier's version.

Bingham, at heart a traditionalist, might have been expected to disapprove of a film so radically altered from Shakespeare's original. Instead he was most enthusiastic and wrote an ecstatic review. He had a single criticism concerning Hamlet's father's ghost: 'Its voice through no fault of the actor has such an indistinct, metallic, sepulchral tone that if you don't already know what it says to Hamlet, spend five minutes reading it up.'

He became, effectively, the editor's right-hand man, exercising that steady presence that flamboyant editors like, and Eade allowed him to range over a number of subjects. A fortnight after his return from Germany, on 11 July 1948, he wrote a veritable broadside attack on the Labour government's Minister of Health, Nye Bevan. The minister had made an extraordinarily offensive comment, condemning the 8,683,858 voters who had voted Conservative, alluding to them as 'lower than vermin' and attacking the non-socialist press in Britain as 'the most prostituted in the world'. Bingham, conservative by nature, was offended not by the cut and thrust of party politics but by the venom and extremism that ill fitted the role of a government minister.

The article, 'The Man Who Hates 8,683,858 People', traced Bevan's career from his first entry into trades union politics, exposing his U-turns, his duplicity and, for good measure, his breaches of parliamentary etiquette. It was a well-crafted and devastating article that reflected not a Tory disposition but rather Bingham's visceral loathing of the extremism under the cloak of Leftist ideology.

The result of the 1945 general election was a surprise only to the most ostrich-like of British voters. Winston Churchill, the very spirit of Britain during the war, was seventy when the war ended, a symbol of an age long past. Much as the First World War had swept the older generation from the stage, the end of the Second World War represented the dawning of a new era in Britain. The Conservative Party had been hustled from power; Labour leaders had long been preparing for this moment and relished the prospect of moving the country to the Left. The wartime Cabinet had included several Labour ministers, but they had hardly been firebrands: Clement Attlee had served as Deputy Prime Minister and Sir Stafford Cripps as Lord Privy Seal and Leader of the House of Commons. By 1948 these two were Prime Minister and Chancellor of the Exchequer. Beyond members of the wartime Cabinet, however, few of the Labour leaders in 1945 had any experience of office; the Conservative Party had held power since 1935.

This inexperience, linked with an inclination to the far Left and too great a sympathy with Moscow, appeared to Bingham to be a formula for catastrophe. The apparent hypocrisy of politicians whom he considered crypto-communists, toying with the principal institutions of British democracy, stirred him to this spirited attack. Legitimate political debate, he felt, was one thing. Bevan, however, disrespectful of the monarchy, scornful of Parliament, embodied all that disgusted him about communism: its intolerance of opposing views, its divisive class hatred. It is no surprise that he wrote his damning article; more remarkable is that the *Sunday Dispatch* printed it.

Six weeks later, on 22 August, there was another opportunity to vent his concerns about left-wing subversion. Under the headline 'General Markos a Failure: Communism Lost a War Yesterday', he brought to bear his knowledge of the communist threat to western Europe. He had seen how the Soviet Union operated in Germany and, clearly, had been watching the activities of ELAS, the Greek People's Liberation Army, with increasing concern.

When the ELAS leader, General Markos, suffered a defeat in the Grammos Mountains, Bingham was exultant. Moscow, he wrote, had fomented guerrilla warfare within Greece, supporting radical groups that stopped short of calling themselves communists, but which were dedicated to the overthrow of democracy in Greece. After the British experience in Yugoslavia, where, despite Tito's growing discontent at Soviet intervention, a communist government was sponsoring 'incidents' with the western allies, there was increasing concern that Greece would fall under the control of Moscow. With the defeat of Markos, Moscow's supposed plan to establish a Republic of Greater Macedonia, including parts of Greece, Yugoslavia and Bulgaria, had been thwarted.

Greece could now return to a peaceful phase of rebuilding without Soviet interference. 'Peace', Bingham wrote, 'may once more come amongst her olive trees.' After five years of German occupation, the Greek government had dealt with the longer-term threat from Moscow. For Bingham this was a sweet victory in a period when Soviet expansionism was setting in train events that led to the Cold War.

The article reflected the author's hatred of communism, condemning its duplicity, lack of loyalty, its opportunism. At his private face-to-face meeting with Marshal Stalin in 1944, Churchill had produced what he termed his 'naughty' document, detailing his proposed spheres of influence after Germany's defeat. He realistically asked for little or no influence in the countries of eastern Europe but he suggested – and Stalin agreed to – considerable British influence in the affairs of Greece. The Kremlin's betrayal of that secret agreement, had Bingham known of it, would only have increased his antipathy to Russian actions in the Balkans.

Such periodic broadsides against the communist threat were interspersed with the many daily tasks and weekly responsibilities that he undertook for the *Dispatch*. Another *bête noire* for him was the inchoate 'nanny state' that made its first appearance under Labour in the late 1940s. As ever, choosing his moment and his weapons carefully, he launched an attack on pettifogging bureaucracy on 20 November 1949. By then, as Labour's reduced majority in the 1950 general election made clear, there was widespread resentment of the manner in which the Labour government, admittedly with the best intentions, had interfered with many aspects of day-to-day life that Britons considered sacrosanct. Bingham was not prepared even to concede that their intentions were good.

He chose as his *casus belli* the recent conviction of one Mr Primmer, a blind man, for selling newspapers in the street. The amount of the fine imposed was small – ten shillings, fifty pence in modern currency – and scarcely a case of imposing punitive damages on the unfortunate Mr Primmer. But this was not the issue that infuriated most. He objected to the court's action on several levels.

John Bingham believed fundamentally that humans have a responsibility to look after themselves if they are able and that the 'nanny state' encourages dependence on the system. The encroachment of the state on the individual's duty to take responsibility for himself or herself was anathema to him. In common with many people who had 'been through' the war, he felt that post-war attitudes failed to emphasise the responsibilities of individuals to society. Society itself had become unduly permissive in some areas and absurdly authoritarian in others.

Moreover, the enforcement of legislation without the exercise of common sense, 'at the taxpayers' expense', would have struck him as offensive.

Ultimately, however, he was uncomfortable merely complaining about the erosion of what he considered fundamental rights and obligations of the citizen in the post-war world. He had spent seven years protecting those rights, defending what he considered to be an enlightened democracy from overbearing authority, and he found the peripheral role of journalism – able to criticise but unable to rectify abuses of that democracy – essentially unsatisfying, the role of a spectator rather than of a player. The role began to irk him deeply.

Another source of frustration for John and Madeleine was more personal: they were struggling financially. There was a modest income from the family trust and, for the moment at least, he was earning a fair salary from the *Sunday Dispatch*. He remembered keenly, however, the years that he had worked there before the war and watched seven editors succeed each other. With each successive editor came sackings, as a 'new broom' was brandished about the office. There was, moreover, a gnawing concern that the newspaper itself might go under – as it eventually did ten years later – and that John, just past that magic barrier of forty, would be out of a job. Without being extravagant, they struggled to make ends meet: school fees for Simon and Charlotte and rent on their flat in Kensington ate away at their income, leaving little for luxuries. In 1949 they were able to afford a family holiday at Saint-Briac in Brittany, but this was far from being a regular event.

Another of his responsibilities at the *Sunday Dispatch* was to act as serials editor. Charles Eade had adopted the serial *Forever Amber* and he charged Bingham with the job of finding other suitable 'bosom and belle' stories that could be serialised for his female readers. To follow *Forever Amber* he chose *Our Dearest Emma*, a romantic work about the relationship between Lord Nelson and Lady Hamilton. The enormous success of that story was on his mind when, over a drink at the Press Club, a colleague commented, 'I'm surprised that Charles hasn't thought of serialising a book about Byron.'

This casual comment gave him pause for thought and, knowing that Byron was a highly suitable subject and that Madeleine knew a great deal about him, he suggested to Madeleine that she undertake the task. At first she protested, 'I couldn't write that historical mush.' Contemplation of their overdraft, however, changed her mind, as serials were netting a cool £100 a week for the writer.

> I began to write the book more or less as a joke [Madeleine wrote later]. It started with a rising storm, great elms swaying in the fury of the wind, and flashes of lightning illuminating the flimsy white gauze of a young girl's dress which clung to her frail form, drenched with the flooding rain. Everything, it will be noted, except a father with a horsewhip.
>
> I wrote 90,000 words and called it *Guilty Splendour*. Charles would have none of that title; he wanted something more catchy. It was dubbed *The Passionate Poet* and embellished with illustrations of girls, girls, girls – and Byron – usually with a canopied bed in the background.

On one matter, however, Madeleine was unmovable: she would not write this 'historical mush' under her own name. In her youth she had been a passionate reader of Sir Walter Scott and she subconsciously chose the name of a Scott character for her *nom de plume*: Julia Mannering, the colonel's daughter in Scott's *Guy Mannering*.

She was soon relieved to have written the story under a pseudonym as the serial was heavily advertised by the *Dispatch*. As she passed huge advertising posters in the Underground she averted her eyes, half expecting a limping, reproachful Byron to be at her heels. On one occasion the novelist Ursula Bloom telephoned to ask John's opinion of her latest novel, *Our Dearest Emma*, which she had written under the name of Lozania Prole, one of her five pseudonyms. Learning that he was not there, she commented to Madeleine that the *Sunday Dispatch* was publishing 'that rubbish about Byron'. Madeleine managed to keep a straight face and agree with her that it was an unfortunate choice of serial.

Encouraged by the reception of *The Passionate Poet*, which was also published as a book, bringing in some more much-needed money, Madeleine wrote a number of other 'bodice rippers' which were serialised in *Woman* magazine. She was justifiably proud when *Woman* paid her £500 for *The Dark Avenue*, a romantic story set in England and France.

Madeleine describes those two years as 'living from overdraft to serial', but there were enough profitable serials to help deal with the next upheaval in their lives. In the early summer of 1950, Bingham had lunch with Maxwell Knight, who, to the detriment of his career, was still complaining to any MI5 officer who would listen that the Security Service was paying too little attention to the communist threat. He knew that Bingham shared his pessimism about Moscow's long-term plans and he invited him to return to 'The Office'. The invitation was both welcome and timely. It was galling to be unable to affect events from a newspaper desk; Bingham wanted to be doing rather than reporting. Moreover, he felt strongly that journalism was a profession for enthusiastic young men and that one was over the hill as a journalist at the age of forty. Since he had recently passed that milestone, Knight's offer was all the more attractive. He asked for time to think about it and returned to Weybridge, where he and Madeleine had rented a house, to talk it over.

The house that they had rented belonged to the financial

editor of the *Sunday Dispatch* and, as Madeleine later recalled, several rooms and the garage were stuffed full with industrial quantities of every kind of alcohol. The drawing room of the house looked like the saloon bar of a pub; so pub-like was it that, despite the landlord's assurance that they could help themselves to as much as they wanted, they felt unable to take a relaxed drink in the house.

On that evening, however, a stiff gin and tonic was called for while they discussed Knight's offer. Madeleine knew immediately that John wanted to accept: he believed that his work in intelligence had been worthwhile and that the Service had been short sighted in its dramatic reduction of staff in 1945. He felt adrift in Fleet Street; this was a chance for him to confront the mounting Soviet threat. Decryptions from the VENONA project, which Britain and the United States had run in tandem since 1943, indicated that Moscow had penetrated American and British nuclear security and stimulated a growing certainty that a Soviet agent codenamed HOMER (later revealed to be Donald Maclean) was operating within the British embassy in Washington. In short, Knight's predictions were proving true and he needed experienced agent runners in Section F4, as Section B5(b) had become in the post-war reorganisation of MI5.

Knight's intentions were twofold. First, and most importantly, he wanted 'that silly boy Jack', as he frequently referred to him, back on his staff. He knew 'from experience' (another of his favourite phrases) that Bingham had the skill of listening – the principal qualification for an agent runner. He was certain that counter-subversion against the Soviet target would require more agents and more agent runners in the very near future. The publication in 1950 of Douglas Hyde's book *I Believed*, the revelations of a senior member of the British Communist Party, had caused a sensation and Knight believed that, at last, both

Whitehall and the general public would recognise the need for expanding his section.

Second, as he was spending an increasing amount of time pursuing his zoological interests, he was thinking seriously about retiring from the department. When that happened, he wanted Bingham to succeed him.

Bingham regarded the second consideration neutrally. Flattered by Knight's confidence, he was prepared to wait and see about promotion. Concerning the first issue, the reality of a growing Soviet threat, his thinking was totally congruent with that of Knight. He had seen at first hand the development of the Soviet influence in Europe; he had observed as a journalist the ratcheting of Soviet pressure in the Balkans, in Italy and at home in Britain. Like Knight, he regarded the ominous sabre rattling of the Cold War as the opening moves in a long and drawn-out struggle. To a patriot, there was effectively no choice. The job needed to be done and he was the man to do it; he had felt jettisoned from the Great Game during the last two years in Fleet Street. He realised that it would require financial sacrifice, not only because the government salary would be less than he was earning at Northcliffe House but also because he would not, with interrupted service, receive a full pension when he retired. But, provided Madeleine agreed, his mind was already made up. Madeleine understood her husband's sense of the futility of his current work; she had been aware of his growing frustration, his sense of being 'on the shelf' since returning from Germany. Her only scruples were financial ones, but fortunately the offer from Knight came on the heels of her profitable sale of serials. She intended to continue writing, and her husband was in the process of completing his first novel, *My Name Is Michael Sibley*.

When Jack came home that summer evening and they discussed Knight's offer, they walked down to the Thames and along the river bank for some minutes in silence. Finally Madeleine asked the simple question – was this what her husband truly wanted to do? The question was almost rhetorical; Bingham's body language answered her question. With some trepidation, but certain that she was right in supporting him, Madeleine gave her approval and 'that silly boy Jack' rejoined his mentor in the business of counter-subversion. This time, however, it was not The Right Club or the blackshirts that would claim his and Knight's attention. The Communist Party of Great Britain, together with the numerous extreme-Left-leaning organisations supported by Moscow, constituted a clear target. A month later, Bingham was back at a government-issue desk with the anonymous address of Box 650, Parliament BO, London SW1 or, for the initiated, Section F4 (Counter-Subversion) of the Security Service – MI5.

CHAPTER 7

RETURN TO MI5 AND DEBUT AS A NOVELIST, 1950-58

Though the Security Service never suspected [Harold] Wilson of being a secret crypto-Communist or fellow-traveller, it looked askance at some of the Communist connections he developed in the course of his Russian travels.
Christopher Andrew, *Defend the Realm: The Authorised History of MI5*

The Security Service that John Bingham rejoined in June 1950 had changed fundamentally from the Service he had left in 1945. Sir David Petrie had retired and been replaced by Sir Percy Sillitoe. The Labour Party was deeply suspicious of MI5, suspecting that the Security Service had been behind the publication of the Zinoviev Letter in 1924. This forged document purported to be a directive issued in Moscow, urging the stepping up of communist agitation in Britain, and had been instrumental in causing the Conservative landslide in the 1924 election. Accordingly, the Attlee government wanted a Director General of whom it approved at the top of the Service. They thought Sillitoe sound, an ex-chief constable who distrusted 'long-haired intellectuals' and 'Oxbridge types', but the new DG was less popular with professional intelligence officers who had worked at MI5 throughout the war and who were appalled at 'having a rozzer at the top'.

The global balance of power had shifted since 1945. The

United States had assumed the hegemony of the west and, when Klaus Fuchs was convicted of espionage in March 1950, Edgar Hoover, Director of the FBI, exasperated at British security breaches, demanded that an FBI agent interrogate Fuchs in London. Sillitoe initially resisted and the Service was soon divided between 'Atlanticists', who accepted American domination of the western alliance as inevitable, and officers who saw Washington as committed to dismantling British influence wherever possible.

The Korean War broke out in June 1950 and there were widespread fears that, since the Soviet Union had successfully exploded a nuclear bomb in 1949, the campaign might develop into the Third World War. The Attlee government, re-elected with a reduced majority in 1950, was committed to British participation in Korea. Foreign Secretary Ernest Bevin was a determined anti-communist and, with the passing of the British Empire, an advocate of American hegemony.

A handful of Bingham's wartime colleagues, including Knight and Himsworth, were still at their desks; Millicent Bagot, the first woman in MI5 to be promoted to officer rank, still dominated research against the communist threat with her encyclopaedic knowledge of Russian operatives. During the post-war decade she was the most important woman in MI5, later immortalised by John le Carré, who based his character Connie Sachs on her. So impressive was her knowledge of the Russian target that Edgar Hoover, although abidingly suspicious of British intelligence, conceded that she was in a class of her own.

In 1948 Attlee had announced to the House of Commons that, by means of a purge procedure, known fascists and communists would be excluded from work 'vital to the Security of the State'. MI5 redoubled its efforts to keep a current database of all Communist Party of Great Britain (CPGB) members and, increasingly

Denis Arthur Bingham, third Lord
Clanmorris of Newbrook (1808–1847).

John Bingham, first Lord Clanmorris of
Newbrook (1762–1821). Portrait by Sir
Henry Raeburn.

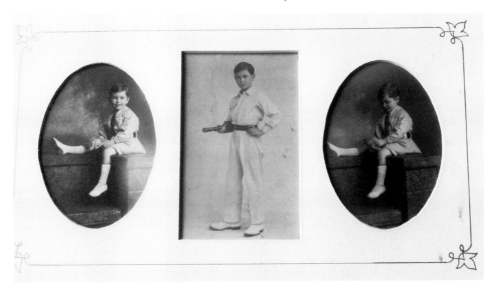

A triptych of the young John Bingham.

Château de la Matholière,
where John Bingham
stayed during 1927–28,
in disrepair today.

The Hon. John and Madeleine Bingham at their wedding, 28 July 1934.

Madeleine Bingham on her wedding day.

John and Madeleine attending the wedding of Madeleine's sister Suzanne, 1936.

Presentation at Court, July 1938: (l. to r.) Lady Clanmorris (Leila), Lord Clanmorris (Maurice), Madeleine, Renée France-Hayhurst, John Bingham.

The Hon. Simon Bingham in the uniform of the 13th/18th Royal Hussars, 1956.

The Hon. Charlotte Bingham and Terence Brady in the 1960s.

John Bingham
and his
goddaughter
Rosy Denaro at
Abingdon Villas.

A self-portrait of John Bingham.

important, to penetrate the Trades Union Congress (TUC) to maintain up-to-date records of communists in leading positions within the unions. By May 1949, Sillitoe felt able to tell Attlee that 'we now [have] quite a number of agents in the Communist Party who [are] well placed and [give] us good coverage'.

The CPGB had been unsuccessful in its bids for presence in the House of Commons, prompting a movement away from open membership of the party towards attempts to subvert the Labour Party from within. In combating this threat, the Security Service had the full support of the Labour Party leadership and the issue assumed centre stage when the Korean War erupted. Communist leaders of the trades unions attempted to disrupt engineering works and strike the docks to disrupt Britain's contribution to the war.

The efficiency of MI5 in covering the CPGB soon led to the dawning recognition by the party that it had been infiltrated. In the wake of this discovery, the upper echelons of the party became far more circumspect about the security of their data. While some valuable information could be obtained about the leaders of the party by telephone checks (Home Office warrants or 'HOWs'), the party kept its records in different places, conscious of the risk of penetration of its King Street headquarters. On Moscow's orders, the party strove to keep its membership lists safe from the prying eyes of the Security Service. Indeed, to maintain even greater security, Moscow encouraged the growth of organisations, notably trades unions, that had no overt link with the CPGB.

Norman Himsworth could report with confidence in January 1951:

The British Communist Party at the moment is led by a group of old men, unable, or unwilling, to pass on the responsibilities of office to younger and more energetic comrades. Never before, perhaps, in the history of the Party has the leadership been so poor, so incapable of carrying the masses with it, as it is today.

Himsworth's assessment was accurate as far as it went. At the time the General Secretary of the CPGB was Harry Pollitt, by then over sixty and in poor health. He remained a devoted Stalinist throughout his life, continuing in that devotion even after Khrushchev denounced Stalin's crimes in 1956. Many party members felt that he represented the past rather than the future.

Knight expressed to Bingham his conviction that the communist threat was a Hydra and that his first task was to assemble his own team of agents. Bingham was quick to adjust to his new role. As in 1940, the enemy was in plain view. His job was to discover its order of battle, to identify areas or organisations which would yield the most intelligence and to penetrate them.

Some agents were already in place, of course, but agents tend to be 'one-man dogs' and the recruitment of agents who owed Bingham their loyalty was his immediate task. Using another of Knight's principles – that among one's circle of friends there was at least one potential agent – he began to build his team.

Most tasks that he had performed for Knight during the war involved listening, a talent with which he was amply endowed. Another talent was vitally relevant: despite not being classically good-looking, having too wide a mouth and the accursed spectacles, he had a remarkable way with women and, believing them to be less conspicuous than men, he concentrated his recruitment efforts on women. All his surviving female friends comment on his magnetic sexuality but it is his son-in-law Terence Brady who describes his technique most bluntly:

Jack was extremely attractive to women. It's very odd how some men do it without doing a thing and Jack was one of them. I think it might have been because he was such a very good listener. He would listen so intently, usually without interruption, then he would take his glasses off, frown distantly, then turn those big eyes on the subject and game over.

From 1950 to 1979 Bingham worked two full-time jobs – at MI5 by day (and frequently by night when clandestine operations such as break-ins were required) and as a novelist in the evenings. On 27 April 1951 the first step towards his second career was taken by his literary agent, Peter Watt of A. P. Watt & Co., in a letter to the redoubtable Victor Gollancz, head of the publishing firm famous for its yellow-jacketed crime list. The letter neatly gives a brief summary of the book's plot and of the somewhat haphazard manner in which it was written.

Dear V. G.

I am sending you a first novel by John Bingham called 'MY NAME IS MICHAEL SIBLEY' which I have much enjoyed reading myself. It is a story of what could happen to an unheroic, indeed rather weak young man and a girl who is no stronger when they come up against the police in a murder investigation. Its great merit lies in the fact that the story could happen to quite ordinary people in real life.

Please disregard as far as you can the state of the manuscript. Mr. Bingham who is a journalist has typed it all at odd times and in odd corners and then as a result of some criticism of a friend of his he rewrote much of it without retyping it all. The impression that the book has been widely shown is an erroneous one.

Yours very sincerely.

Peter

The manuscript was read by the firm's chief reader. Jon Evans was a first-class literary analyst whose imprimatur carried great weight at the publishing house. A well-known figure, he was, like Victor Gollancz, a committed socialist as well as the author of *The New Nazi Order in Poland*, which the Left Book Club published in 1941. No less committed to Gollancz the man than he was to Gollancz the firm, he died peacefully at home in the 1980s with a manuscript on his lap.

Evans was impressed by the novel and, subject to a single alteration, was in favour of publishing it. His reader's report summarises the plot with great sensitivity:

> I cannot recollect ever having read a murder story told from this angle before – seen entirely through the eyes of an innocent man whose behaviour is making him appear more and more guilty. And even if it has been done before (and I suppose it probably has), it is done excellently here.

Bingham immediately made the change that Evans requested. He had, he wrote, been 'inclined to feel that a slightly sardonic enigmatic end might have more "bite" than the usual petering out into living happily ever after'. But, rewriting the last three pages, he commented that he would 'rely upon the decision of that very experienced firm ... as I am only a writer, not a touchy genius'.

Victor Gollancz himself, a complex but direct man, found the title too long and suggested a simpler blunter title. This discussion went to and fro within the firm and with the author. In the event, the original was retained and the machinery to publish *My Name Is Michael Sibley* ground into action.

The novel is compact and tightly written. The protagonist Michael Sibley is largely drawn from the author's early life: his time at Cheltenham, his early career as a journalist in Hull and his return to London. It opens with a sense of impending disaster worthy of a Greek tragedy. On a clear evening, the sort of evening when all seems well with the world, Michael Sibley is rejoicing in being alive when two policemen call on him to question him about his friendship with John Prosset, who was murdered over the previous weekend.

Sibley is innocent of the crime but, as the story progresses, the reader learns not only that he had held a consuming hatred for Prosset since schooldays, but also that he had considered killing him when Prosset seduced his fiancée, Kate Marsden.

Sibley is less than candid with the police, and at each subsequent interview, by varying degrees of equivocation or simple untruths – 'boxing and coxing' as the police inspector refers to it – he casts suspicion on himself and is eventually charged with the murder. Ultimately acquitted, he achieves 'emancipation' when, having changed his name, he becomes a worthy member of a community in the Cotswolds, chatting in the local pub with the village policeman.

Although not a thriller in the traditional sense – the murderer is never definitively identified – the book is thrilling. The reader is led through every stage of Sibley's equivocations and evasions, his weakness of character. Opposite Sibley is the relentless police inspector whose method of questioning, while undoubtedly realistic, shocked a British public who still believed that their 'bobbies' were affable and genial protectors of justice.

Michael Sibley was an immediate success, eliciting ecstatic reviews from many sources. In the *Manchester Evening News*, Julian Symons described the book as 'Really first-class. Extremely exciting. Mr Bingham, astonishingly, is able to maintain the point of tension reached early in the book right to the last pages.' Perhaps the most insightful review came from John Connell of the *Evening News*, who wrote:

Extremely exciting, with a quiet breathless grip on the reader's emotions and interests from the first page to the last. It has a deceptive simplicity of construction and an unassertive deftness in the manner in which the story unfolds which I found utterly admirable ... The suspense is the book's dominating quality.

Thus did John Bingham achieve the ambition that he had held since Cheltenham days: to publish a novel. It was a novel, moreover, that reflected his early life, as significant portions of the book are autobiographical. Wrestling with his own early lack of self-confidence, his own perceived inadequacies, he succeeded in crafting a straightforward yet subtly nuanced plot, adding what he called 'the fluffy stuff', and creating realistic characters in a threateningly real world.

During 1950 and 1951, efforts in MI6 and MI5 to discover the identity of HOMER intensified and by May 1951 the Security Service was determined that there was enough evidence against Donald Maclean for him to undergo hostile interrogation on 28 May. On 25 May, Maclean, together with fellow Soviet agent Guy Burgess, fled to France and ultimately to Moscow. Clearly they had been forewarned and the hunt began for the 'Third Man' who had alerted them. The ripple effect of the scandal permeated the Service.

Bingham was occupied with two tasks: building his team of agents and capitalising on the success of his novel with a second book. The recruitment of agents takes various forms and can be divided into two broad categories: agents already in place and penetration agents. Of these, the second is more reliable as the loyalty of the agent is, if not assured, less questionable than that of an agent recruited or 'turned' by virtue of the position that (s)he occupies. Within the category of penetration agents there are agents who are permanently dedicated to the mission and the 'occasionals', recruited for specific information-gathering tasks. While most of his penetration agents were female, the majority of the 'occasionals' were men, often businessmen, who made trips behind the Iron Curtain. All information that they brought back about the countries they visited was added to Bingham's database as he built up a picture both of communism in general and of specific conditions in different eastern European countries.

Journalists are particularly suited to the role of 'occasionals'. Trained to gather information effectively and accurately, accustomed to travel in the course of journalistic assignments, they perform a valuable role for both major branches of British intelligence. With his many Fleet Street contacts, Bingham had worked both sides of the street: after meeting Max Knight in 1939, he had reported to him on the activities of certain journalists at the *Sunday Dispatch* before he officially joined MI5; after rejoining, he resuscitated several journalists to perform specific jobs for him.

One businessman with connections behind the Iron Curtain was Louis Denaro, a family friend who had once dated Madeleine. In the 1950s, Louis was Assistant Managing Director of International Nickel ('Inco'), an Anglo-Canadian company that traded in nickel and other metals. At the time there was an embargo on sales of nickel to Iron Curtain countries from the USA and Britain, but Canada had a quota system in force and because Louis had a Swiss, rather than British, American or Canadian, passport, he was free to travel widely, attending trade fairs in Brno and Poznan. Maureen Johnston, Louis's secretary between 1957 and 1961, recalls the assignments that he performed:

> Louis would go from one country to another and write a report ... about the state of the country, who was asking what, how the

countries were being developed, just like marketing research, but obviously things that were of interest to Jack ... The reports that came back were what we would now call market research, but they were trying to find out what weapons were being developed, what the nickel would be used for. Louis was looking for things that would be of interest to the government here.

The information that Louis supplied was a plethora of different facts. Apart from intelligence regarding nickel and alloys that might be used for weaponry, he would report on the frequency of trams, on the cost of a bar of chocolate or a newspaper. No scrap of background information on an Iron Curtain country was unimportant.

Moreover, one thing led to another. Because Inco was on a quota system, there was frequently a surplus of metals that could not be sold to eastern buyers. A Czech entrepreneur named Emil Smidak reached an agreement with Louis to buy the surplus and made a considerable fortune. Smidak, too, became an agent, furnishing Bingham with information about Czech industry. Later, when Smidak applied for residence in Britain, Bingham became concerned that he might have recruited a double agent and had him thoroughly investigated before his residency permit was granted.

It was on women, however, that his network depended. Wartime experience had shown him that men tended to brag whereas women were better able to keep secrets. In 1952 he recruited his longest-running agent, whom he used to penetrate the communist threat for over two decades.

Elizabeth Mary Julia Pirie, known to her family as 'Elizabeth' but in her covert life as 'Julia', served in the Auxiliary Territorial Service, the women's branch of the British Army during the Second World War. She volunteered for a posting to France after D-Day and advanced into Germany with the 21st Army Group.

Returning to England, she worked with the Duchess of Atholl, chairman of the British League for European Freedom. This was an organisation that decried Soviet domination of eastern Europe, a fact which makes the next step in her career the more bizarre: she applied to work for the CPGB and became personal assistant to John Gollan, General Secretary of the party. From this vantage point she was able to feed back to MI5 valuable information concerning a wide variety of subjects: the layout of offices within the King Street headquarters, which rooms were used for which meetings, the general *modus operandi* of the party's headquarters and, most importantly, that there existed a printed list of all members, open and secret, of the CPGB.

Julia Pirie was a cool character. When she died in 2008 at the age of ninety, her obituary described her as 'a small, dumpy woman with the appearance of a confirmed and rather matronly spinster ... the most unlikely of spies' and continued 'but her unassuming demeanour masked a sharp intellect and the powers of observation essential for the task of a secret agent'. Throughout the quarter of a century that she worked to Bingham she would meet him at the Oval cricket ground, where she would pass information to him. A by-product of these meetings was that she developed a love of cricket that she retained until her death.

Victor Gollancz had been cautious and had commissioned a relatively small print run for an unknown author's first novel. To his surprised delight, the book went into its second printing, which also sold quickly. Bingham's association with Victor Gollancz and his staff became increasingly warm as he began work on his second book. Confident that he had another successful plot in his mind, he began crafting *Five Roundabouts to Heaven*, another novel written in the first person that provides a host of clues about his early life. By July 1952 the manuscript was in the hands of Gollancz and his staff.

He had received an advance of £100 for *Michael Sibley*; now this was increased to the princely amount of £150 for his second book. V.G.'s daughter Livia Gollancz, looking back on this generosity nearly sixty years later, reflected that this was most unusual as her father was notoriously parsimonious with his firm's money, preferring to lose an author than be over-munificent with advances. John Bingham was a rising star at the Henrietta Street offices.

V.G. himself made this clear in an encouraging letter after reading the manuscript. Once more, however, he was dissatisfied with the title – as were most of the Gollancz staff – but Bingham held firm. From Saint-Briac in Brittany, where the family was on holiday, he responded to Gollancz on 2 August 1952:

> It was very nice of you to bother to write and tell me that you liked 'Five Roundabouts to Heaven'. While I naturally hope that the public will endorse your views to our mutual profit, it is only fair to say that whatever happens to the book nothing can now take away from me the enormous pleasure and self-confidence given to me by the mere fact that a man of your experience has found it readable. This is the sort of thing that a writer remembers, or should remember, all his life.
>
> As to the title, I have lived so long with 'Five Roundabouts to Heaven' that I find it extremely difficult to begin, even, to think of another ... Before finally deciding on a change, however, you may care to consider the reasons why I chose it. They are as follows:
>
> 1. It bears some relationship to the plot.
> 2. It is so completely incomprehensible as to be, I had hoped, mildly intriguing.
> 3. It gives nothing away.
> 4. It is rather in the line of modern titles.
>
> I am quite prepared not only to bow, but to bow willingly,

to those with greater experience in these things; and I can well see that the title is somewhat clumsy from the point of view, for example, of single-column adverts etc.

Again, many thanks for your letter.

By October the book – under its original title of *Five Roundabouts to Heaven*, as V.G. had relented in his opposition – was ready for printing. Although less autobiographical than *Michael Sibley*, the book drew directly from personal experience and, like *Michael Sibley*, can be used selectively as a source for Bingham's early life. Philip Bartels, an ostensibly happily married man whose career has stalled since he returned from the war, falls in love with Lorna Dickson, a mature but still young woman who lost her husband in the Burma campaign. Believing that his wife would be devastated if he were to leave her, he reaches, by reasonably logical analysis, the regrettable but necessary conclusion that he will need to kill her if he is to be free to marry Lorna. From the most compassionate of motives, he plans and sets in motion a carefully thought-out murder. We must all die sometime, Bartels reasons. It's not when you die but how you die that matters. Accordingly, he goes to great lengths to be sure that his wife Beatrice will suffer no pain and no fear when she takes the poison that he has left for her.

Meanwhile his best friend Pete Harding, to whom he has introduced Lorna, wants her for himself. By sowing doubts in her mind he induces her to end the affair with Bartels, which she does on the night that he has planned Beatrice's death. The tension leads to an inevitable yet still surprising denouement after Bartels realises that Beatrice may die for nothing.

The book is similar in construction to *Michael Sibley*, employing several of the same devices: a first-person narrator, the interspersing of different chronological sequences in the narrative, the clear identification of one character with the author. The principal differences between the two early books are that in *Five Roundabouts*, the narrator does not represent Bingham himself, and that the style is more sophisticated in its use of flashbacks leading to the main thrust of the narrative. The second book is greatly more ambitious and polished than the first.

Five Roundabouts also introduces the reader to a vitally important stage of the author's life. In this book he recreates the magical quality that Tigy retained for him and introduces us to his first experience of falling in love, both with the château and with 'Ingrid', whom he met there. The nostalgia that the principal character feels for that year is perfectly credible, principally because Bingham was writing from his heart.

Once again the critical reception verged on rapturous. K. John of the *Illustrated London News*, who had been complimentary about *Michael Sibley*, called it 'brilliantly suspenseful and ingenious, expertly told and a distinct advance upon its forerunner'. John Connell in the *Evening News* spoke of 'masterly technical accomplishment – but accomplishment harnessed to the service of an important idea, and not wasted on mechanical trivialities'.

A thoughtful and balanced assessment came from *Punch*:

> Mr Bingham allows an unfair share of omniscience to his first-person narrator, and he is annoyingly given to shunting back and forth in time, but his story has such momentum, his characters are so convincing, that one gladly forgives his faults and surrenders to his spellbinding.

With two successful novels under his belt and a confident relationship with Victor Gollancz, Bingham felt able to spread his wings, to become more creative, to rely less on autobiographical material. For the next fourteen years he probed in his imagination the psychology of murderers and criminals, and wrote six books. He rarely had difficulty with devising plots, into which he inserted authentic scenes of police interrogation, of which *Michael Sibley* gave the first example. In his third book, *The Third Skin*, he abandoned the device of a first-person narrator and constructed the simplest of plots, concentrating on the psychology of hunter and hunted in a police investigation. He determined to take time to perfect the book, working and reworking his manuscript.

While the author may at this point have relaxed the pressure on himself to complete the book quickly, this was not true of his publisher. A year had passed since his second success and Gollancz was not inclined to see a thoroughbred horse remain in the stables. On 9 October 1953 he wrote a short sharp reminder to his author:

> This last couple of days I have been trying to sketch out next year's programme, and have been wondering whether you have an idea whenabouts you may be delivering another novel (which I shall read as eagerly as the rest of your public will). I am not trying to hurry you, but I should like to have an idea.

Despite his assurance, V.G. was indeed trying to hurry Bingham to bring his third novel to market and, through knowledge or by intuition, he was right to do so. By abandoning the autobiographical style and the device of himself – or a character that was partially himself – as a narrator, Bingham had cut the cable that connected his own persona so vividly to the narrative and to the emotions of his characters. He was venturing into new territory and was finding the transition heavy going.

As ever, the plot for *The Third Skin* is direct, disarmingly simple in concept, but he left the world he knew, the world of an elegant château in the Sologne or of a provincial newspaper office, and tackled a *demi-monde* of which he knew nothing: the lower-middle-class world of post-war 'teddy boys' in south London. It was a long way from the Bangor Castle ballroom to the dance halls of Hammersmith and the West End. It was not a journey that the heir to the barony of Clanmorris had undertaken in his own life; undaunted, however, he attempted it in his fiction.

Through October and November he struggled with the new environment he had adopted. Perturbed by the growth in juvenile delinquency, he was determined to write a more socially conscious novel. For an introduction to this unknown milieu he turned to Graham Greene's 1938 book *Brighton Rock*. Compounding his view that Greene's characters were not 'deep' was his scepticism about the character of Pinkie in *Brighton Rock*. He simply did not believe that a petty crook could think as profoundly as Greene had made him think. Normally an avid fan of Greene, he felt that *Brighton Rock* was flawed because it was artificially profound.

His third novel would be more realistic, less sophisticated. On the other hand, he needed to inject the voice of reason as a bellwether of sanity in a world that he felt was going rapidly to the devil. After several rewrites and adjustments to the principal characters, he arrived at a balance that worked.

The plot is as direct as those of his first two novels. Les Marshall, a weak, posturing youth, brought up by his mother in Streatham after the death of his father, falls in with a crowd of petty criminals who frequent the London dance halls. His desire for a girl in the group is exploited by Ron Turner, her boyfriend, to lure Les into driving the getaway car in a burglary. In the course of the burglary, Turner kills a nightwatchman. The net begins to close around Turner and Les himself only escapes the gallows when he is run down and killed by a newspaper van. Turner shoots and kills a police sergeant before he is arrested.

The weakness of Les Marshall is in sharp contrast to the

resilient determination of his mother Irene and the rational calm of Inspector Vandoran, who heads the police investigation. Once again, the book is not a traditional thriller. It is the systematic building of the case against Les Marshall and his mother's resolution to save him that give the book its chilling realism.

Irene Marshall and Inspector Vandoran represent decency and common sense. Despite his determination to bring the criminals to justice, Vandoran is painted as a thoroughly decent man, not above applying aggressive pressure in interrogation. After the plot has reached its conclusion, the reader is unsurprised that the divorced Vandoran and the widowed Irene Marshall decide to step out together.

Inspector Vandoran is a character of whom Bingham was justifiably proud. There is much of himself in his creation and, later in his career, when he was developing the character of a shrewd police superintendent, it was to Vandoran that he returned.

The Third Skin was the last of the books published by Gollancz on the original three-book contract. V.G., reluctant as ever to pay extravagant advances even to his favourite authors, yielded marginally, allowing the £150 advance on publication to become £100 down, with the balance upon publication. But, with a vigilant eye on precedent, he refused to alter the written contract. Nevertheless, Bingham had for the first time received a cheque for £100 before the presses began to turn – a benevolent omen.

Published in 1954, *The Third Skin* was well received. Norman Blood of *Time and Tide* called it 'a most accomplished piece of work', and the *Yorkshire Observer* spoke of 'a fascinating story, a human document that evokes pity and terror'. The *Sunday Times* reviewer, however, identified the single flaw in the book, commenting 'that Mr Bingham has chosen a milieu with which he is not sufficiently familiar'.

So began a year of change for the Binghams. It began propitiously, but by the end of 1954, amid a multitude of disappointments and sadnesses, the exhilaration of the New Year had quite vanished. During that summer John and Madeleine veered dangerously far from their comfort zone of Kensington, buying a large house in Reigate and moving in September. The plan was that Madeleine's parents would move into part of the house and share some of the costs. A sensible idea in abstract became a nightmare in reality. The company engaged to pack belongings and move them from their flat in Iverna Court, Kensington, failed to keep their side of the contract; finally, after several annoyances, the house was ready and their possessions were moved into Reigate. On the following day Clement Ebel died.

Madeleine was distraught. Her father had been a rock-like symbol of continuity in her life, an ever-present, ever-competent male who got things done when she needed. Practical, ambitious, permanently optimistic, he had been a vital presence in the family. Without Clement, her husband would have to fulfil many more roles. Madeleine blamed herself for her father's death because she had persuaded her parents to uproot themselves. She declared the Reigate house intolerable; she worried about the future without Clement to protect her, foreseeing financial catastrophe. Unable to sleep, she expressed incessant self-hatred, finally agreeing in late October to seek psychiatric help.

John, while sympathetic, was quite unused to emotion on this scale. Ever practical, however, he wrote a factual summary of events to Gollancz, apologising that his father-in-law's death and his wife's temporary derangement would necessitate a slight delay in the delivery of his manuscript. Things were further complicated by Madeleine's having submitted a manuscript entitled *Humphrey* to Gollancz. He was concerned that, if V.G. should refuse it, this would cause further distress; he urged the publisher that, should he not wish to accept it, he might compliment her on the work but say that for policy reasons he could not publish it. Gollancz, replying on 26 October 1954, said that his firm would not be able to publish *Humphrey*, agreeing to couch his refusal in the diplomatic manner suggested. As for John's next book he was generosity itself, writing:

> Oh, please don't worry for a single second about the date of delivery. It is only that we like to know in advance, so that we can get out our publicity a good six months before a book comes in; but the exact date is of little importance. The important thing is that the book should be as good as possible! So let it be a month late, or two months late, or three months late, just as you like; don't let it be less good by hurrying.

The winter of 1954–5 was difficult for John and Madeleine. Their relationship had always been fond and there is no doubt of Bingham's affection and respect for his wife. Reigate is close to London, but Kensington, closer to the West End and its theatres, was her 'manor'. Deprived of her father and cut off from her favourite social milieu, she continued to hate the Reigate house, both as a physical entity and as a symbol of Clement's demise.

Nor were things easy for her husband. The defection of Guy Burgess and Donald Maclean in May 1951 had caused widespread alarm in both MI5 and MI6. Since May 1954, a Royal Commission in Australia had been investigating the spy ring revealed by Vladimir and Evdokia Popov when they defected from the Soviet GRU. There was a certainty at the Security Service that a 'Third Man' – not to mention a fourth, fifth or sixth man – existed at a high level within either MI5 or MI6 or both. Emotional distress within the family could not have come at a more inconvenient time.

The penetration of the CPGB was bearing fruit. Party officials assumed that MI5 had them under electronic surveillance and frequently moved important meetings to different rooms that were harder to bug. Their chosen venue for key meetings was a small, windowless basement room; Julia Pirie communicated this to Bingham and Operation TIE PIN was mounted.

For this operation, the entire staff of A Branch surveillance, the 'Watchers', were employed. Pirie had reported that a coal chute led down to the room from under the pavement. While an MI5 technician attached a bug under a false door and fitted it to the top of the chute – a noisy business – the Watchers rambled past the office, ostensibly groups of tipsy revellers, making enough racket to drown the noise of the work being performed.

A further success followed with the execution of Operation PARTY PIECE, described by the official historian of the Security Service, Professor Christopher Andrew, as the most important operation in the Cold War. Arthur Spencer of MI6, who became a close friend of Bingham's during the 1950s, was seconded to MI5 and recalled in 2011 the operation that flowed from intelligence provided by Pirie. 'Without PARTY PIECE,' Spencer claims, 'in June 1955, Britain would have become a Communist state.' He continues:

> For some time F4 had tapped the phone of a notorious Communist couple named Berger, as well as those of the CPGB head office ... eventually one significant item was heard. It referred to 'the files'. What files were there, so important that they had to be kept in a private house, away from the CPGB office, where they could have been snatched if the Security Service raided it? We dearly wanted to know.
>
> Len Burt of Special Branch said that if we wanted to get the files by burgling the Bergers' house, he would put his local CID officers to surround the place and prevent anyone interfering!

This must be the only time police offered to protect burglars. We thanked him but said we didn't want to take the files away but to copy them, which we couldn't do until we knew that the Bergers were going away for long enough for us to copy them.

Spencer recruited an agent, the underused secretary of a barrister friend, and could not believe his luck when the Bergers, more concerned with a few pounds a week extra income than the security of their house, advertised for a lodger. His agent applied and was accepted. Now it was simply a matter of waiting until the Bergers went away. After a month or so they accepted a weekend invitation to the West Country and Operation PARTY PIECE was launched.

Bingham confirmed through Pirie that such secret files existed and that they were, indeed, stored away from King Street in the home of a sympathetic family. Arthur Spencer's agent put it about that she was holding a party while the Bergers were away for the weekend; the CID protected the Bergers' house and a team in the West Country watched the house where they were staying. The MI5 team wore small pieces of white cardboard on their lapels as identification; anyone not wearing the cardboard was politely intercepted and told that the Bergers were away, so there was no point in visiting the house, where, anyway, a party was being held by their lodger. All went smoothly and over 1,000 files were copied with about 4,000 entries previously unknown to Special Branch or MI5.

Bingham's section was charged with accumulating evidence of counter-subversion and handing that evidence to a higher level, at which the decision would be taken whether or not to inform Special Branch and have a suspect arrested. This constitutional nicety was, however, circumvented in PARTY PIECE and other operations in which the Service needed to acquire evidence by less lawful means. In short, when a burglary was called for.

Burglaries were often central to Bingham's operational tactics. Peter Wright in *Spycatcher* speaks of MI5 agents who 'for five years ... bugged and burgled our way across London at the state's behest while pompous bowler-hatted civil servants pretended to look the other way'. On 28 August 1971, Bingham's son Simon had married Gizella Maria Zverkó, whose family had escaped from Hungary after the 1956 rising. Gizella remembers the burglaries as thrilling for her father-in-law. 'He told me once that he loved breaking into houses,' she recalled, 'when they were trying to suss out if people were "plants" or if they were genuine.' Early in Terence Brady's friendship with Bingham's daughter Charlotte, he called at the house one evening to be greeted by Charlotte, who confided that 'Papa is just off on a burglary'. Without revealing to his family whom he intended to burgle or why, he allowed the burglaries to become something of a family joke; in this way he was able to share some of the clandestine nature of his work without compromising its essence.

It was March 1955 before Bingham could write to Gollancz announcing that his fourth book would be ready by the middle of the month. This time, diplomatically, he suggested three titles to the publisher: *The Inspector Listens*, the title that he preferred, *The Paton Street Case* or *Behind the Silence*. Gollancz, direct as ever, chose the second, the most factually descriptive of the three.

By this stage John Bingham had acquired a reputation for a certain cynicism about police methods. As a skilled interrogator himself, he knew where and how pressure could best be applied in a police interview and he had not shied from depicting it with utter frankness. H. R. F. Keating in *Whodunit?*, his encyclopaedia of crime and thrillers, singled this out as the most remarkable quality of Bingham's writing.

In an attempt to dispel this image of disdain for the police force, he had attempted an ambitious theme – that of a police inspector whose efficiency is tinged with compassion. He had hinted at this before in his creation of Inspector Vandoran in *The Third Skin*, but this time, as he wrote to Gollancz with a certain hyperbole, 'it is definitely a detective story, but highly topical in one aspect – dealing with something which has not, I believe, been touched upon in fiction before. I have tried to combine authenticity with humanity, no easy task when dealing with a machine like the police force.'

Peter Watt had succeeded in raising the ante from Gollancz for his client's fourth book: the parsimonious publisher was now prepared to part with £175 as an advance. Bingham was delighted, but it was hardly a sum to convince his bank manager that his evening job was viable by itself. Royalties were arriving regularly, however, and Penguin Books expressed an interest in reissuing his early works. Fortune, if not smiling, was certainly not baring her teeth.

When *The Paton Street Case* was published in October 1955 it was well reviewed, if not as enthusiastically as his earlier books. A review in *Time and Tide* described it as 'a superb detective story', while the *Times Literary Supplement* commented generally that 'Bingham is one of the more rewarding detective novelists'. Having scaled great heights in his first three novels, he was now expected to bring off a masterpiece every time, for, as *British Weekly* opined, 'Bingham is a master of his art'.

Dodd, Mead, Bingham's American publishers, were optimistic and published *The Paton Street Case* as *Inspector Morgan's Dilemma*. As the book conformed more to preconceived lines of popular American fiction (murder, detection, plot twists, solution), it received more praise than *Michael Sibley*. 'Exceptionally good: absolutely the top,' trumpeted the *News Sentinel* of Knoxville; 'tense and well-written' was the judgement of the *Oakland Tribune*. After a rocky start, Bingham now had an American following.

Once again, he had woven a tight plot, deviating from his previous books in making the detective inspector the protagonist. For the first time, he wrote from the more conventional perspective of the hound rather than that of the hare. A key point in the convoluted story comes when the inspector allows a suspect to remain at large, to the amazement and dismay of his sergeant, who advocates pulling him in immediately. When the suspect vanishes and kills himself, the sergeant is vindicated.

After a further twist it emerges that the suspect was innocent and the inspector carries the weight of responsibility for his suicide. That is the effective climax of the book, as the final twists are unconvincing and the plot shuffles rather than rises to its end. Overall, it is a success, but it is not difficult to understand why critical praise was muted after its earlier rapture. Like each preceding book, it was ambitious: it tackled the issue of murder in a subtly unconventional manner. No aficionado of his work would have turned away; many, however, will have scratched their heads.

The year of 1956 was a milestone, personally and professionally. On 28 May the formidable Allen Lane of Penguin Books signed an agreement to reprint *Five Roundabouts to Heaven* with an advance of £125 and royalties of 7 per cent. While this did not represent undreamed-of wealth, the very acceptance of a book by Penguin was an important step forward. It was a seal of approval of the author himself and a reasonable assurance that future books would be well received.

The Binghams were now established at 24 Abingdon Villas, close to Kensington High Street, immediately christened 'Dingley Dell'. Madeleine at last had the right house in the right place for her to live the literary life she craved. The house was purchased from Lady Margaret Douglas Home for £8,500 by the Clanmorris trust in the summer. Although elegant and structurally sound, it was in a run-down state. As family money was tight, Madeleine and Simon redecorated the entire house themselves before Simon left for National Service. Having won a place at Queens' College, Cambridge, he would go up to the university to read Classics in October 1958; in the meantime he was slated for National Service in the 13th/18th Royal Hussars. Charlotte was at school at The Priory in Haywards Heath. American sales were encouraging. Peter Watt sold *The Paton Street Case* to a German magazine for £250 and to an Italian publisher for £285.

At 'The Office', the aftershocks of the Burgess and Maclean affair seemed at last to have subsided and Section F4 was confident that it had successfully penetrated the CPGB. Perhaps the most valuable information from Julia Pirie was based on her observation of the politics within the party. Although her boss John Gollan was nominally the General Secretary, he had little real power. By the late 1950s the greater threat was the disruptive element within the TUC, used by Moscow to subvert British industry.

This truth was supported by the decline in membership of the party. The slide began in March 1956 when it was revealed that, at the 20th Congress of the Communist Party of the Soviet Union the previous month, Nikita Khrushchev had denounced Joseph Stalin, who had died in 1952. The new leader referred to a regime of 'suspicion, fear and terror' built up by Stalin. To destroy 'the Stalin cult', he revealed details of the purges in the late 1930s and the assassination of prominent Bolshevik politician Sergei Kirov in 1934.

These revelations caused dismay among many communists, but greater erosion was to follow. When the national uprising against Soviet domination of Hungary broke out on 23 October, the Soviet Politburo initially responded in *Pravda* that there would be greater equality between the Soviet Union and its satellites, adding, 'The Soviet government is prepared to enter into the appropriate negotiations with the government of the Hungarian People's Republic ... on the question of the presence of Soviet troops on the territory of Hungary.'

On the same day, however, the Politburo acted directly counter to that communiqué and on 4 November launched a devastating attack that crushed the rebels in three days. Popular disgust at this savage suppression caused widespread defection from the party.

With their lives more peaceful and with some sense of anticipation, the Binghams planned a holiday, their first proper break for five years. John had two novels fermenting in his mind; two years had passed since his last book and he intended to surprise his readers with his next offerings. He would submit the manuscript for the first of these, a disturbing work he called simply *Marion*, then they planned to drift down the Adriatic coastline for some much-needed rest and relaxation. Once he returned, he would start work in earnest on the second novel.

For the first time, however, he hit a roadblock at Gollancz when Jon Evans, the publisher's reader, turned in a sharply critical report on *Marion*. In the past there had been minor issues that needed to be resolved. This time, however, two readers raised fundamental questions about structure and sequence; even the basic plot was questioned. In his previous novels Bingham had shown great skill in fashioning the storyline, and this had compensated on occasion for occasionally pedestrian writing; gripping plots had carried him through. Now his forte was being doubted.

There was also disagreement between his English and American publishers about almost every aspect of the book. The Americans, critical of the title, changed it to *Murder off the Record*, an annoying development as Bingham planned to use that title for his next book. He suggested an alternative, *Sweet Poison*.

For the American market, moreover, Dodd, Mead wanted to cut 35,000 words of the early chapters and to expand the more dramatic, action-packed finale. Victor Gollancz, on the other hand, thought the early chapters far superior to the hurly-burly of the ending. Publishers on both side of the Atlantic found the book too long and urged cuts; the problem was that they wanted to cut radically different parts.

Bingham strove to keep both sides happy. His friendship with V.G. and his wife Ruth had developed in the five years that they had worked together and it was relatively easy to settle differences of opinion, either in the Gollancz offices or over the dinner table at Abingdon Villas. He agreed that 'there was something wrong somewhere, and I didn't know what'. As far as the demands from Dodd, Mead were concerned, they would be partially dealt with, but it was the English-approved version, preserving the early chapters, that would go into print. He recognised that the first version of 110,000 words was too long for a paperback edition at that time and, with his eye on the future market, he agreed to edit the manuscript to 80,000 words. All this he proposed to do in the six weeks before leaving for Italy on 3 June. He took a week's leave from 'The Office' and delivered the finished version to Henrietta Street on 14 May.

The result is a book that is haunting, cunningly woven, but unbalanced. The plot is disjointed and unconvincing, depending on improbable coincidences and frantic, illogical deduction. It has great tension and, naturally, it includes a trademark police investigation as a suspect's innocence is called into question by a wealth of circumstantial evidence. And it does introduce the deeply disturbing Marion, a thoroughly unscrupulous and immoral woman who, as Evans pointed out, is not actually central to the plot. Yet Bingham named the book after her, betraying perhaps an obsession with the character. In a letter to Dennis

Wheatley the following September he refers to 'poor Marion, the bitch', adding that 'I've an even worse bitch in my next book, to be published in November: I expect people will say I've been crossed in love – illicit love, since I'm married. Oh well!'

None of Bingham's books provoked such widely differing notices as *Marion*. A review in the March 1958 issue of *Books and Bookmen* echoed what other reviewers had praised in his earlier work, referring to the now familiar interplay between police and suspect, saying that 'Bingham's forte is the impact of a murder on the lives of ordinary people like you and me.' *The Observer* was elusively Delphic, prophesying that 'with careful plotting he may yet stun us with a masterpiece'. Equally ambiguous was Francis Iles, who wrote in the *Manchester Guardian* that 'at his best [John Bingham] is the most distinguished and exciting of our crime novelists today'.

Julian Symons of the *Sunday Times*, a consistent admirer, gave the most perceptive review: '*Marion* fades badly about halfway through, when we realise that the circuitous way in which the story has been told is really unnecessary, but it revives with a stormy finish.'

In early 1958 Pan Books agreed to publish *Marion* in paperback with an advance of £300. At about the same time Penguin Books expressed an interest in *Michael Sibley* and an agreement was signed in the summer for its reissue in the prestigious green paperback.

With V.G.'s firm, relations continued to be both professional and increasingly friendly. Victor and Ruth Gollancz were frequent visitors at Abingdon Villas and the two couples talked of meeting in Venice in the summer. During the first three months of 1958 Bingham revised his sixth book, *Murder Plan Six*, several times, crafting it with perhaps more care than he had employed since his very early work. The result is a unique story, certainly bizarre, curiously compelling and with a singular twist: one of the characters is Victor Gollancz, to whom he dedicated the book.

The dedication expresses Bingham's gratitude that the publisher had taken a chance in publishing his first crime novel and had, in the intervening time, become a friend, offering help and sympathy to a new writer. Gollancz, he wrote, shared with him the belief that the thriller could be elevated from its lowly status into at least 'the middle branches of the literary tree'. Crime, he wrote, is with us all the time and it deserves to be treated as an important element of modern society. Detectives, no less than doctors, are professionals who have specific responsibility for dealing with issues that confront society. Crime novels, Bingham believed, should be more realistic in their treatment of murder and other criminal behaviour. It is unrealistic to create amateur detectives who perform their miracles outside the force.

On occasion, Bingham wrote, he had been accused of being 'anti-police'. He rejects the accusation, praising the force for performing 'an exacting and often dangerous job so well, always considering the legal jungle, festooned with red tape and restrictions, in which they must operate'.

It is a moving dedication, warm in its praise of the publisher and crisp in its statement of Bingham's purpose. Even as he wrote it, however, he must have been sure that the book itself would be controversial.

For eighteen months he had worked on his sixth book. In March 1958, while congratulating his author on the sales of *Marion*, which, he said, were 'piling up quite a nice total', Gollancz pressed him to deliver 'that wonderful new thriller'. But Bingham was not to be hurried. Accepting that delay would hold up publication until after the autumn, he trimmed the book to a precise 200 pages and delivered it to his publisher on 2 June to coincide with Victor's return from a two-month holiday.

Bingham was very pleased indeed with the result. Not without reason, as *Murder Plan Six* stands among his books as perhaps the most experimental. It succeeds as a crime story; it is delightful as a pen portrait of a publisher for whom the author had a deep-seated professional and ethical admiration.

He had formulated the structure to build up tension for its own sake, the reader being unsure exactly where the tension originated. The *Oxford Mail* responded well with the comment, 'You can't deny that the new stories from off-beat writers like John Bingham are always an exciting experience – his latest, *Murder Plan Six*, certainly is.' This review must have pleased the author enormously. Violet Grant, an outspoken reviewer in the *Daily Telegraph*, also found much to like in the book and posed a central question: 'Far-fetched? Well, perhaps, but as usual Mr Bingham gets his story across with the maximum tension and conviction.'

Less complimentary was the usually positive Julian Symons in the *Sunday Times*:

From the very talented Mr Bingham a disappointment. *Murder Plan Six* is a most esoteric book in which a crime novelist gives to his publisher an account of his reasons and plans for murder in a series of tape recordings. Not even the fact that the publisher is Mr Victor Gollancz (in the book as well as on the title page) can save the story from dullness.

The exposure and status of the book were greatly increased when Alfred Hitchcock adapted it to create 'Captive Audience' for *The Hitchcock Hour* with James Mason and Angie Dickinson. The production was well reviewed in *TV Times* on 29 March 1963.

There was one new and encouraging thread in the reviews. Not only did the *Evening Standard* reckon it to be 'a thriller of a very high order', but, quite suddenly, Bingham found himself being compared with Agatha Christie, whose books at that time stood in a firmament of their own. The reviewer at the *News Chronicle* deemed him 'a much better hand at the novel of murder than Agatha Christie', while the *Daily Telegraph* wrote that 'Bingham is as original as Miss Christie is orthodox'.

This was heady praise. The book had been a long time maturing, germinating in his mind as both an original crime story and a tribute to the way in which his career had been furthered by Gollancz. The device of including the publisher as a principal character, at first sight bizarre, clearly appealed to readers. If he had entertained doubts about his future career as a novelist – or, more specifically, whether he could maintain an adequate steady income if he were to leave MI5 – these doubts now appeared to be dispelled.

CHAPTER 8

THE GENESIS OF GEORGE SMILEY, 1958-66

I can remember my father reading the novel and saying 'David has put me in his book. He's made me awfully plain. I really don't think I'm as ugly as that.' But he was exactly like Smiley. When I first watched Smiley I just couldn't believe it. It was like watching my father on screen.

Charlotte Bingham, quoted in the *News Letter* (Belfast), 15 March 2001

In 1958 David Cornwell (John le Carré) joined MI5. He had many of the right qualifications for the spy world: a childhood spent with his father, a brilliant fraudster often, but not always, one step ahead of the law; a public school education; a First in Modern Languages from Oxford; excellent French and fluent command of German; experience with Army Intelligence in Austria during his National Service. Le Carré brought to Counter-Intelligence a cornucopia of talents and experience into which the black arts of espionage could be introduced.

His early years are captured in his sometimes hilarious, sometimes heart-breaking novel *A Perfect Spy*. Abandoned by his mother when he was five; sent to Sherborne School, an institution that he despised; experienced at fighting his own corner – he had spent a year at the University of Bern in the late 1940s, when he was seventeen – and with two years of teaching at Eton behind him, he seemed to have done a great deal with his twenty-seven years.

Maxwell Knight had urged Bingham to succeed him but the latter strenuously resisted promotion, pointing out that his skills lay as an agent runner, not as a manager of agent runners. The administrative nature of such a job did not appeal to him; his agents were loyal to him and he reciprocated that loyalty.

Thus Bingham occupied the position of *primus inter pares*, the senior and most respected of the agent runners in the area of counter-subversion. Simon Clanmorris recalls that, much later, le Carré described for him how Bingham had been a skilful field operator who took enormous care of his agents, most of whom were women. He met them frequently, in some instances daily, and had an almost pastoral responsibility towards them. They rewarded him with personal, as well as professional, loyalty. In Bingham's role as a senior agent runner within the section, it was natural that he should take le Carré under his wing and instruct him in the operations of the section and, if he went on leave, would allow le Carré to handle his agents in his absence.

A friendship developed between the conventional middle-aged, relative old-timer – nearly fifty when le Carré came to the Security Service – and le Carré, twenty-three years younger, something of an iconoclast, already possessed of an interesting curriculum vitae. Bingham became a mentor for the younger man, on one occasion suggesting ways in which le Carré might handle a difficult situation in which a female agent, working for a target organisation, had been 'blown'. Bingham suggested an elaborate deception, in the course of which the officers of the target organisation were led to believe that the agent had been the unwilling recipient of letters from an investigative journalist, interested to find out more about the work she was doing. By leaving the letters, created by the forgery department of MI5, in her handbag when she went to lunch – whereupon they were promptly read by her employers – the agent deflected any suspicions that she was reporting to the Security Service. Naturally enough, the newspaper for which the 'journalist' had supposedly worked denied all knowledge of the matter. In due course, le Carré withdrew his agent without her being compromised. It was an ingenious deception that impressed the young le Carré and one which he recalled to Simon Clanmorris fifty years after the event.

Bingham invited his new colleague home to meet his family, and soon David and Alison Cornwell (known as 'Ann') became regular guests. Madeleine describes their early friendship:

> My husband ... had been back in Intelligence some seven or eight years when The Office produced a new recruit – David Cornwell. He was a good-looking fair young man at that time, in his late twenties, intelligent and very funny, an ex-schoolmaster from Eton, with a nice wife and two small children.
>
> Jack liked him very much, for David had the same sense of humour as many of the old Fleet Street chums, sharp and knocky. He had an Oxford degree and spoke excellent French and German. He seemed a most promising recruit for The Office, and well set to rise in the profession.

The salary scale for civil servants in the 1950s was far from generous and the Cornwells sought ways to supplement the income of a junior member of the intelligence team. They had married young and were struggling to make ends meet. In a 1963 interview with *The Guardian* le Carré described their early relationship, saying that as soon as he met Ann he knew that she was the right girl for him. When he came out of a lecture, he told his interviewer, he gave his notes to Ann, who went through the set books and created files and card indices. When le Carré won his first-class honours – an achievement of which he claimed to be more proud than any other – he attributed his success entirely to her.

Madeleine felt concerned for Ann, worrying that her absolute devotion to her husband left her vulnerable. According to Madeleine, 'she used to look at him as if he were some amazing piece of good luck which she had never thought would come her way. It was like something in a women's magazine.' Perhaps with the benefit of hindsight, Madeleine wrote that she thought it was a mistake. Although she was in favour of good and loving wives, she felt that 'adoration, stark and unveiled, is seldom good for anyone'.

One plan to supplement le Carré's salary was to take in a lodger at their Battersea flat. Madeleine recalls that when this gentleman was about to return to Africa, he offered to cook them a typical African dinner. Ann returned home in the afternoon to find 'corn all over the floor in the loo with a live chicken pecking it up'. The blood of a freshly killed chicken was, apparently, essential for the authenticity of the dish. Ann's surprise was exceeded only by her husband's horror when, after a spirited chase around the flat, the chicken was eventually caught and beheaded. Much as they had enjoyed their paying guest, they decided that they should seek another source of extra income.

Le Carré was putting ideas together for his first novel. By that time Bingham had published six crime stories, and he offered to introduce le Carré to his agent, Peter Watt, and to Gollancz. Both agent and publisher were impressed by le Carré's first book, *Call for the Dead*, in which the reader meets his most enduring and most successful character, George Smiley.

In the 1950s men were rigidly divided into two groups: those who had fought in the war and those who had been too young. Bingham fell into the first category, le Carré into the second. Bingham, twenty-three years older, represented another era; he was a standard-bearer of a generation that younger men tended to scorn as old fashioned. However much le Carré may have admired him, he fell on the other side of that great divide, The War.

This is reflected in a curious and engaging way. Highlighting the generational difference is the nickname that the novice writer awarded to his mentor: he dubbed him 'le Carré' ('the Square' in French). Yet, to emphasise the closeness between them and because intelligence officers were prohibited from publishing under their true names, he adopted Bingham's first name and the nickname he had awarded him to form his own *nom de plume*, 'John le Carré'. That name appeared for the first time on the cover of *Call for the Dead*.

Bingham was greatly amused and flattered by le Carré's choice of pen name. He was an avuncular figure, a man who took great pleasure in encouraging men younger than himself and, doubtless, it is that quality that prompted le Carré to pay him such a tribute. It is not, however, for the *nom de plume* but for the character of George Smiley that the association between the two full-time intelligence agents and part-time writers will be long remembered.

Early in the book we are introduced to Smiley. The importance that le Carré gives to his first substantial character is clear from the very first lines. The opening chapter, entitled 'A Brief History of George Smiley', paints him in striking, surprising, colours. He is described as overwhelmingly ordinary, physically plain, ill dressed, married to Lady Ann Sercomb, an exotic aristocrat who periodically leaves him, at the time of writing having eloped with a Cuban racing driver. Smiley sees himself as discarded; a man without fortune, rank or noble regiment; a plebeian who made a brief appearance on the aristocratic stage.

Despite his unimpressive physique, Smiley is an accomplished intelligence officer. Le Carré allows him to discourse at length on his infallible methods of interrogation; his intellect is never in doubt; he has clearly had 'a good war'; his interrupted service with 'the department' mirrors that of John Bingham. Above all, his patriotism is absolute. He is cunning, resourceful, compassionate. So clear is the identification with Bingham that it is remarkable that it lay suspected but unconfirmed until le Carré admitted it during a radio interview in 1999.

For a long time le Carré did not admit publicly that he had used Bingham as the model for Smiley. Among the Bingham family, however, there was, from the outset, no doubt about Smiley's origin. So certain were they that Madeleine wrote a memoir entitled *Smiley's Wife*, recounting the experiences of being married to an agent runner.

Bingham's sole objection to the George Smiley that le Carré created in *Call for the Dead* was based not on Smiley's ethics but on his physical appearance. 'David has written a book about me,' he commented, good-naturedly adding that le Carré had made him unreasonably ugly. Thus far, at least, he was not uncomfortable with the equivalence of himself and the fictional version. He and George Smiley were ethically congruent.

It is John Bingham's ethical stance, his complex cocktail of values, that can be traced in his written work. Many, indeed most, of the clues are there. They belong to the moral teething period, the years in which, already physically mature, he began to develop his ethical muscles.

His son Simon comments that his father was undistinguished, academically and athletically, in his youth. Yet by 1950 we find a resolute, self-confident defender of Britain's character. His first job, working for the *Hull Daily Mail*, had, in his own words, made a man of him; the Second World War and its aftermath had strengthened his inherited values. During the 1950s he furiously rejected most post-war trends and values, embracing only a few, and those few always tempered by his pre-war assumptions and beliefs. It is small wonder that his young colleague nicknamed him 'the Square'.

The friendship continued. Bingham was amused by the notion of being Smiley and would refer to himself in the third person as 'Smiley' in letters to le Carré. There are differences between the two, of course. Whereas Smiley is described as short and fat, the original was of above average height and stocky; while Smiley, in le Carré's description, wears expensive but ill-fitting clothes, Bingham was always decently, if conservatively, dressed. His suits were always bought off the peg but they did at least fit him. Yet these differences are of minimal importance against what later emerged as fundamental differences of ideology. The split between the two writers began in 1963, after le Carré published *The Spy Who Came In from the Cold*.

Until then both had written only murder mystery stories. When we meet Smiley in *Call for the Dead* he is working in 'the department'. The investigation that he conducts plays out like a police drama in which the background of spying is second-ary. When we meet him again in *A Murder of Quality*, his life in intelligence is behind him, no more than a convention in the story.

But in his third novel, not only Smiley but the whole intel-ligence service is painted in morally ambiguous colours. In *The Spy Who Came In from the Cold*, one side is as immoral as the other: both are prepared to send innocent people to the gallows to preserve their assets. A complex conspiracy is devised to entrap a thoughtful, ethical East German official in order to ensure the safety of his superior, a brutal former Nazi who has been turned by the department.

The department has no regard for whomsoever it may destroy along the way. The two sympathetic characters – Fiedler and Liz Gold – are both calmly cast aside to their deaths. The central character, Alec Leamas, sacrifices himself out of disgust for the despicable conspiracy. In the final scene, after an East German agent has double-crossed Leamas and shot Liz Gold as she scales the Berlin Wall, we see Smiley, a leading conspirator, on the 'right' side of the wall, urging Leamas to jump. Calmly, Leamas looks down at him, turns around and climbs down on the 'wrong' side, where he is promptly shot.

Thus far at least, questioning such indifference to the rightness and decency of 'our' side, John le Carré was treading on danger- ous ground but had stayed just the right side of John Bingham's ethical line. Two years later, however, with the publication of *The Looking Glass War*, he crossed that line, not only seriously offend- ing Bingham but also incurring the wrath of the mandarins of British intelligence, who once more saw one of their own cash- ing in on his secret experience.

The thrust of *The Looking Glass War*, in which a superannuated agent is sent to certain death in East Germany, is that incom- petence and infighting are endemic in Whitehall and a serious threat to the efficacy of British intelligence. Turf wars cripple an ill-conceived, faultily mounted operation. Cynicism reigns in MI6 while incompetence hamstrings MI5. It is a good story, skilfully told, but it reveals a notional schism in Whitehall and appears to derive directly from le Carré's experience; he, unlike Bingham, knew at first hand the operating styles of both MI5 and MI6.

There are several versions of how the friendship between the two was affected by the publication of *The Looking Glass War*. Naturally enough, the most graphic version is that told by le Carré. In the introduction to the 2000 Simon & Schuster editions of three of Bingham's books, he accounts for the split plausibly.

He describes himself, in Bingham's eyes, as a literary apostate who had soiled the good name of the Security Service. Protests that he was merely engaged in a literary conceit, he argues, were ineffective in the face of Bingham's sense of having been betrayed, along with the Security Service. He had become, he concludes, 'a shit' in Bingham's eyes.

He adduces, moreover, other differences. While Bingham was fundamentally an MI5 man and therefore, despite having performed work in collaboration with MI6, overwhelmingly concerned with hunting down communists in Britain, le Carré had, after only two years, transferred to the more glamorous MI6. He implies in his explanation of the rift that an MI5 man could scarcely comprehend the intricacies of Pure Intelligence. He paints Bingham as a good and fiercely loyal agent runner, devoted to his agents, and protests that he could never have cast Bingham in a role that involved the kind of cynical sacrifice of agents performed in *The Spy Who Came In from the Cold* or *The Looking Glass War*. Such praise aside, he clearly believed that Bingham, mired in counter-espionage, had the luxury of a one-dimensional morality.

In le Carré's view, the war of 1939–45 had caused Bingham to adopt fixed positions, tenable while Britain was fighting the evils of Nazism, but impossible to maintain in the more nuanced battle between capitalism and communism. Le Carré, by contrast, was more alert to the demands of espionage in the 1960s with the greater subtlety of deception that it required.

Le Carré's explanation of the split is partly true, although he attributes the damage to the friendship to differences of ideology alone. Simon Clanmorris recalls that his father, embracing the ethic of his generation concerning the sacrosanctity of marriage, felt that le Carré was treating Ann, his wife, rather badly. Indeed, the couple divorced in 1971 after several years of disharmony.

He also adduces a second more down-to-earth reason: that Madeleine was extremely and enduringly envious of the enormous financial success of *The Spy Who Came In from the Cold*. This is an understatement.

John was content to deliver a stinging rebuke to le Carré in his foreword to his 1966 book, *The Double Agent*. Distressed that *The Looking Glass War* had painted the rival intelligence services MI5 and MI6 as brutally inhuman, and compared their efficiency in a manner very favourable to MI6, damning the antiquated methods of MI5, he felt that such writing, accurate or not, could do no good to either service. He responded in terms whose meaning would have been clear to any insider who knew them both.

The foreword is a broadside against critics of the intelligence services who, Bingham surmised, were driven by political motives or wishful thinking. By painting MI5 officers as either incurably cynical or incompetent dissolutes they were doing immeasurable damage to the reputation of the Service and undermining the morale of its officers. Such criticism, he believed, could do nothing but encourage the enemies of democracy.

This was an aspect of le Carré's writing that continued to baffle Bingham. Certain that le Carré was not in any way a communist sympathiser or fellow traveller, he simply could not understand why he appeared, in Bingham's view, to be providing encouragement to the opposition, the KGB.

There was also a personal bone to pick. For John Bingham, loyalty was an absolute; he was concerned that his protégé lacked this quality. He had made the introductions between le Carré, his agent and his publisher, and there seemed to be a satisfactory working relationship between all parties. After the publication of *The Spy Who Came In from the Cold*, however, it was clear that le Carré was in a position to demand far better terms than Gollancz was offering.

Encouraged by the success of his third novel, le Carré made greater demands for rights to his future work. John wrote to V.G. that le Carré had been riding his agent, Peter Watt, very hard to obtain better terms. When Watt suffered a stroke and died in July 1965, Bingham speculated that 'David may be slightly blaming himself, justly or unjustly, for poor Peter's demise', revealing later in the letter that le Carré had 'left Peter two or three weeks before the latter had his stroke'.

In fact, he cleaned house completely, dismissing Peter Watt as his agent and deciding not to proceed further with Gollancz, choosing Heinemann instead for his next two books. As John wrote to Victor Gollancz, 'I expect you are now rather relieved you didn't get *The Looking Glass War* and all the tie-up for subsequent books, and at no mean price.'

Watt was a heavy smoker and a copious drinker, a man who enjoyed many of the luxuries of life. He was also by no means poor and had been in indifferent health for a year, so it was unreasonable even to hint that the shock or disappointment at losing a star client could have provoked his death. The very mention of such a possibility, however, indicates that Bingham felt le Carré's departure from his literary agent was a serious matter.

Contact between the two writers was sporadic between 1963 and 1969. Le Carré left MI6 in February 1964 to devote himself full time to writing. He also travelled extensively, including several trips to the United States, where he had been lionised after the success of his third and fourth books. At a meeting in a Wimpy Bar between trips, he compared literary success to being involved in a car crash. Bingham listened carefully and sympathetically but offered no advice. The problem was le Carré's to solve in his own way.

In 1965, shortly before *The Looking Glass War* was released, le Carré was again in London and the Binghams dined with him.

Madeleine recorded that it was a pleasant evening, 'like friends who have met after a long separation'. After the meal, Bingham observed that 'David has not changed much'. But, as meticulously polite, self-effacing and unassertive as Smiley who eats an appalling meal with undrinkable wine at a roadhouse restaurant without a hint of protest, Bingham found le Carré's exchanges with the wine waiter unsettling. He was concerned that his friend could have lost a sense of humility. When the *Daily Express*, about to serialise *The Looking Glass War*, quoted le Carré as commenting that his American press tour had been 'like running for President', he was cynically amused. Receiving a pre-publication copy, he was unable to agree with the *Express* that 'the book has suspense, poignancy, humour at times, and an uncanny quality of grim realism as the blunders of a run-down Intelligence Department send agents to tragic and unnecessary deaths'. Instead, he commented laconically to Madeleine, 'I suppose it is better to foul one's own nest by remote control *after* one has left it.'

Even so, it is clear from his diaries that his friendship with le Carré was not irreparably damaged. He records lunch with him on 15 November 1965 and makes a note to contact him four weeks later. Madeleine, on the other hand, continued to be envious of le Carré's success. This envy swelled as George Smiley became an increasingly popular character and the name of John le Carré became more and more often cited as the authentic voice not only of the spy novel but also of the real world of intelligence. Because the secret world is secret and because le Carré's novels do such a convincing job of portraying a covert world – with a plausible jargon of lamplighters, scalphunters, pavement artists and assorted participants – his books have been accepted as realistic portrayals of intelligence and, given the enforced silence of real-life spymasters, le Carré has become a familiar consultant to the media on all things to do with espionage.

Madeleine's recurring complaint that le Carré was not qualified to speak as an expert on MI5 or MI6 as he had spent so
little time in intelligence is unworthy. The secret world holds a
fascination for the press and their reading public and, with so
many juicy spy scandals coming to light in the 1970s, it is natural
that journalists would seek comments from an intelligence expert
– someone who had actually experienced that milieu. Whether
or not le Carré's world of espionage is accurate in all respects,
it was readable and very plausible. He is an excellent researcher
and highly accomplished at 'the fluffy stuff'. While MI5 and MI6
pursued a policy of absolute silence, it was natural that he should
become the 'inside voice' of the secret world.

Although offended by the treatment of the Service in *The Looking
Glass War*, Bingham, having delivered his rebuke the following
year, was able to maintain the friendship. For Madeleine, her
feelings were stoked by every new book from le Carré and every
success on the screen. The first film was *The Spy Who Came In
from the Cold*, with Richard Burton as protagonist Alec Leamas
and Claire Bloom as Liz Gold. This was a huge success when
it was released in 1965. In the following year Sidney Lumet
directed *The Deadly Affair*, an adaptation of *Call for the Dead*, in
which James Mason played Smiley, and four years later came
The Looking Glass War, with a young Anthony Hopkins playing
Avery and Sir Ralph Richardson as Leclerc, the putative head
of MI5. Madeleine could not accept that le Carré was collecting substantial royalty cheques and income from sale of the film
rights, while her husband received a mere £175 from Gollancz
as an advance for *The Double Agent*.

Ironically, the mentor–pupil relationship that Bingham and le
Carré had formed in 1958 had become inverted by the middle
of the next decade. After writing *Spy*, le Carré never looked back.
With the exception of *The Sentimental Lover*, which was largely

ignored, each of his novels added geometrically to his fame. The publication of *Tinker, Tailor* in 1974 fixed him in the firmament of celebrated espionage writers.

By contrast, after two triumphs in 1965 and 1966, Bingham never regained the stature that his early books had conferred. Le Carré soared while Bingham strove to create an espionage novel as successful as *Spy*. The greatest irony is that it was to George Smiley, modelled largely on Bingham, that le Carré owed his success.

CHAPTER 9

MI5 AGENT RUNNER AND NOVELIST, 1960–69

When we did something wrong he could be very frightening. I suppose if it was your job to terrify communists, it was not too hard to terrify children. I don't suggest for a minute that he was cruel or a bully. He never shouted or threatened or hit us. He simply withdrew intimacy until he felt we had learned our lesson.

Charlotte Bingham, interview with the *Daily Mail*, 9 February 1999

On 23 June 1960, John and Madeleine gave a party at Abingdon Villas for Maurice's eighty-first birthday. It was a beautiful day; the scent of the lilies was as never before and Maurice was happy with his family around him. He and Leila returned to the hotel where they were staying and, on their way to dinner, Maurice joked about the food and promptly collapsed. He died the next day.

Madeleine noted with acerbity that none of the Ulster Binghams came to the funeral. His obituaries were brief; his life had contained little that was noteworthy since the Boer War.

John thus became the 7th Baron Clanmorris of Newbrook in the County of Mayo. The 6th and 7th Barons had been fond of each other, albeit in a somewhat formal manner. John was dutiful but, in all substantial ways, very different from his father. The 6th Lord Clanmorris had cut an archaic Edwardian figure, monocle firmly in his right eye – the trademark monocle that, according to Charlotte, the Binghams wore to suggest short-sightedness as they cut acquaintances in the street.

Madeleine's pen portraits of her parents-in-law are often unflattering. She had not forgotten being treated as an interloper and fortune hunter at Bangor Castle; Maurice and Leila's grudging assistance when Simon needed urgent medical help still rankled.

Bingham's accession to the title made little difference to his financial position. Since the 1920s the assets of the family had been held in a trust whose entail would end with his heirs; from this trust he received an annual allowance of £1,500. For the new baron there was no castle, no fortune to allow a leisured life. The future heralded more of the same – working two jobs to make ends meet.

If *Murder Plan Six* had been a tribute to Gollancz, his next book carried in its title a tribute to another mentor. During the war the operatives of Section B5(b) of MI5 had been known as 'Knight's Black Agents'. Now he proposed to remember his old boss in his seventh novel, *Night's Black Agent*.

This has a complex plot, a strange motivation and a villain who is irredeemably evil. Far less credible even than its predecessor, set in the fjords of Norway, it draws on the author's knowledge of the area from fishing visits in the early 1930s. The denouement is the pursuit and destruction of the villain in the Norwegian mountains.

Despite straining credulity, the book is compelling and was well received. Writing in the *Sunday Times*, Julian Symons endorsed it, saying, 'Bingham is the perfect exemplar of the New Wave in crime writing ... Recommended with all the warmth at my disposal.' Nor was Symons alone. Penguin Books soon agreed to a £350 advance for the paperback rights, the highest advance yet for a Bingham paperback.

At 'The Office', meanwhile, Bingham extended the reach of Section F4. During the late 1950s the deliberately Edwardian image of Prime Minister Harold Macmillan had increasingly become a target for satire. The established order in Britain was under attack by playwrights like Arnold Wesker, whose first play, *The Kitchen*, had been produced in 1957. Although most publications such as *Private Eye*, which launched in 1961, were more satirical than revolutionary, the expression 'class struggle', with menacing Marxist overtones, was in common parlance; concern grew among MI5 officers that the youthful idealism of satirists could easily be exploited. Bingham created a subdivision within F4, called simply 'F4/ARTS' (inevitably referred to as 'FARTS') and sought agents to penetrate suspected subversive elements.

Madeleine's 'theatricals' gave him access to the acting profession but not to the New Left within it. When Charlotte met her future husband Terence Brady in 1964, however, Bingham scented a potential agent, as Brady rubbed shoulders with the anti-Establishment group of actors who had created *Beyond the Fringe* four years earlier. Mild by modern standards, as the first show designed to lampoon the established order in Britain, it was seen as subversive by the Establishment.

This group of young actors were certainly not communists, but they represented a novel challenge to Conservatives in Britain. Terence had taken over from Peter Cook when the show was playing in London and, soon after he met Charlotte, he was approached by her father:

> Most oddly he once asked me to work for him. Madeleine had worked me up into a high old state of anxiety shortly after I had met Charlotte by warning me that Jack had a very powerful job and that if he ever found out anything about me that was contrary I would live (or perhaps not live) to regret it. I hadn't a clue what

he did and no one of course could tell me. Then one day I was
invited to have lunch with Jack. I thought the agenda was going
to be about my love for his daughter but not a bit of it. After an
extremely stiff gin and tonic (Jack abhorred weak drinks) he made
it perfectly clear I had his approval then he asked me to work for
him. He said he wanted me to 'spy' on my fellow actors and tell
him which ones were red, pink or blue. He explained briefly how
he saw the threat of Communism and subversion and said that I
must be aware that quite a few of my peers were dangerously Left
... He said all I had to do was watch, listen and report, however
little or however much. I didn't have to think about it. I refused
even though I thought there goes a big black mark against me.
He asked me very kindly why I couldn't do it and I did my best to
explain my feelings about loyalty, my friends, my job and my own
political position, which was the least important reason. I finally
told him I simply could not work undercover most of all because –
as I explained – I had too much imagination and would bring him
in a lot of nonsense. He found this very funny, told me not to think
another thought, to have another drink, and the subject was never
brought up again. But we think he did get some of the profession
to work for him – in fact we are almost certain that he did.

In *The Honourable Schoolboy*, John le Carré devotes one chapter
to the techniques of agent running. Craw, the Australian journalist, extracts intelligence from his agent Phoebe Wayfarer by
constant attention, congratulating her even when the intelligence
is worthless. One day, he is sure, she will deliver the goods. Such
was Bingham's method as he acquired his team of agents – at
least nine of whom were active at the end of the 1950s.

    These were the agents whom he met regularly, often daily, for
debriefing. There were, doubtless, countless others who had a
working brief to report to him anything that helped him fill gaps

in the picture of the communist target, but it was on the stable of regular agents that he expended most effort. Their welfare was his principal concern and his diaries are full of notations of expenses incurred in ensuring their comfort. One agent had a penchant for drinking Dubonnet, and he would meticulously record the small amounts expended in indulging that habit. Charlotte remembers a police officer who would visit their house in Abingdon Villas regularly with handfuls of parking tickets incurred by his agents in the course of their work. He would dutifully settle these on his agents' behalf.

Later, as a novelist, he described his career as 'slogging away for twenty-five years' and it was that quality of persistence that served him well as an agent runner. He had no desire to be among those whom John le Carré in *Tinker, Tailor* described as 'silk shirt agents'. He understood the need for pertinacity and patience along the long road of penetrating the CPGB and the trades unions.

Occasionally, however, there were windfalls, such as the bonanza of intelligence that brought a form of closure to the Burgess–Maclean affair. In December 1961 Anatoli Mikhailovich Golitsyn, a KGB major assigned to the Soviet embassy in Helsinki, defected to the CIA. Interrogated by the CIA's James Jesus Angleton, Golitsyn provided intelligence that finally identified Philby as the Soviet 'mole' responsible for alerting Maclean. The long-standing belief of Philby's guilt among officers in both MI5 and MI6 was vindicated. Armed with this, Nicholas Elliott of MI6 travelled to Beirut in late 1962 to obtain a confession from Philby; he succeeded in obtaining a verbal confession but Philby vanished on 23 January 1963, defecting to Moscow before a second planned meeting.

After the initial British enthusiasm at the intelligence he brought, Golitsyn posed as many problems as he solved.

Christopher Andrew considers him an 'unreliable conspiracy theorist', discounting many of the defector's theories of Soviet global strategy. Additionally Andrew comments that Golitsyn actually misled MI5 in his assertion that there were five Soviet agents, known in Moscow as the 'Magnificent Five', all at university at the same time, working inside British intelligence. In taking this statement literally, he argues, the search for the other members of the Soviet spy ring took several wrong directions.

The MI5 interrogation of Golitsyn was handled principally by Arthur Martin of Section D1, who flew to the USA in 1962. In early 1963, after a series of disagreements in Washington concerning the value of Golitsyn's assertions, the defector asked to be resettled in England, and he arrived in London in July. At this point MI5 undertook more searching interrogations conducted by several officers, including Bingham.

From the outset there was disagreement among MI5's officers. Martin, according to Andrew, was 'a skilful and persistent counter-espionage investigator ... but he lacked the capacity for balanced judgment and a grasp of the broader context'. Martin continued to maintain that Golitsyn's revelations were accurate and invaluable; a second interrogator, very likely John Bingham, commented that his 'knowledge ranges over a wide field but nowhere has it any great depth'.

This difference of opinion caused a rift within MI5 between believers and sceptics. Soon afterwards a senior MI5 officer leaked that the Soviet defector was in London, whereupon Golitsyn departed abruptly for the USA.

He left behind him several tantalising assertions. First, he confirmed the intelligence from VENONA that pointed to Philby as the 'Third Man'. Second, he asserted that Harold Wilson, the leader of the Labour opposition, was a KGB agent. Third, he set in train the destructive search for a Soviet agent at the very top of MI5 that led to wild accusations and counter-accusations over the next decade.

Amid the controversy surrounding this intelligence, Sir Roger Hollis, MI5's Director General since 1956, proposed a full assessment of Golitsyn and his intelligence; Bingham was commissioned to research and write his biography. In February 1964, however, Yuri Nosenko, claiming to be a deputy depart- ment chief within the KGB, defected to the CIA from Geneva. He was spirited to Washington, kept in solitary confinement and subjected to hostile interrogation lasting over three years.

This unusually harsh treatment resulted from Golitsyn's asser- tion that the KGB would send an officer, ostensibly defecting to the west, to discredit the intelligence that he supplied. Nosenko appeared to fit that profile. Whether or not Nosenko was a true defector, he created a serious division of opinion between the FBI and the CIA and deep rifts within MI5. Hoover believed that Golitsyn was unreliable and that Nosenko was genuine; Angleton remained convinced that Nosenko was the planted 'defector' that the CIA had been warned of.

The second of Golitsyn's claims concerned the leadership of the Labour Party, involving two strands which would, if true, constitute a major threat to national security. While the Labour Party was in opposition from 1951, Harold Wilson worked to establish himself as a future leader of the party. During his tenure at the Board of Trade in the Attlee government of 1945–51 he had developed contacts in the Soviet Union, and after 1951 he travelled frequently to Moscow as a representative of a company importing timber from the USSR. These commer- cial trips had political overtones as Wilson strove to demonstrate that he was able to deal with Russians. The Security Service noted these visits and, after Golitsyn's defection, opened a file on Wilson. So sensitive was the issue that the file was opened in the name of 'Harold John Worthington' and kept out of the mainstream registry.

Following the Labour Party's election loss in 1959, Wilson led an attempted coup to replace Hugh Gaitskell as leader, but was roundly defeated. Three years later Gaitskell suddenly died from an attack of *Lupus erythematosus*. Golitsyn claimed that Gaitskell had been assassinated by the KGB in order to clear the way for a more Leftist Wilson government. Startling though this allegation was, its credibility depended on the assumption that there had been a long-standing plan to assassinate Gaitskell, as Golitsyn had defected two years before the Labour leader's death. As Wilson had challenged Gaitskell in 1960 and Golitsyn had defected in the following year, it was just plausible that the KGB had formulated a plan when Wilson's bid to unseat Gaitskell failed. Since Golitsyn had not spoken of such a plot before Gaitskell's actual death, his claim was generally discounted within the Service.

The third important piece of intelligence to flow from Golitsyn concerned the spy ring that included Burgess, Maclean and Philby. The assertion that 'The Magnificent Five' had been at university together involved the Service in a fruitless search to find two other individuals who fitted the exact description given by Golitsyn. When, in April 1964, the American Michael Straight confessed that he had been recruited at Cambridge by Anthony Blunt, Arthur Martin, promising immunity, succeeded in extracting a confession from Blunt. In the same year John Cairncross, a Treasury official and another Cambridge alumnus, also admitted that he had spied for the Soviet Union. Cairncross, however, had not gone up to Cambridge until 1934, by which time Philby and Maclean had already graduated. In fact, the Security Service had successfully identified all five members of the ring but, because of Golitsyn's assertion that the five had been contemporaries at university, continued to look for other agents. This was to lead to even greater disruption.

Arthur Martin remained convinced that there was another Soviet agent in a senior position in the Service and an investigation of Graham Mitchell, Hollis's deputy, began. Martin and Peter Wright, another senior officer in the Service, became suspicious of the Director General himself, but were unable to produce evidence that could be used in a prosecution. Both Mitchell and Hollis were subsequently cleared of suspicion. These turbulent events did not involve Section F4 directly, but the atmosphere of suspicion surrounding the internal investigations was deeply damaging to the morale of the Service.

After Gaitskell's death Wilson ran successfully for the leadership of the Labour Party and, with the Conservative Party discredited by the sex–spy scandal involving John Profumo, a change of government was inevitable. Within the Service there was widespread anxiety not only that its cosy relationship with Macmillan's government was to end but also that the country was to be led by a man suspected of dangerously close relations with the Soviet Union.

The new Labour government in 1964 perceived MI5 as a right-wing organisation and Wilson immediately sought to reduce its influence. The Prime Minister, according to Barbara Castle, was obsessed by the belief that the intelligence services were plotting to unseat him.

There were at least two plots to remove Wilson. The first of these was planned in May 1968 and appears to have gone no further than a discussion between Cecil King, the chairman of International Publishing Corporation, Earl Mountbatten of Burma, Sir Solly Zuckerman and Hugh Cudlipp, King's colleague on the board of the *Daily Mirror*. King had been conducting an editorial campaign to remove Wilson and on

8 May 1968 he openly suggested to Mountbatten that the latter be prepared to assume control of the government after a military coup. In his memoirs, *Walking on the Water*, Cudlipp described the meeting.

Once the group was assembled, Cecil King launched a tirade against the Labour government and, in particular, against the Prime Minister. The national situation was grave, he claimed, and immediate action was needed before the entire edifice of government collapsed and the armed forces were compelled to intervene to stop bloodshed. The only way to avoid this apocalyptic outcome was to form a national government with a universally respected figure such as Mountbatten at its head. Would Mountbatten, he asked, be prepared to serve at the head of a new administration to forestall anarchy?

Zuckerman, violently uncomfortable at the direction the meeting had taken, replied that such discussion amounted to treason; he and Mountbatten promptly departed.

With a mere six months until his sixtieth birthday, Bingham felt mixed emotions as he surveyed the British political scene. The country lost prestige when Wilson was forced to devalue the pound in 1967, and the illusion that Britain could maintain its position as a world power – an illusion that many of Bingham's generation had stalwartly clung to – was revealed as untenable. Disenchanted by the American handling of the war in Vietnam, a younger generation was making its presence felt across the country, busily rejecting perceived archaic values – the very values that Bingham had defended since the 1930s. The year of 1968, the year in which he was slated to leave the service, ushered in a novel set of challenges for MI5.

Throughout the early 1960s there had been a steady flow of defectors from the Warsaw Pact countries. There had also been spy scandals within Britain, but Bingham argued plausibly that the west was winning the war of ideologies. For twenty years the attention of the Service had been trained on the Soviet Union, and he looked forward to retirement in the reassuring knowledge that he had contributed materially to the defence of the realm. Such complacency vanished amid the events of 1968.

On 17 March 1968, 10,000 demonstrators gathered in Trafalgar Square to protest against the Vietnam War. A splinter group of 3,000 attempted to storm the American embassy in Grosvenor Square in what the BBC described as 'a bloody riot such as Britain has never before witnessed'. Further demonstrations against the war followed on 7 July and 27 October, when a total of 25,000 demonstrators marched and 6,000 of them, led by the Maoist Britain-Vietnam Solidarity Front, were met by over 1,000 policemen outside the American embassy.

These demonstrations were more than matched by students and workers in Paris who took to the barricades in a widespread strike. MI5 officers followed events across the Channel assiduously and Section F4 was alert for signs of similar coordinated student uprisings in Britain.

On the night of 20–21 August, Soviet tanks rolled into Prague to suppress the 'Prague Spring', democratic reforms introduced by Alexander Dubček. Amid protests from around the world, the Soviet Union moved against Prague with more than 250,000 troops, removed Dubček and bolstered the position of the Czech Communist Party.

Concerns over these events were dwarfed by a more immediate threat closer to home. On 27 April 1968 the first civil rights march was staged by Catholic groups in Ulster. A second march was organised for 5 October but was banned when the Apprentice Boys of Derry, a Protestant organisation, announced that they would march the same route on the same day. In defiance of the government ban, the Catholic civil rights group held their march and were roughly handled by the Royal Ulster Constabulary. Riots ensued in Derry; the Catholic minority in Ulster, spearheaded by Bernadette Devlin and the People's Democracy group, stepped up their protests.

On 6 November, Home Secretary James Callaghan asked the Director General of MI5, Sir Martin Furnival Jones, for an up-to-date appreciation of the prospect of IRA violence in Ulster. Professor Christopher Andrew, author of the official history of MI5, comments that the Security Service was astonishingly ignorant of the situation. Security in Ulster was handled by the Royal Ulster Constabulary, while on the British mainland Special Branch was responsible. MI5 had managed to stay clear of an issue that was generally regarded as insoluble.

The appreciation submitted by MI5 was profound, but rested on the age-old misconception that the issue was essentially local, involving friction between nationalists (Catholic) and unionists (Protestant). Memorably, they reported that 'the security problem in Northern Ireland is simple. It springs from the antagonism of two Communities with long memories and relatively short tempers.'

Although accurate in tracing the differences between the communities to historically different religions (a flight attendant once famously advised passengers that they were arriving in Belfast and should set their watches back 300 years), the assessment overlooked the most important fact. The Provisional Irish Republican Army ('PIRA') believed that, ultimately, unionists would accept Home Rule; the true enemy was not Protestant Ulster, but England. PIRA was not conducting a local vendetta but a war of national liberation.

In late 1968 and early 1969 – just as Bingham was due to retire – a series of riots and pitched battles in Belfast and Londonderry convinced the Service that greater attention should be paid to the threat of violence on the mainland and, somewhat belatedly, a section was established to counter this threat. In her autobiography *Open Secret*, Stella Rimington, later the first female Director General of MI5, records that 1968 and 1969 saw the threat of terrorism develop in Britain and marked the beginning of a sea change in MI5's direction. A far greater threat was posed by terrorism 'on our own doorstep' at the end of the 1960s, she recalls. This, combined with the rise in international terrorism, led to a reduction in the resources allocated to fighting the Cold War. The changed emphasis, in turn, caused a fundamental shift in the culture of the Security Service.

In retrospect, it was inevitable that Bingham would be retained past retirement date and become involved in the problems of Ulster. He had family and contacts there and, although his attempts at an Ulster accent were notoriously dreadful, he was the obvious officer to gather intelligence on the spot. Repeating his wartime *modus operandi*, he made several visits to Northern Ireland over the next six years, spending hours in pubs and cafés, listening to the opinions and prejudices of locals. He claimed that he had never met people as intransigent as Ulster unionists – this from a man whose great-grandfather founded the first Orange Lodge.

Bingham had left the *Sunday Dispatch* in 1950 and returned to MI5 for a variety of reasons, not least the declining circulation that heralded the paper's demise. In fact, the *Dispatch* had struggled on for a further eleven years before it gave up the fight and closed in 1961.

Since his first newspaper job in Hull he had enjoyed, even romanticised, the camaraderie of a newspaper office. In 1963 he completed *A Case of Libel*, in which he paints that camaraderie boldly, highlighting the way in which a less than sensitive editor can destroy the *esprit de corps* essential to a good paper.

His descriptions of the functioning of the newspaper's office are compelling; this, after all, was his meat and drink. The matter of the libel, too, is convincing and cleverly drawn. The last seventy pages of the book, however, are devoted to an unconvincing, bloodless liaison between the newspaper's lawyer and the woman libelled before the story reverts to the final closure of the paper. The writing lacks the objectivity of his better work and the imprecise characters of the latter half of the book detract from the sensitive characterisation of the early chapters. It is easy to understand why he felt compelled to write it, less clear why it had to be so long.

Advertised by Gollancz as 'a straight novel by John Bingham', it is a vital part of a biography of its author but was largely discounted by his growing coterie of readers. On 12 June 1962 he wrote to Victor Gollancz foreseeing this, knowing that the publisher's reaction would be that 'a crime writer should stick to his clues and leave other and cleverer people to write non-crime books'. Admitting that 'it is not great literature', he commented: 'It is a story I have often wanted to write, so I suppose it had to be done.' He did, however, reassure his publisher that 'I shall now revert to crime, to your relief.'

It was a final tribute to a profession he had greatly enjoyed, that he had celebrated in *Michael Sibley*. It was a rite of passage, an epitaph for a world that was changing. In the new world order, newspapers would ever after play second fiddle to television – a development Bingham despised.

While her father was writing *A Case of Libel*, Charlotte too had begun to write. Her disparate qualities – rebelliousness tinged with an ethical conservatism, liberally seasoned with irreverence and iconoclasm – combined when she took up her pen. At the time, according to Madeleine, Charlotte's idea of working was to take a temporary job, collect her wages on Friday, then ask

Madeleine for a loan on Tuesday. Madeleine decided that this was an unacceptable routine and spoke to John about getting Charlotte a proper job. He found her a job at 'The Office', where she worked in the Cork Street and Grosvenor Street offices.

Another cause of friction was Charlotte's tendency to invite girlfriends to stay the night at Abingdon Villas. They slept on the drawing room floor until one night when John returned late and stumbled on a sleeping girlfriend. 'I will not have this house turned into a DP camp,' he thundered. Charlotte was uncertain what a DP was, but she grasped the gist of the outburst.

One evening, Charlotte commented to Madeleine, 'I must have been out with about 300 men and I haven't met a super-man yet.' Madeleine urged her to start a book with just that sentence (which she did), and John gave her advice: 'Write as you speak – amusingly – and write the truth. And never finish a sentence with a series of dots.'

Armed with this less than comprehensive blueprint, Charlotte began to write, slowly and painstakingly, like her father; she finally gave the finished book, *Coronet Among the Weeds*, to her agent. He gave it to Heinemann, who sold it to seven countries at the Frankfurt Book Fair. Charlotte was launched.

Coronet is a delightful work, the autobiography of an eighteen-year-old, which parodies the debutante season and was for a time mandatory reading for every eighteen-year-old English girl. Charlotte's debutante season had cost £250 but she made about £20,000 from her account of it. 'Overall, a good investment,' Madeleine commented.

There are many parties in the book – both debutante balls and less reputable events. One of the latter, held at Abingdon Villas, resulted in the destruction of John's beloved garden. With charming irreverence, Charlotte describes how, the following morning, her father was 'one minute looking for greenfly and the next he was standing around with all this earth'. On seeing the carnage, Bingham, her mother informed her, was 'very hurt'.

Throughout the book Charlotte maintains the pose of being a disinterested teenage observer of her family. In one passage she perfectly captures the conspiratorial way in which father and daughter viewed Madeleine. Her father would come out from the cinema imitating the lead character in whatever film he had just seen – stiff-upper-lipped if he watched a war film, acting the part of Hannibal after a film about the Punic Wars. Madeleine, by contrast went on being herself. 'If you're being Hannibal,' Charlotte teased her father, 'you don't want to be asked to go and get someone's slippers.'

In *Coronet* we see the familiar relationship of rebellious, frivolous, iconoclastic daughter shocking conventional, moralistic mother; between father and daughter there is an adoring mockery. The reader meets a father who would prefer to eat nothing but bread and dripping, if he could get away with it; who would prefer drinking whisky with the domestic help in the kitchen to mingling with the 'weeds' at Charlotte's parties. They are tender images, lovingly drawn.

Charlotte's success with *Coronet* was immediate. She became the darling of the press, who pursued her for interviews, snapping endless photographs of her in a variety of poses. The best of these was a posed photo that appeared in *LIFE*, showing father, mother and daughter, the three writers, at work in Abingdon Villas, which was striking and imaginative, if unrealistic.

Charlotte loved the attention and would invite reporters to meet her at the Ritz. Ever practical, Madeleine pointed out that this incurred considerable costs for the newspapers and suggested that she give such interviews at home. Some members of the press hinted that Bingham was in some way benefiting from his daughter's success. 'All I do is pay for the whisky,' he replied.

At about this time *A Case of Libel* was published. Having succeeded to the title, he was now 'a decadent peer' in the eyes of the press. One reporter wrote of his new book, 'While his daughter makes thousands of pounds with the help of publicity, Lord Clanmorris is attacking Fleet Street.' Bingham wrote to the editor, pointing out that he wasn't attacking Fleet Street in *A Case of Libel*: he, as an ex-newsman, was very sympathetic with the lot of reporters. The offending reporter promptly telephoned to apologise, explaining that he had only read the blurb of the book.

Throughout this heady period of Charlotte's success John maintained his dispassionate objectivity. He was delighted for his daughter, despite ruefully commenting that she had made, with one book, twice as much money as he had made from ten years of writing.

Bingham had promised V.G. that he would return to crime and he was as good as his word. In the spring and summer of 1965 he polished and delivered to Gollancz the manuscript of *A Fragment of Fear*, the book that definitively re-established him in the front line of psychological thriller writers. V.G. immediately recognised the book's potential and organised a massive launch, accompanied by endorsements from as many 'big names' as could be corralled to the cause. Gollancz identified the book as the one that would sell to American readers and agreed personally to take on the promotion of the book to American publishers. In the certainty that film rights could be sold profitably, he sent a draft copy to Alfred Hitchcock, who had already used *Murder Plan Six* and *Five Roundabouts to Heaven* on his television show *The Hitchcock Hour*.

Back home in Britain, John le Carré, approached for an endorsement, duly obliged, writing:

Not just Vintage Bingham, but his Great Year. He gives an example of the classic crime novel; the tension within is expressed by the tension without. In a nightmare world, he handles his characters with compassion and sincerity, but also with alarm.

A Fragment of Fear was one of Bingham's personal favourites. The treatment is stark: how an individual can be trapped inside his own mind when everyone around him, for varying but quite acceptable reasons, believes that he is unbalanced. He expected an unrestrained response to the book but admitted that he was unsure whether it would be positive or negative. In the event, with minor dissent, it was acclaimed as a most successful original. The biggest problem that faced him when he wrote it was how to finish it and he is not entirely successful in his resolution, as the *New Statesman* pointed out: '*A Fragment of Fear* adroitly takes up the theme underlying *The Lady Vanishes* – someone who knows he's stumbled into a mystery but can't persuade anyone else to believe him ... The resolution of the plot is ludicrous but while it lasts the story won't let you go.'

From other reviewers, acclaim came without that damning qualifier. Any doubts about John Bingham's continued presence at the top of the crime writers' tree were dispelled. Critics were unanimous in praising this 'Vintage Bingham' and, once again, comparison of his work with that of Agatha Christie appeared, this time in the review from the *Times Literary Supplement*: 'John Bingham is, in contrast to Miss Christie, essentially a modern writer concerned, in *A Fragment of Fear*, to show how easily the sanity and substance of the individual can be lost in other eyes.'

The review in the *Sunday Times* on 14 November 1965, moreover, was read by E. P. Dutton, a New York publishing house, which contacted Gollancz the following day to buy the American rights. James MacGibbon, handling publicity at Gollancz, was also confident of an advance of £1,000 from Penguin for the UK paperback rights. The publisher had certainly stirred up interest in the book, which he saw as a potential blockbuster. Four months later Victor Gollancz's prescience bore even riper fruit. Universal agreed to buy an option on *Fragment* for £1,000 with a further £10,000 payable when filming began. After a mid-season slump, John Bingham was once again a thoroughbred at the peak of his form.

There were several reasons why he needed to re-establish his position in the mid-1960s. His early success with his first two novels and, to a lesser extent, with *The Third Skin*, had seemed to be the harbinger of fame and wealth, but neither had come in the quantities he had hoped for. Royalties were steady but unspectacular. As an experienced fisherman, he knew that he had failed as yet to 'land the big one'.

If that knowledge caused him distress, it was accentuated by the plaudits accorded to le Carré and to Charlotte, two writers close to him. For them success had been more immediate and had been accompanied by financial rewards beyond his dreams. However much readers admired Bingham's work, Victor Gollancz, meticulous guardian of his firm's assets, was still offering advances of £175.

In 1965, therefore, he decided to stray into uncharted territory; the taste of the era appeared to be spy stories and he knew he had at least one good spy story in him. The first thing to do, therefore, was to speak to his literary agent Peter Watt, for despite their fifteen-year acquaintance, Watt had no idea of his MI5 connection and he, after all, would want to know that his client knew whereof he wrote. Meeting Watt outside his office, Bingham confided in him. His agent was genuinely shocked and, as he spluttered, he was sworn to silence. Still spluttering,

Watt took his leave and slid off to the Garrick Club for a restorative bracer.

Stood at the bar was a friend who seemed concerned at Watt's appearance. Reassuring him that he was not ill, Watt stammered, 'Had the most awful shock. Author of mine. Known him for years. Just told me that he belonged to MI5.' The friend expressed his sympathy but made a mental note. Watt had not known that his confidant was an MI5 agent; the quiet, reclusive Bingham had agents everywhere. Within five minutes of pledging his silence, Watt had chosen a Bingham agent to confide in.

When he started writing his first spy novel in 1965, Bingham's sights were set on rivalling le Carré's success. He stated as much to V.G., writing, 'I do not know how the sales of this one will go, but I do know that the next one ... will, or should, if I can do it right, do as well as *Spy* – provided I can get it past the "gnomes of Whitehall".'

The second goad to drive him to greater success was very different and much closer to home. After the publication of *Coronet*, Charlotte had become such a celebrity that when Penguin Books were preparing for the release of *Murder Plan Six* in paperback, their blurb referred to 'John Bingham, immortalised as the amiable father of Charlotte in *Coronet Among the Weeds*', hardly a description to please the author of nine novels. For reasons professional, reasons personal and reasons financial, therefore, he was training for the big fight when he began work on *The Double Agent*.

The year of 1965 was a turning point in many ways. John and Madeleine became grandparents for the first time when Charlotte's daughter was born; John, after much reflection, decided that he could reconcile with his conscience the idea of publishing a novel with an espionage rather than a crime theme.

He finished work on *The Double Agent* and delivered it to Gollancz. All in all, everything was well in Abingdon Villas. It was with a spirit of optimism that the Bingham family entered 1966.

The ever-watchful V.G. stood on precedent in the matter of an advance for *The Double Agent*, granting only the customary £175, but his publicity machine compensated for such parsimony. Trumpeting it as 'Bingham's Masterpiece', it drew attention to a complex plot, filled with the normal ingredients of a spy thriller, but emphasising the blend of 'terror, real and implied', and 'chillingly horrifying revelations of human behaviour' that give the book its cutting edge.

When Bingham turned his hand to writing spy stories in 1966 – having first obtained clearance from 'the gnomes of Whitehall' – he was greatly more reticent than le Carré about the operations of MI5 and MI6. Indeed, it is almost as if in obtaining any detail of how agents were run, one is pulling teeth from the author. Le Carré's portrayal of the world of intelligence may be completely fictional, but to paint any detailed picture, accurate or not, was something that Bingham was not prepared to do. The most bizarre feature of *The Double Agent* is that the *modus operandi* of the KGB is depicted with many more descriptive flourishes than that of the KGB's British counterpart, where the writing is matter-of-fact. He is laconic, guarded to the point of oversimplicity.

Despite this shortcoming, the book was an immediate success. The critics' response was enthusiastic, confirming for Bingham the direction he had taken. After hesitating for several years about the ethics of writing anything even tenuously connected to espionage, he pulled off a sizeable success without betraying secrets or operational detail.

One of the most glowing reviews came from Susan Hill of the *Coventry Evening Telegraph*:

John Bingham has never got the treatment he deserves. He has been one of our best detective story writers for years, he has an eager and admiring circle of readers, but he has never 'hit the big time' in the sense that many one-book men (and lesser-book men at that) have done.

Equally pleasing was recognition from his peers at the Crime Writers' Association. *The Double Agent* was runner-up in the 1966 CWA Merit Award and the book was highly praised by the Association, who called it 'by far his most successful'.

In record time the paperback rights were sold to Panther Books, and in January 1967 John Bush at Gollancz could boast to E. P. Dutton in New York that 'we have done exceptionally well with *The Double Agent*, selling 50 per cent more than any other Bingham'. While it would never rival *Spy*, it was a vindication of a long-ruminated decision to attempt another genre.

Pleasure in the success of *Double Agent* was dimmed by the death of Sir Victor Gollancz at the age of seventy-three on 8 February 1967. He had led a remarkable life: nephew of two knighted professors, he came from a distinguished Jewish family in north London, was educated at New College, Oxford, and had founded his publishing firm in 1927 at the age of thirty-four. A devotee of several humanitarian causes, he had mobilised British public opinion in favour of decent treatment of German civilians after the Second World War and been instrumental in the founding of War on Want, a crusade against hunger worldwide, in 1951. His death was a blow to everyone who worked for the company; for forty years it had been guided by the firm hand and dedicated vision of one man.

V.G. was succeeded at his firm by his daughter Livia. The success of *The Double Agent* enabled her to be more generous in September 1968 when the terms for Bingham's next book, *I Love,*

I Kill, were negotiated. His status now justified an advance of £300 and a more complex agreement. On the following day the paperback rights were sold to Panther for the customary 7.5 per cent and a £500 advance.

When it came to printing *I Love, I Kill*, however, there were two obstacles: first, Jon Evans, the Gollancz reader, admitted that he had been 'thoroughly bored by the greater part of the book', a statement that must have caused some hesitation in the firm's publicity department. Second, the main character, an ambitious actor who fights his way to the top of his profession, systematically using and discarding his friends and colleagues, was considered by the firm's legal department to bear too close a resemblance to Richard Burton. The lawyers cautioned Gollancz that it might be considered libellous.

At all events, the legal team withdrew their objection and the publicity machine was cranked up to promote the book. Despite the best efforts of the Gollancz team, the book did not perform well. It had several of the trademark Bingham features, such as extended police interrogations, but the milieu in which it was set did not come naturally and the description of principal charac-ters and their behaviour (what Bingham called 'the fluffy stuff') was unconvincing.

The realistic nature of the theatre setting was generally praised. The *Times Literary Supplement* was a touch equivocal about the book but commented that 'the background is theatri-cal and realistically so'. Overall, critical reaction was mixed and the reviewer of the *Irish Times* was not alone in opining that this was 'far from Mr. Bingham's best'.

As it was a story about the theatre in which a murder occurs rather than a murder mystery, the *Irish Times* was right in its judgement. While, as ever, Bingham is interested in the psychol-ogy of the murderer, that interest is more superficial than in his earlier books. It almost seems that he wanted to move away from murder as a theme, possibly eager to capitalise on the success of *The Double Agent* with another spy story. It is certain that his heart was neither in attending the theatre nor in writing about it.

At this point in his writing career, Bingham seems to have been at a crossroads. He had concentrated on realistic crime, almost exclusively murder stories, in his early books. At first he had been disappointed in le Carré when he turned from murder as a subject to all-out espionage in 1963. Once Bingham himself had crossed the Rubicon with *The Double Agent*, however, he wanted to repeat its success. With that as his objective, he returned to the theme of espionage for his twelfth work.

CHAPTER 10

DISAPPOINTMENTS, 1969–79

We always knew that we could work with John Bingham, and that really was adequate for us. He wasn't what I'd call one of our star authors, but he was certainly one of our top writers.
Livia Gollancz to the author, July 2011

The 1960s were anathema to Bingham. He found himself living in a country politically and culturally alien to him. Depressed at the Labour victory in the 1964 general election, he was appalled when Edward Heath became leader of the Conservative Party in the following year. British politics seemed to be polarising. Sceptical of modern trends, he was shocked by the Labour government's attitude to the Service and doubtful that a Conservative government would provide solutions to the country's malaise.

The year of 1969 began amid industrial turmoil as the government strove to curb the power of the trades unions. Popular discontent mounted as 'the pound in your pocket' lost purchasing power. At 'The Office' he soldiered on and, in the evenings, busied himself with his second spy novel, *Vulture in the Sun*.

He had hardly begun writing when his mother died on 3 June. After a number of illnesses in her later years, her death came as no shock. Nonetheless, she was the last direct link to two sides of his family – in Cape Town and Bangor – and her death represented a break with the past. Mother and son had grown apart, despite Bingham's regular weekly visits to her after Maurice died. Bingham had begun to see himself as a relic of the pre-war years. Leila had married Maurice a few years after the end of the Boer War and had remained an Edwardian figure, far more remote from her son's generation than Bingham felt from his post-war colleagues. Nonetheless, now aged sixty-one, Bingham felt trapped within the Service and yearned for a break.

The opportunity was provided when Columbia Pictures and producer Paul Dehn arranged to shoot the film version of *A Fragment of Fear* in Pompeii. Dehn had worked with le Carré on the immensely successful *The Spy Who Came In from the Cold*, starring Richard Burton and Claire Bloom, and on *The Deadly Affair*, an adaptation of *Call for the Dead*, with James Mason and Maximilian Schell. The cast for *A Fragment of Fear* was also impressive, headed by two icons of the 1960s, David Hemmings and Gayle Hunnicutt.

For a month John and Madeleine spent whole days and nights together in Italy. They had been married for over thirty-five years, yet this was their first extended period alone together, without the intrusion of agent welfaring, miscellaneous burglaries and the other activities that had kept John away from home. Madeleine was ecstatic at the novelty of daily breakfast and dinner with her husband and frequently referred, in later life, to the magical quality of those weeks, willing him to find time to recreate them. Two ladies staying in the same hotel in Vico Equense observed them together and decided that they were a couple who had met late in life and just married. Amusingly, when the four became friendly, Bingham established by careful but apparently casual questioning, that the ladies were in fact from MI6.

The film was released in September 1970 and was a modest success, driven largely by the status of its lead actors. Since starring in *Blow-Up* in 1966, Hemmings had become a huge box-office draw, while Gayle Hunnicutt had acquired a reputation as a sultry sex symbol and had starred with James Garner in *Marlowe* in 1969.

Madeleine had for a long time taken an interest in John's writing and had served periodically as his informal editor. In the late 1960s, one can sense her increased involvement in his work. She adapted *Michael Sibley* for the stage and in 1969 she did the same for *The Double Agent*, producing two versions, a two-act play and a three-act play. Charlotte and Terence collaborated on this venture and submitted the screenplay to Thames TV. On 12 May 1969, *The Double Agent*, starring Brian Blessed and Leonard Rossiter, aired in the ITV Playhouse series. It received mixed reviews across the country; the most negative note was sounded by the *Daily Telegraph*, who dismissed it as 'monotonous, stock characters, too low key'. In truth, there were too many spy stories on the market.

Since Livia Gollancz had taken control of her father's business, firmer and crisper memoranda circulated at Henrietta Street; the firm's *modus operandi* was tightened. In 1970 Bingham was requested to complete an 'Author's Biographical and Publicity Information' form, a task that clearly irritated him as his responses to questions are often frivolous. He left the 'Name in full' and 'Permanent address' fields blank, for example, presumably reckoning that if the firm did not know these details, something was amiss.

He and Livia got on well enough. Forty-some years later, Livia talks of him with great warmth. 'He was a very pleasant man and easy to work with,' she recalls. 'I used to dine with him and his family when they lived in Abingdon Villas.' She also implies that a different kind of editor might have been firmer with him, when she talks of her time as his editor:

I think our firm really suited writers like John Bingham, the basic editing. Of course there are different sorts of editors – take Diana Athill at Andre Deutsch. She was the total opposite of me. I would check a book for obvious errors and then do all the jobs necessary to publish it.

Bingham reciprocated that friendship; his letters to Livia are warm and friendly. He signs off with 'All the best, dear / Love, John'. In the spring of 1970 he delivered the manuscript of *Vulture in the Sun*. A modern, espionage-based Romeo-and-Juliet story, it is set in Cyprus and provides a snapshot of the intricacies of espionage and counter-espionage between west and east. The plot is dense and, in the view of Jon Evans at Gollancz:

> [All the characters] seem to be very much in the dark about what everyone else is up to. It's one of those yarns in which it is abso- lutely impossible to see the wood for the trees – and the trees for the undergrowth. One has to be content to take things as they happen.

Both Evans and Livia felt that *Vulture*, while not up to Bingham's normal standard, had the potential to sell, and it was published in the spring of 1971. Panther Books quickly bought the paper- back rights with an advance of £350.

The book had been delayed by several events: first, Leila's death and what Bingham obliquely referred to as 'other compli- cations' in the autumn of 1969. Then the filming of *A Fragment of Fear* intervened, setting the release date back further. By the time the book appeared in print, the reader gains the impression that the author was rather bored with it; it does not move at the pace of earlier work. Pedestrian passages, which Bingham would previously have improved, stand out starkly. It is not, by any means, his best work.

Reviews were mixed. Faithful Bingham fans – Violet Grant in the *Daily Telegraph* and Anthony Price in the *Oxford Mail* – were enthusiastic, commenting that with 'the precisely drawn island setting [accurately delineating the Turkish and Greek areas] he builds up the plot like the master craftsman he is, and the end comes with a nice unexpected twist' and describing the book as 'well contrived, always believable – a wholly satisfying spy mystery'. But there were dissenters: the *Guardian* reviewer hit the mark with the comment 'Enjoyable and credible, if a bit on the slow side', while the most disparaging review came from the *Huddersfield Examiner*, focusing acutely on the weakest element of the book:

> It is a deliciously complicated story of cross and double- and treble-cross and by halfway through one is not at all sure about whose side anyone is on. But somehow, and most unusually for a Bingham story, one doesn't awfully care.

The indifferent reception to *Vulture* is particularly sad, as it was to be the last book that John Bingham published with Gollancz for ten years. Livia Gollancz, looking back at that period of his career, admits that there were questions about sustainability:

> There may have been a falling-off of quality in his later books. But I wasn't the sort of editor to make him rewrite a book ... I think, as with many writers, his early novels were the best he wrote. They generally are.

Meanwhile, as discontent grew in Britain with endless industrial disputes, Wilson's government suffered a series of reverses at by-elections and the Prime Minister called a general election in May 1970. In a surprise win, Edward Heath's Conservative government was elected with a working majority, a victory that was greeted with delight by the more conservative officers of MI5.

For the second half of the 1960s the Labour government had perceived the Service as a tool of the Conservative Party and periodically attempted to limit its powers. The aloof management style of Sir Roger Hollis and his successor Martin Furnival Jones further encouraged the view that MI5 was run by reactionary Tories and that it would benefit from a breath of fresh air. The struggles between reactionaries and younger 'Atlanticists' that John le Carré depicts in *Tinker, Tailor* and *Smiley's People* were played out in real life on the Whitehall stage. Morale within the Service suffered and, as Christopher Andrew maintains, by 1974 it had fallen to a level 'lower than it has been ever since'.

In the early 1970s MI5 was engaged in a running feud with the Foreign Office over the increasing KGB presence at the Soviet embassy. Despite the claims of the Security Service that this was a growing threat, the Foreign Office downplayed the importance of the increasing number of Soviet 'diplomats'. Reginald Maudling, who became Home Secretary in Heath's government, was critical of the Service, arguing that fading morale necessitated bringing in an 'outsider' to replace Furnival Jones when the latter retired.

The new Heath government, determined to demonstrate that it and not the Left ran Britain, was embroiled in a series of disputes with the TUC and demanded more intelligence on the activities of union officials, a demand that was passed to Bingham. Furnival Jones responded to Maudling that the function of the Service in a democracy was to involve itself in matters of national security and that to gather intelligence to assist the government in an essentially political battle would be to exceed the Service's powers. This position, while strictly correct, further divided opposing camps within the Service.

The prestige of the Service was increased in the following year, however, when Oleg Lyalin, a KGB officer in London, defected and provided evidence of the presence of over a hundred illegal KGB operatives in London. Amid much fanfare, 105 Soviet intelligence officers were expelled from Britain on 25 September 1971. The natural result was an increased Soviet dependence on the CPGB and the trades unions. Against the odds, Bingham's experience was once again valuable currency. On the other hand, the insistence by the Director General that the Heath government was improperly requiring the Service to operate beyond its charter led to furious recriminations. Amid this controversy, Maudling pressed harder for an outsider to succeed Furnival Jones. The memory of the last outsider who took the chair, Sir Percy Sillitoe, still haunted the corridors of the Service, however, and Furnival Jones successfully argued for his deputy, Michael ('Jumbo') Hanley, to succeed him in 1972.

Bingham still made frequent trips to Belfast. Using a network of contacts supplied by a relation, he gathered a mass of useful background information about Ulster, but this would be of limited use once the PIRA turned its attention to acts of terror on the mainland. On 30 January 1972, thirteen unarmed civil rights protesters were shot dead in Derry by British soldiers. The incident, which came to be known as 'Bloody Sunday' and the 'Bogside Massacre', ensured that PIRA would take the fight to England.

On 8 March 1973, two car bombs exploded outside the Old Bailey, causing one death and 150 injuries. In 1974 the campaign continued with bombings in Guildford on 5 October (5 dead, 65 injured), in Woolwich on 7 November (2 killed) and in Birmingham on 21 November (19 killed, 180 wounded). By 1974 PIRA had exploded forty bombs in London and claimed thirty-five lives.

Their activities were checked in December 1975 when, fleeing after an attack on Scott's restaurant, four members of PIRA's Active Service Unit were pursued and trapped in Balcombe Street, Marylebone. These four, who claimed responsibility for the Guildford and Woolwich bombings, were captured after a six-day siege of the flat where they holed up, taking two hostages. When this was televised on BBC News on 12 December, Bingham was ecstatic at the outcome, pointing at the screen and exclaiming to Madeleine, 'My men, my men', as Special Branch officers arrested the four.

Less than four years later that triumph would turn to tragedy. When PIRA exploded a bomb on Earl Mountbatten's yacht off the Sligo coast on 27 August 1979, it was clear that Britain had not succeeded in containing Irish nationalist terrorism. When Bingham heard the news, he was shattered. He sat in front of the television 'howling like a wolf'.

In 1968 George Hardinge, an accomplished editor of crime fiction, moved from William Collins to Macmillan. Hardinge was obsessively interested in 'whodunits' and brought a new seriousness and expertise to the publishing of a genre which many publishers found slightly beneath their dignity. At Collins he had been Agatha Christie's editor and had formed the Crime Club, to which many leading crime writers of the era contributed work. At Macmillan, he immediately created the Crime List and, with the help of Julian Symons, a crime writer with fifteen novels, a Gold Dagger Award (1957) and an Edgar Award (1960) to his credit, set about attracting new authors to the Macmillan stable.

Symons became a family friend and, at his urging, Bingham decided to become a Macmillan author in the new Crime List. He had been impressed by the efficiency and the terms that he received at Panther Books, in which Macmillan had a substantial shareholding. Loyalty to Gollancz had been anchored on his respect for and friendship with Victor; although he had excellent relations with Livia, the bond was not as tight as before.

He did not immediately sever his relationship with Gollancz. During 1971 he discussed plans with Hardinge and Symons and they agreed that he should write and Macmillan publish a book in a different genre. That would introduce him to the Macmillan team and allow him to decide which publisher he would work with in the future.

Bingham proposed that he write an account of a series of murders committed in the suburbs of Glasgow in the 1950s. It would be his only non-fiction work, focusing on the bringing of the killer to justice as much as the crimes themselves.

On 11 July 1958, Peter Thomas Anthony Manuel, convicted of 'capital murder and murder done on a different occasion', had been hanged at Barlinnie Prison in Glasgow. Serial killers always generate hysteria among newspaper reporters and there had been widespread fear in the Glasgow suburbs as Peter Manuel struck apparently at random, driven by the sheer lust to kill. He killed at least nine people – according to his confession while awaiting execution, he killed nine more – between 1946 and 1958.

Bingham had met Detective Superintendent William Muncie of the Lanarkshire County Police, who had been involved in the series of cases, and had become interested in the story. He now planned a factual book describing the crimes. With his experience as a journalist, his profound knowledge of police procedure and his ability to tell a thrilling tale, he was ideally fitted to the job. His agent agreed that Macmillan, rather than Gollancz, should be the publisher.

The project was soon underway in late 1971 and he spent considerable time in and around Glasgow. The book, titled *The*

Hunting Down of Peter Manuel, was published in June 1973. As a piece of objective reporting, it is masterly. It is also a gripping read, as Bingham's sense of the dramatic, never exploited or overused, makes for a compelling study of the murderer. He does not fall into the trap of attempting to analyse, explain or interpret Manuel or his actions. There are few literary flourishes, merely first-class reporting, bound together with tension-building devices, into a 224-page report.

The book received consistently good reviews from several publications. Most reviewers contrasted the non-fiction book with his work in crime fiction, and the reviews were almost unanimously in favour of his new direction. There was praise not only for the careful exposition of the facts but also for the style and objectivity of the writing.

The most perceptive of the reviews was written by C. P. Snow for the *Financial Times.* In a sensitive and comprehensive analysis of the book Snow wrote:

> It is well-known that John Bingham has written some of the best spy-stories and thrillers of his generation. Of their kind, *Double Agent* (spy-story) and *Five Roundabouts to Heaven* (thriller) are as good as have been done. I mean they don't belong only to their kind, they are serious additions to literature ... Bingham has many of Simenon's qualities ... on the other hand, he has a much more interesting mind than Simenon, whose ruminations appear to be either prosy or excessively credulous. Bingham is very seldom either.

Snow spoke with confidence as he was a family friend, a frequent guest at Madeleine's literary salons in Abingdon Villas. While he was friendly with John, Snow was frequently an outspoken critic and praise from him was praise indeed. His name undoubtedly helped to help 'plant' the review, but the review would certainly have been impartial.

The financial results of *Peter Manuel* were also gratifying – an advance of £500 on signing and a further £500 on publication. Sales were brisk in the first year and 2,217 copies were sold. In future years it performed steadily, never reaching spectacular levels but helping to establish Bingham as a serious writer with a third genre of book. Sales were respectable enough to convince Macmillan and Bingham that a three-book series in his more familiar area of expertise would be worthwhile.

His day job, however, was becoming more demanding. Sir Michael Hanley, the new DG, immediately came under pressure from Heath to increase penetration of the TUC. In time-honoured bureaucratic tradition, Hanley proposed that a committee be established to assess the internal security situation in Britain.

As the dispute over the role of the Security Service and the legal basis for the government's increasingly shrill demands for action to curb the power of the unions reached a crescendo, Heath called an election for 28 February 1974 on the issue of 'Who Governs Britain?' On election day, the aim of union leaders Arthur Scargill and Mick McGahey to bring down the Conservatives was fulfilled. Harold Wilson, abidingly suspicious of MI5 and its supposed links to the Conservative Party, was returned to power.

Bingham now busied himself with *God's Defector*, the first of the three books to be published by Macmillan. Madeleine, eager that he should benefit from his new publisher's greater reach, involved herself more in his work. An early manuscript of *God's Defector* has several additions and alterations in Madeleine's handwriting. These suggest a difference between their respective plans for the book, and a fundamental one: whether it should be a spy story or a crime story. Madeleine clearly favoured the latter while John inclined to the former.

Both Ducane from *The Double Agent* and Vandoran from *The Third Skin* are versions of John Bingham – the agent runner and the voice of compassionate common sense. There are elements both of police work and of the Security Service in *God's Defector* and the book could have been slanted in either direction. In the event, there is a curious conflation of the two earlier characters. The literary ruse is hardly credible and there emerges an unconvincing character who makes just one crossing of the stage.

The plot, however, is ingenious. A Catholic priest loses his faith and in leaving the Church is no longer bound by the secrecy of the confessional. He is, however, privy to a number of secrets, some of which could, if publicised, be damaging to state security. Different individuals, for different reasons, become interested in ensuring that the priest remains silent. This tenet of the book had a personal association. Bingham had adopted the Roman Catholic faith before marrying Madeleine; during the 1960s, according to Hervé de Moncuit, he used to attend Church of England services. Towards the end of his life, however, he reverted to Catholicism.

The response from critics was mixed. Violet Grant of the *Daily Telegraph* enthused, writing, 'I've never read a book of this kind which carries more conviction', and H. R. F. Keating was equally complimentary in his review for *The Times* with: 'Situations are Bingham's forte, and this is a humdinger. Priest goes atheist with beltful of explosive confessions. Whitehall Intelligence moves in. Read on.'

Those, however, were the exception. Maurice Richardson in *The Observer* spoke of 'atmosphere laid on with a fog machine' and the *Birmingham Post* stated frankly that 'John Bingham ... has occasionally played it too cool in his stories but in *God's Defector* he is not at his best.'

Macmillan had designed a superbly striking dustcover for the book and hoped for impressive sales. They had again given a significant advance (£350 on signing and £700 on delivery) and they were disappointed when over three years the book sold just 3,275 copies. Neither the character nor the book was the hoped-for success. The blending of spy story and crime thriller allowed it to fall between two genres. Thus a highly original idea disappointed in execution. Despite the book's fairly tepid reception in Britain, however, the German magazine *Stern* bought the serial rights.

Bingham was depressed at the nature and the result of the February 1974 election. The choice, as he saw it, was between Harold Wilson, whom many of his colleagues believed to be a communist agent, and Edward Heath – 'Ted the Red' as he occasionally referred to him – who, he believed, was pursuing industrial policies that could only benefit the Left. Britain's world role, moreover, had been attenuated by Wilson's slavish devotion to Washington.

Bingham was not alone in his distrust of Wilson. According to senior MI5 officer Peter Wright (although he subsequently qualified the assertion), up to thirty of his fellow officers were anxious to remove Wilson, two of whom blustered that 'Wilson's a bloody menace and it's about time the public knew the truth ... We'll have him out, this time we'll have him out.' Wright also claimed that he was approached by a group wanting to take matters further by replacing the Prime Minister with a military government.

The second plot to unseat Wilson was developed in 1974 and had a far wider membership than the first. This once again had the goal of placing Mountbatten at the head of a temporary government and was supported by military leaders and by several stalwart Right-leaning aristocrats. John Bingham became involved in penetrating the latter elements of the group.

It is unclear if any coordination existed between the different groups of plotters, but one of those involved appears to have been his distant kinsman and namesake, John Bingham, the 7th Earl of Lucan. Simon recalls that his father was active in penetrating the group that Lucan moved in. The 7th Earl was a fixture at the Clermont Club, a gambling house in Berkeley Square owned by his friend John Aspinall. Allegedly, a group of Clermont *habitués* including Lucan and Aspinall met to discuss a *coup d'état*.

The family link between the two John Binghams was so distant that it cannot have been the reason for the assignment. Far more likely is that one of his agents had an *entrée* into the Clermont Club set and that he used this agent to penetrate the group of plotters. To infiltrate an agent into what was notoriously a man's world in which women were not welcome, he will have used one of his many 'occasionals', probably a wealthy aristocrat. Unfortunately, no official evidence has surfaced to cast light on the nature or progress of the 1974 plot; the intelligence amassed by MI5 remains classified.

Wilson remained in office from March 1974 until his abrupt resignation on 5 April 1976. Soon after his resignation he summoned two BBC journalists, Barrie Penrose and Roger Courtiour, to his London home and requested them to investigate a number of plots that he alleged had been launched to discredit him and topple his government. The most bizarre of these, involving the South African security agency BOSS, turned out to be insubstantial, but Penrose and Courtiour became convinced that there had been plots to unseat Wilson and that several MI5 officers had been complicit in at least one of these. This was supported by Peter Wright, who, in his book *Spycatcher*, writes of a cabal of MI5 officers who sought to discredit Wilson by leaking stories linking the Prime Minister and his political secretary, Marcia Williams, in an adulterous affair.

The 1970s were not the finest years of the Security Service. After the successes of the 1960s, with the series of Soviet defections that Bingham later referred to in his letter of 2 October 1979 to John le Carré, concluding that 'I don't think we did too badly', his last years in MI5 were fallow. The focus of attention had shifted; the nature of counter-subversion became politically motivated. The Service that he had joined, a close-knit group of men with military backgrounds, had faded away and been replaced by a different hierarchy. Younger, hungrier men and women (itself a major departure), trained along American lines, disdained the doctrines of men they saw as outdated Cold War warriors, blind to the more subtle alignments of the modern world. The split between the Soviet Union and China had dispelled the old myth of a communist monolith and when, in February 1972, President Richard Nixon made his historic state visit to the People's Republic of China, the schism between 'old' and 'new' officers in the Security Service widened.

Bingham increasingly questioned the congruence of his current role with the purpose he had embraced in 1950. Letters to family and friends, depressingly headed 'The Slaves' Galley', look forward to a life beyond the Service. Yet, with the governance of Britain in the hands of a man whom MI5 had suspected of being a Soviet agent and whose intimates included men with highly questionable links to the Warsaw Pact countries, he must have felt more than ever that retirement would amount to desertion of his post. Accordingly he soldiered on through three years that saw the departure of Harold Wilson, industrial chaos under his successor James Callaghan, and a final shift to the Right when Margaret Thatcher became Prime Minister in 1979.

Meanwhile, he continued writing. He was determined that his three-book contract with Macmillan should be noteworthy and, one year after the publication of *God's Defector*, in 1977, *The Marriage Bureau Murders* was released.

This is a puzzling book, universally described as 'black', 'chilling' and 'dark' by critics. Maurice Richardson in *The Observer* lauded it as 'Bingham's blackest and best for some books', which can be read either as an endorsement or as an adverse assessment of the more recent works. A similarly ambiguous review came from Patrick Cosgrave in the *Daily Express*:

> John Bingham is tempted neither by mystery nor by exotic locations. Bingham's Sidney Shaw sets up a marriage bureau after his wife abandons him – as a cover for murdering women. Bingham gets his effect from the straight unemotional way he describes pebble-glassed, feeble, ineffective Shaw going about finding a psychopath to do his killing for him while maintaining an unobtrusive business front. There is plenty of tension. It is an utterly chilling book.

The book is certainly chilling but its crafting is rudimentary and the entire plot unlikely. The *Daily Record* commented that 'it's a notch below Mr Bingham's usual high standards. Too woolly by far,' while Edmund Crispin in the *Sunday Times* lamented that 'Mr Bingham has done better than this, the nadir of his books, and we must hope that he will have regained his customary form in the next one'. Unfortunately, the reading public took heed of the negative reviews and *The Marriage Bureau Murders* sold fewer than 3,000 copies in 1977 and 1978.

Bingham's last year in the Security Service saw a form of closure to the scandal that had been fermenting when he rejoined MI5 in 1950. The search for HOMER had led to Donald Maclean and, in turn, to the 'Third Man', Kim Philby, in 1961. After Philby's escape and defection to Moscow, the hunt for a 'Fourth Man' had focused on Anthony Blunt, a friend of Burgess, suspected of pro-Soviet sympathies. Despite eleven interrogations by Arthur Martin and Jim Skardon of MI5, Blunt admitted nothing of importance and the investigation stalled.

In 1963 Michael Straight, an American who had been a near-contemporary of Blunt at Cambridge in the 1930s, revealed that he had been recruited to the Soviet cause in the 1930s by Blunt, at the time a don at Trinity College and, more recently, the Keeper of the Queen's Pictures. Armed with this information, MI5 again approached Blunt in April 1964 to extract a confession. Faced at an interrogation with the choice between exposure and immunity in return for a full confession, Blunt promptly chose the latter option. He admitted to having become a Soviet agent in 1934 and to having passed secret material to Moscow during the Second World War. In accordance with the agreement, MI5 kept secret Blunt's activities and his involvement in the defections of Burgess, Maclean and Philby.

The secret remained safe within the Service for fifteen years until Andrew Boyle, in his book *The Climate of Treason*, dropped broad hints that Blunt had been the 'Fourth Man'. Cannily, Boyle stopped short of naming him, but word circulated in Fleet Street that 'Maurice' was none other than Blunt. *Private Eye* took up the story in its issue of 28 September 1979, expanding on it in its 8 November issue. Soon the identification was common knowledge and Edward Leadbitter, the Labour MP for Hartlepool, announced to Downing Street his intention of asking Margaret Thatcher in the House of Commons to confirm or deny the identification.

The Prime Minister, in characteristically direct fashion, confirmed that Blunt was the 'Fourth Man' and that this had been established by MI5 in 1964. The story had all the elements of an appetising scandal. Blunt, educated at Marlborough College and Trinity, Cambridge, was a member of the Establishment, and thus the popular press lost no opportunity to attack. He was, moreover, a homosexual, a fact that dovetailed neatly with a juicy spy story. Thirdly, his position as an adviser to the monarch – and, incidentally, his remote kinship with the Queen Mother – brought Buckingham Palace into the widening gyre of scandal.

From the viewpoint of the Security Service the revelation was a disaster. Traditionally, Ministers of the Crown steadfastly refused to answer questions relating to the intelligence services, claiming the overriding importance of national security. Sir Bernard Ingham, Thatcher's press secretary, speculated that the Prime Minister broke with that tradition in order to demonstrate to the press, the Security Service and the public at large that she alone was running the country. Whatever the reason, she was forthright. Responding to Leadbitter's question on 15 November, she catalogued Blunt's activities, frankly describing the role of the Security Service in obtaining and then suppressing the facts. At a stroke she removed the mantle of secrecy under which MI5 had long operated and fed the popular press the information that the Establishment had protected one of its own.

The reaction was hysterical. Blunt was stripped of his knight-hood by the Palace and denounced as a 'pansy aesthete' (Malcolm Muggeridge, *Evening Standard*), as 'a treacherous Communist poof' (John Junor, *Daily Express*), 'the spy with no shame' (*Daily Mail*) and 'this evil arrogant poseur' (*Now!* magazine). The story provided a feeding frenzy for every branch of the press and very soon broader questions were being asked about how a confessed Soviet spy had been allowed by the Security Service to maintain his position close to the Royal Family for fifteen years.

Under savage attack from the press and virtually accused as

co-conspirators, MI5 was in a state of siege. In the eyes of the public it had effectively been party to a cover-up, demonstrating the worst fears that the Security Service was a reactionary organisation that would preserve the reputation of its members, whatever the public interest – an accusation that had surfaced in other connections during the 1970s.

For Bingham, the Blunt affair was a sorry saga in which the Service was unreasonably pilloried. It had been in the country's interest in 1964 to contain the knowledge of Blunt's Soviet connections: wide public knowledge of the treachery of a member of the Royal Household would have been unnecessarily disruptive. Moreover, Blunt had not handled any sensitive material since the war, at which time Britain and the Soviet Union had nominally been allies in the fight against fascist Germany. For MI5 to suffer opprobrium fifteen years after the event seemed unreasonable, evidence of how values in the country had suffered by the late 1970s. Yet now there was 'a certain amount of flak flying around' and it was Bingham who, in his role as liaison with Fleet Street, had to handle damage control. It was his last official assignment with the Security Service. Although, as he predicted to Livia Gollancz, 'emergencies' might require his services on occasion (as indeed they did, intermittently, for the next three years), he would from 1 January 1980 be free of distractions and able to concentrate full time on his work as a novelist.

It is tempting to compare John Bingham's last years in the Security Service with the position of George Smiley in MI6 towards the end of his career. In three novels – *Call for the Dead, Tinker, Tailor* and *Smiley's People* – Smiley's actual tenure is uncertain and equivocal, but his devotion to the cause is beyond doubt. In the two later books, more particularly, when Smiley has achieved the status of a wise elder, he is dragged back to his desk by emergencies. It is a short step from the identification of

John Bingham as the model for Smiley to extrapolate that he was himself kept in play by national crises and that this formed part of the character that le Carré created.

The shift in MI5 strategy kept Bingham in the Security Service after his sixtieth birthday, and five years later the election of the second Wilson government offered a timely reason for retirement. Smiley's disdain for the Labour Party's suspicion of the intelligence services, as depicted in *Smiley's People*, neatly reflects Bingham's view. Yet once again – in 1974 as in 1968 – his sense of duty kept him in harness. When he wrote to Livia Gollancz on 3 December 1979 that he would 'finally retire' from MI5 on 31 December, his sense of imminent liberation is palpable. 'Things', he commented blandly, 'should be easier.'

He had returned to MI5 at the age of forty-one, believing that journalism was a profession for men on the younger side of the milestone of forty. Although post-war Britain, impecunious and cynical, differed fundamentally from that country, the font of reason and common sense, that he had described in the *Sunday Dispatch* in 1938, his commitment to its defence was as powerful as it had been throughout the war. That commitment never wavered, although in the 1960s he periodically asked himself whether his role in that defence was achieving its purpose. It is a curious irony that, when the shift of strategic emphasis began in 1968 – the very year when he was due to retire – despite the downgrading of the importance of counter-subversion, he was seen as a necessary and experienced safe pair of hands to keep the section in operation. Counter-terrorism assumed more importance and status than counter-subversion but Bingham, the experienced old-timer, was retained while the Service regrouped.

For a further eleven years, even as the constitutional position of the Service became an increasingly political issue when the enemy came from within rather than from Moscow, Bingham maintained an unswerving antipathy to communism, but the see-saws of government – and government's interpretation of the Service's function – forced him to question whether he was in tune with the Security Service in the Heath and Wilson years; younger officers, many of them women, occupied the high ground of planning; morale slipped lower and lower in the early 1970s; the so-called Women's Revolt of 1972, when the Service's female officers demanded equal rights with their male colleagues, made him feel acutely that he was a relic of a distant era. When Harold Wilson, an avowed enemy of the intelligence services, returned to office in 1974, Service morale was at an all-time low. After Wilson's resignation, relations between James Callaghan, the new Prime Minister, and Sir Michael Hanley, MI5's Director General, collapsed. The long-threatened action to bring 'a breath of fresh air' to the Service followed in 1979 when Callaghan dismissed Hanley and appointed Sir Howard Smith, a career diplomat, to be the next Director General.

Through countless shifts of purpose, the very *raison d'être* of the Security Service during the years from 1950 to 1979 changed fundamentally, generally in directions that would have been distasteful to John Bingham. It is idle to speculate how his life might have unrolled if he had been able to retire in 1968, pointless to wonder how his career as a novelist might have developed. He was a patriot and a trouper; the show had to go on.

CHAPTER 11

SMILEY TRIUMPHANT, 1974-82

I don't think we do too badly in Britain, considering how little intrusion there really is into the private lives and liberties of a vast population.
John Bingham in a letter to John le Carré, 2 October 1979

Eight years had passed since the release of Bingham's first espionage novel, *The Double Agent*, when John le Carré completed the book that will certainly persist as his most successful work. George Smiley, central character in *Call for the Dead* and *A Murder of Quality*, shadowy schemer in *Spy* and *The Looking Glass War*, strode to centre stage in *Tinker, Tailor, Soldier, Spy* and, for as long as the Cold War continued, yielded that dominance to no other fictional spy. Studiedly complex – and the more admired because of its complexity – John le Carré's *chef d'oeuvre* has delighted his devotees for nearly forty years.

It was galling for Madeleine when, with the release of *Tinker, Tailor* in 1974, George Smiley became a household name. Now le Carré's success was demonstrably the result of the characterisation of her husband, yet not a penny of le Carré's royalty cheques found its way to the Bingham household accounts. In the same year another film was released with Diane Keaton starring as Charlie in *The Little Drummer Girl*, adding fuel to Madeleine's resentment. But the crowning insult, in Madeleine's eyes, came four years later when Alec Guinness portrayed

George Smiley in the massively successful BBC television series of *Tinker, Tailor.*

It is in *Tinker, Tailor* that the character of George Smiley comes of age. His appearance in le Carré's first novel introduced the figure; now that figure acquired substance and depth. And in every important feature, every characteristic, Smiley is the essence of John Bingham.

In his 1986 book *Taking Sides: The Fiction of John le Carré,* Tony Barley analyses the character that le Carré created. His conclusions could have been written about Bingham as much as about Smiley. Of his 'squareness' he writes that critics and reviewers commented on the nostalgia that is inherent in Smiley's character, the implied association with an earlier and more powerful Britain. Smiley finds much of post-war Britain distasteful; his own generation has left the stage and Smiley himself is a superannuated relic. Moral values have been corrupted and he is periodically brought out of retirement to reimpose the lost virtues on the Circus.

Writing of interrogation, Barley again identifies a famous talent of Bingham and brings it to the fore in Smiley, stressing Smiley's skill as an interrogator, a talent that is superbly described by le Carré. Cross-questioning, Barley notes, is insistently present, whether covert, restrained, casual or deliberate and aggressive.

Even in the use of work names we see Bingham's shadow in Smiley's choice of *noms de guerre.* Barley points out that Smiley's frequently used work name 'Standfast' springs from John Buchan's novels. Buchan was one of John's favourite writers and the notion of standing fast fits congruently with le Carré's own descriptions of the man he knew in the 1950s.

Turning from strengths to perceived weaknesses, Barley refers to Smiley's meeting with Karla in New Delhi in *Tinker, Tailor* and how Smiley appears foolish and sentimental. In *Tinker,*

Tailor Smiley comments that his behaviour with Karla contrasted a feeble, western liberal with a rigorous and disciplined communist. While Smiley is painfully aware of his ideological weakness and his dialectical failure in his attempt to 'turn' Karla, he is adamant that he would prefer to be a feeble western liberal than to be Karla, whose determined ideology terrified him. While it was Tony Barley who described Smiley's ethos, it is easy to imagine that descriptive judgement coming from Bingham himself.

While le Carré continued to maintain a public silence about the origins of his now iconic character, insiders were all too aware of the influences on Smiley. When the series was about to air and Alec Guinness's face was released as Smiley, John's former secretary telephoned him to say, 'I've just seen you on the front of the *Radio Times*.' Bingham was amused by the comment; Madeleine's reaction was very different, entitling one chapter of a memoir she was writing 'The Spy Who Came into the Chips'. She could not help herself comparing the two men – le Carré had spent a mere two years at MI5; her husband had devoted the better part of his life to it. Le Carré had accumulated property in Hampstead, in Cornwall, in Switzerland; she was left alone in an empty house in Abingdon Villas each evening while her Smiley worked until past midnight welfaring his agents. Bingham had remained scrupulously reticent about operations in MI5; le Carré had trumpeted them about; whether his tales were accurate or fanciful, to her he had rejected the rules that her husband lived by.

For many viewers Guinness simply *was* Smiley. We might know little of him – he appears first at an Oxford interview with Jebedee of All Souls, thereafter he simply is – but there is no facet of George Smiley that comes as a surprise to us. We understand both his ruthlessness and his humanity, his unsatisfactory relationship with his wife and his consuming loyalty to his agents.

He is a constant throughout the trilogy, neither changing nor developing. Alec Guinness captures perfectly the quality that Inspector Mendel identifies in *Tinker, Tailor, Soldier, Spy*. On the surface, Smiley is as vulnerable as a hedgehog crossing the road, but at the end of the day it is Smiley who remains intact. Mendel reflects that, despite his humble manner, Smiley is as stout and firmly rooted as an oak, the only tree unharmed when the storm subsides.

Solid, sound and, above all, square – David Cornwell's nickname for John Bingham.

In his writing, Bingham is straightforward and honest in setting out his moral precepts. He neither preaches nor glorifies. Human emotions, motives, private ethics, the stripping away of posturing down to the 'third skin' are elements of life that he experienced during and immediately after the war, and which remained at the forefront of his mind after he returned from Germany. Sympathetic yet detached, he acquired a remarkable objectivity that helps us to understand his subsequent career. And, incidentally, that of George Smiley, whose parallel life he led.

That objectivity, the ability to penetrate human motive with precision and clarity, helped to make Bingham a most effective interrogator as well as an eerily perceptive writer. His certainty of his own values never tempted him to oversimplify human motivation, which he was always careful to regard as variegated and subject to change. Comfortable in his own skin, he was ever alert to the possible discomfort of others. His light-hearted description of interrogation to Charlotte is simple and revealing: identify the target's needs or fears; make the target believe that those needs will be gratified or those fears allayed if questions are answered; hey presto! If the interrogator has identified the fears and needs correctly, the desired answers will be forthcoming.

This calls for extreme sensitivity, clear perception, combined with a ruthless determination to obtain the desired end. As Charlotte recalled, her father never needed to shout at his children or express his anger violently; he simply withdrew intimacy until he felt that the necessary lesson had been taught.

Aficionados of John le Carré's work could point to several instances of Smiley's sharp sensitivity as an interrogator. Perhaps the two outstanding and very different examples are his lengthy interrogation of Rickey Tarr early in *Tinker, Tailor* and the masterly turning of Grigoriev in *Smiley's People*. In the latter the build-up of tension, the urgency to complete the process before Grigoriev's absence is noticed, contribute to the drama. Grigoriev is bundled into the interrogation room where Smiley, speaking German, demands calm with a single word, '*Ruhe*'.

Allowing Grigoriev space for his weaknesses, to wallow in his own discomfort, Smiley gives him the stage, but Grigoriev is too small to fill it. When Smiley finally speaks, it is without drama or histrionics. In the manner of a long-serving commissar, he questions Grigoriev, using the time-honoured technique of eliciting answers as a prelude to ensuring obedience. He assumes a manner that is ponderous and remote, almost indifferent.

Smiley applies pressure, working relentlessly on Grigoriev's fears – fear of his wife Grigorieva, fear of being revealed as an adulterer, above all fear of the department of the KGB that had enlisted his services. Throughout, according to Toby Esterhase, Smiley was in control, delicately but firmly shepherding Grigoriev, submitting him to his will.

Both Bingham's children have commented on their amazement at Alec Guinness's performance as Smiley in the television series; the resemblance to their father was uncanny – despite the fact that the two never met. From the simple foibles, such as polishing his spectacles on the fat end of his tie, to his gait, facial mannerisms, deep, mellifluous voice and his ability to withdraw, to vanish into a crowd, this George Smiley was remarkably close to their perception of the original.

It was, in fact, Smiley's ability to vanish imperceptibly into a crowd that stimulated the final overt clash between Madeleine and le Carré. In an interview the latter described Smiley as 'forgettable'. The word was intended as a compliment: to possess forgettability, after all, is a huge asset in the secret world; MI5's agent-running course teaches 'the ability to merge into the background, to be unmemorable'. For le Carré's detractors, however, Madeleine leading the charge, this was an insult that deserved a spirited riposte. On 14 September 1979 a female agent at MI5 wrote to le Carré and in a lengthy diatribe commented:

> I am writing to you now as I heard your remarks about Smiley as the 'most forgettable man you had ever met'. I was with the 'forgettable man' at the time, so he heard it too. ...
>
> This man whom we both know has given every help, compassion, and staunch friendship to all who have been honoured to know him. He has never failed anyone through all the 25 years I have known him. He also has a quality ... of unswerving loyalty to his friends and colleagues ... Just let me say that 'Smiley' is a marvellous help, companion and friend and to many of us he is the most 'unforgettable' man in spite of your hurtful and cheap gibes.

Madeleine was delighted when she saw the letter and could refer to it in her own barbed note to le Carré, who promptly appealed to Bingham to intercede on his behalf.

Quite reasonably, he pointed out that it was absurd for Madeleine to object to 'forgettable'. To the man in the street, forgettability might be thought degrading, but it was an essential quality for success in the covert world. He stressed that Smiley was created out of affection to Bingham, his model, and that the affection had endured. Although he clearly found Madeleine's pettiness irritating, he, for his part, wanted to put the quarrel behind them.

Bingham was content to accept the olive branch and replied that he accepted 'forgettability' in the spirit it was offered but admitted to being genuinely puzzled by his colleague's apparent disloyalty to the department:

The Slaves Galley, 2.10.79

Dear David,

Thanks for your letter and enclosure. Smiley has never minded being called a Forgettable Man, and has even regarded it as a mild professional compliment to a man who can merge into the general background. He thinks that that and keeping a low profile are quite useful traits.

On the other hand, to be perfectly frank – always difficult for Smiley – he has often been puzzled as to why you have so frequently and harshly attacked his mob, directly in interviews or obliquely in books. (Troops don't normally improve by, in effect, being called a lousy lot of bums, and inefficient or ineffective to boot.)

You are far from being pro-Soviet Russia or pro-Communist, but I would think the attacks gave comfort and even pleasure and glee in some places. Puzzling to simple souls like Smiley – perhaps his only really unsolved mystery.

All organizations have weak points, including the KGB, as the flood of defectors and some of our British (unpublished) successes could clearly show. I don't think we do too badly in Britain, considering how little intrusion there really is into the private lives and liberties of a vast population.

Kind regards – your favourite 'homosexual fantasist',

Ayatoller [*sic*] John

Despite the friendly tone of the letter, he could not resist insert-ing a sting in the tail. Le Carré had given an interview to Philip Oakes in September 1977, when *The Honourable Schoolboy* was published, and had taken a broad swing at his former colleagues, as Oakes's article revealed:

> The principal characters in the book are spies and spymasters, and their victims people he knew well when, as a Foreign Office hand, he was privy to the tactics of agents great and small. 'I really loathe the games they play,' says le Carré. 'The game justi-fies their very existence. They're all fantasists talking endlessly about the team spirit, which I take to be a euphemism for homo-sexuality, and reiterating the myths they create around themselves as monotonously as banging a ball against a wall.'

Such talk pandered to the growing egalitarian society that Britain was becoming, offering a swipe at public schools, the Establishment and the Service, appealing to the age-old myth that all public schoolboys were closet homosexuals, snobs and incompetents perpetrating an outdated class prejudice. The suggestion that he and his colleagues were 'homosexual fanta-sists' had made an impression and Bingham was able to use it in that counter-thrust two years later.

The extent of his good humour, however, was more than matched by Madeleine's continuing malice. In 1975 she had published an engaging book, *Peers and Plebs,* and she was plan-ning to publish a sequel. First she gave it the working title of *Peers and Plebs II* but in 1979 she changed this to *Smiley's Wife,* rewriting it substantially to include a savage attack on le Carré. It was a full-scale offensive in which three chapters were devoted to the assault. It was written and rewritten, worked and reworked, polished and repolished to cause the maximum embarrassment to le Carré. Fortunately for all concerned, but to the fury of Madeleine, MI5 reminded her that she had signed the Official Secrets Act in 1940 and, therefore, publication of the work was subject to their approval. Madeleine explained the sequence of events in this way:

> This autobiography was recently accepted for publication by Hamish Hamilton, who published my biography of Beerbohm Tree and the recent *Earls and Girls*.
>
> Because my husband John Bingham who, of course, figures in the book, worked for many years as a senior officer in British Intelligence, I first submitted it to the Text & Broadcasting Committee; this is the body which issues 'D. Notices' to prevent publication of sensitive material.
>
> The D. Notice Committee gave the book a provisional go-ahead. Hamish Hamilton announced it in their autumn catalogue.
>
> Then the D. Notice Committee changed its mind. They reminded me that I had signed the Official Secrets Act ... and they warned Hamish Hamilton against publication of the book.
>
> The explanation given to me by the D. Notice Committee was that a very high official had decided against publication not because the book contained any official secrets but because it set a precedent: authors with inside knowledge of British Intelligence might start writing about it...
>
> To save Hamish Hamilton embarrassment I asked for the book back. Although I have by no means withdrawn it from publication either here or in the US.

Madeleine was justified in feeling frustrated by the stated official position for it is riddled with inconsistencies. A 'D' Notice was the only means by which the Security Service could forbid publication and could be used only in the national interest where sensitive material was concerned. Far more likely is that John, aware of the furore that publication would stir up, used his influence to have MI5 prevent the book's publication. It is easy to imagine him suggesting that its publication would do no one, least of all the department, any good. Better simply to obstruct it and it would die a natural death. If so, he chose the wisest course in suppressing a vituperative and malign *ad hominem* rant.

He was not immune to the human emotion of envy, although the extent of his feeling was greatly less intense than Madeleine's. He was doubtless fascinated that George Smiley had become a cult figure among lovers of espionage novels and he had the notion of developing the character of Ducane as his equivalent of George Smiley, based on the same model – himself.

Throughout their acquaintanceship Bingham retained affection for le Carré. He was periodically concerned that his fame had corrupted him and was ever puzzled that sometimes his books appeared to question the ethics of intelligence work. On occasion – as in the preface to *The Double Agent* – he rebuked him, but it was as much in sorrow as in anger.

Madeleine's bitterness, on the other hand, knew no limits. After her tangle with MI5 over the publication of *Smiley's Wife*, she dashed off a comedy whose title embodied her derision of le Carré. The BBC had followed the 1979 television version of *Tinker, Tailor* with a serialisation of the third and final Karla story, *Smiley's People*. Madeleine, resenting le Carré's success and now equally at loggerheads with MI5, wrote *Smelly's People*, a farcical, outdated story about a Polish defector whose memoirs were banned by MI5. This, like *Smiley's Wife*, fortunately remains buried in the archive.

How should we interpret and understand the three-cornered relationship between Smiley, his original and his creator? First it must be said that Smiley possesses qualities that Bingham did not share: a distinguished author of monographs on minor German poets, he enjoys dining rights at Lincoln College and demonstrates an intellectual concern with moral issues. These are all qualities that belong to the other half of the Smiley equation, Vivian Green, who was chaplain at Sherborne while le Carré was there and Rector of Lincoln College when he was an undergraduate. He made an enduring impression on le Carré as the single tolerable element of his time at Sherborne and was duly filed away as a potential character.

Le Carré always had a notion of what Smiley would be. He was, one may speculate, looking for ethical and practical consistency, a character that would be meek and, despite his cunning, naive in the jungle of Whitehall. George Smiley was to be surefooted operationally, certain of the verities of his profession, yet uncertain, permanently puzzled by challenges outside his area of competence. One cannot imagine Smiley replacing a tap in the bathroom, yet he would immediately have seen, like Bingham, the mechanics necessary to protect le Carré's blown agent at MI5. His origins must be unclear, yet he must have aristocratic connections. He must arrive on the pages of le Carré's work as a finished product, rock-like, as Inspector Mendel saw him.

One can imagine le Carré's delight at finding the perfect model in his office when he joined the Security Service in 1958. Here was the son of a baron, bemused by the changing society around him, dedicated to his job, supremely confident of the rightness of his cause, yet analytical enough to have reached his ethical posture logically. He had imagined a deep mellifluous voice; Bingham supplied it. He imagined a man whom women fussed over; Bingham had a string of female agents devoted to him. He saw endearing personal mannerisms; Bingham polished his spectacles on the fat end of his tie. Truly, John le Carré must have exclaimed 'Eureka!'

By the time that the two met, John Bingham had become the perfect model for Smiley – and, equally importantly, he was done with becoming. Just as Smiley is unchangeable on the pages of John le Carré, so his model appeared as the finished product. The uncertain young man of the 1920s had returned to his true vocation in the 1950s. Just as George Smiley was diverted from an academic career into his rightful *métier*, so John Bingham found his way back to agent running almost by chance in the post-war years. Smiley should be fluent in German; Bingham was. Smiley should be outwardly mild, yet possess a commanding presence when it was needed; we need look no further than Charlotte's description of her father's authority to find that quality.

The young Bingham had been assaulted by an impressive array of reasons to doubt himself. His father, the eldest son and heir, had failed to achieve distinction, while two of his uncles were decorated war heroes. His uncle by marriage was awarded an OBE in 1919 and elevated to the peerage as Lord Glentoran in 1939. Meanwhile John was burdened with uncertainty about his own ability. He considered himself physically unattractive, toad-like; he wore thick spectacles, an imagined defect that he regarded as the very hallmark of a feeble person. Despite his physical strength, which he refers to in *Michael Sibley*, and which Charlotte Bingham mentions, notably in *Daughters of Eden*, a book written as a tribute to her father, he did not see himself as physically impressive.

Yet, by the time he appears to George Smiley's creator, he has come to terms with himself and has the ethical and practical consistency that le Carré sought for Smiley. Having been a passionate anti-fascist, he has become equally passionate in his efforts to hunt down disruptive communists. While he has an array of criticisms of post-war Britain, he is certain of its fundamental decency, of its underlying values, believing them to be shared by all Englishmen. He was deeply involved in the activities of the Allied Control Council. Le Carré had a similar experience, interviewing and processing displaced persons in Austria between 1950 and 1952. The latter's experience is described in his largely autobiographical novel *A Perfect Spy*.

In his fictional account le Carré inverts the sequence of events around this time. His hero Magnus Pym is recruited into secret work during his stay in Bern, goes up to Oxford where he performs tasks for MI5, then does his National Service in Austria. The real-life John le Carré, however, spent those two years in Austria before going up to Oxford in 1952. Could it have been that, at some point between 1950 and 1952, Bingham met le Carré, perhaps in connection with their similar work in Germany and Austria and, at that point, he recruited him as an undergraduate agent who could keep an eye on extreme left-wing groups at the university? This mission is described in a frank, sometimes hilarious account of Pym's activities in *A Perfect Spy* and gently satirised in le Carré's later book *Absolute Friends*.

Whether or not le Carré was recruited in the early 1950s and whether or not it was Bingham who recruited him, the latter's influence on him, even as far as unwittingly bestowing his *nom de plume*, is certain. The character of George Smiley was introduced to le Carré's readers in *Call for the Dead* and developed in *A Murder of Quality*. He then lies fallow, emerging unchanged to dominate the pages of le Carré's central work, the *Quest for Karla* trilogy.

Once Smiley's epic battle with Karla is resolved, le Carré's uses for him are diminished. The end of the Cold War and the tearing down of that graphic symbol, the Berlin Wall, put an end to Smiley's presence on le Carré's stage. Even so, le Carré himself could not consign Smiley to the flotsam of the

Cold War. Instead he brings him back for a cameo appearance in 1990 in *The Secret Pilgrim*. Ned (he of no surname and of *The Russia House*) invites Smiley to a dinner of probationers at the Circus's training school. A wistful but ever-incisive Smiley offers the young spies wisdom, tempered by experience and that ever-present doubt. This is vintage Smiley. Introduced as a legend, he protests mildly that, far from being so, he is merely a plump, elderly gentleman who makes an appearance at the end of the meal. In his final curtain call, Smiley's simple directness bears a remarkable resemblance to that of John Bingham.

At one point Smiley touches on ends and means, urging the cadet spies not to be all things to all men, warning them that, once one accepts that the end justifies the means, one pays a certain price. It is a plea for honesty, even in an intrinsically dishonest profession.

If Bingham could have heard Smiley thus, then perhaps le Carré and he would never have parted company. The problem was, as le Carré pithily puts it, that he had become 'a shit' in Bingham's eyes by questioning the professed values of the department. Fitting the means to the end is one thing – regrettable but necessary. Questioning the ends themselves, suggesting that the west is as flawed and hypocritical as the east, that democracy is as unprincipled as totalitarianism, is beyond the pale. As soon as Smiley shows his doubts, gives rein to cynicism or questionable practices, Bingham and Smiley diverge. Smiley, when he meets Karla in Delhi, appeals to Karla that there is as little moral value on one side as there is on the other. Both Smiley and Karla, he argues, have the ability to see through the value systems of the other side but, now that Karla is going home to an almost certain death at the hands of a firing squad, perhaps the time has come to set aside the differences between east and west. The great visions of our youth no longer apply, pleads Smiley. Bingham would have found that behaviour offensive.

In making the identification between Smiley and Bingham, le Carré refers to the latter's operational skill and deep love for his country. Thus far, there need be no issue between the two. But when Bingham's patriotism became somehow diluted by Smiley's apparent ethical uncertainty, there was some distance between Smiley and his model. Le Carré, Bingham felt, had called into question the values that the latter held most dear, the very values, in fact, that had formed the character of Smiley in the first place.

Bingham was able to depersonalise the rift, unlike Madeleine, whose fulminations against le Carré became increasingly personal. On one occasion she actually recorded a conversation about their friend, presumably so that she could have an exact record for her memoir, *Smiley's Wife*. Although Bingham was certainly aware that the conversation was being recorded and may, therefore, have been cautious in his comments, the exchange is revealing and it confirms many of the tentative notions expressed above.

I know you don't agree but I think part of his [le Carré's] trouble is that he is a perfectionist. If people such as literary agents, publishers, intelligence organisations are not perfect – they are pretty good stinkers ... I must say I am completely puzzled about why he is always attacking British intelligence, either directly in interviews to the press – particularly in America where, of course, his views are quite welcome – or obliquely in his books. I don't understand why he does it. He must know, as he is very intelligent, and he's not pro-Soviet or pro-communist, that this attitude of his gives comfort, pleasure and, indeed, glee to people who, I am sure, he genuinely regards as his opponents in eastern

Europe. I am sure they enjoy reading these books. It gives a great deal of discomfort to our own agents, and to those people in the intelligence services who are trying to keep up the morale of these agents. Many of them are leading very difficult, trying and sometimes dangerous lives, and it doesn't help to tell them that they are a lousy lot of inefficient no-goods.

It was of course this question that Bingham posed to le Carré in his letter during the 'forgettable man' storm. It continued to bother him that someone who had worked for British intelligence could 'let the side down'. In the dialogue with Madeleine, Bingham swoops back several times to this question: why does le Carré write in a way that demeans British intelligence and can, therefore, only be of comfort to Britain's enemies? He isn't a communist, so his behaviour is the more incomprehensible. Over Madeleine's *ad hominem* comments, he speculates dispassionately:

I suppose one could put forward this possibility. He made a success with the book *The Spy Who Came In from the Cold* which, I suppose, did not show British intelligence as ethically the tops. It was a success and maybe he found that by attacking the intelligence services he gained a certain amount of publicity because the media have always been slightly narked – intrigued anyway – that they could not publish or weren't allowed to publish stuff about the intelligence services here. Now, for the first time, someone had broken through, and actually said nasty things about the British intelligence services … He had gained a lot of publicity and he thought to himself, 'Well, this is a good thing and I'll do this for my next book.' And that worked. I don't think he necessarily believed it up to then, but after a while it could be – with the continual run of success and applause, particularly in America, where they are always delighted to hear anything wrong with

British intelligence – he thought – well, no, he didn't think; possibly he was no longer thinking straight – he was in a groove that he couldn't possibly break out of without condemning the things he had said before. That's a possibility, although it's not necessarily true ... I think that, fundamentally, he is a basically patriotic sort of man, but he's got bogged down in his own smear campaign and he can't get out of it.

Throughout the conversation he strives to understand why his protégé could have pursued this approach when he became successful. How, he wonders, could le Carré have despised all intelligence officers except Smiley?

His books are devoid of love for people – or even affection. Except for Smiley. Even if you think people are comic in their reactions – as they often are – I agree you still ought to be able to penetrate and reproduce their true feelings. The officers he draws are false to truth – and to life. He was my friend – probably still is – but I deplore and hate everything he has done and said against the intelligence services.

That about sums it up. David will never be happy.

The detachment, the understanding of human moral frailty, of a man's tendency to believe his own press releases – these are qualities worthy of George Smiley. And their complexity is more plausible than le Carré's explanation that Bingham simply dismissed him as 'a shit'. Like Smiley, Bingham, the professional intelligence officer, was profoundly puzzled and he sought an explanation that fitted the facts. Le Carré had now achieved success but described success as a road accident. Like Smiley, Bingham probed, and concluded that 'David will never be happy'.

One important postscript must be added. An inalienable fact about George Smiley is that he has a bizarre marriage to the mercurial Lady Ann Sercomb. For the fictional character of Smiley his cuckolding is a vital appendage. That was emphatically not the nature of John and Madeleine Bingham's marriage. Madeleine always stressed the need for complete trust, particularly given the clandestine nature of her husband's job. She was neither of aristocratic lineage nor partial to love affairs with Cuban racing drivers. Ann Smiley may have been described as George's 'bitch goddess' on account of her frequent desertions and Smiley's continued willingness to take her back, but that description, despite the acrimony that infected later relations between Madeleine and John le Carré, could never apply to Madeleine. Arguably, it was that characterisation of Smiley's wife – a woman different in almost every way from the real Mrs Bingham – that sharpened the latter's anger at le Carré.

Such then is the background to the identification, the nature of the rift that divided mentor and disciple, and the simple incomprehension that continued to separate them. As we proceed through John Bingham's written work, we encounter Smiley-isms and ponder how George Smiley might have behaved. This is hardly surprising as it was the model for Smiley that was writing, sometimes in the first person. It is interesting, in passing, that in the autobiographical sections of his work he is highly critical of himself; only in the second period of his writing, notably in *The Double Agent*, do we find his good qualities embodied, in the character of Ducane, and his description of that character is restrained. From the works of John le Carré we can extract many qualities that made Bingham – and Smiley – so remarkably sound and consistently ethical.

Smiley also stands alone in le Carré's work. Whereas many characters from the Karla trilogy return in different guises in later post-Cold War works, George Smiley is never injected into a later character. Like Bingham's agents, he was a 'one-man dog'. Apart from a description of Rosalind from *As You Like It* in *The Little Drummer Girl* as a woman with many people under her hat (following Toby Esterhase's description of Smiley in *Smiley's People*), there is not a hint of an ersatz George Smiley once the Cold War is over.

On the other hand both writers are congruent in their description of Bingham's 'squareness'. Whether we are reading of Smiley's bleak failure to comprehend the complexities of modern life or chuckling at a Bingham-esque rant about a new-fangled kettle or a pinball machine (*My Name Is Michael Sibley*) or enjoying a sideswipe at modern youth and contemporary advertising (*The Third Skin*), one cannot help glimpsing Smiley.

For both Bingham and Smiley, life was more complex than it need have been. As *Michael Sibley* ends with Sibley ensconced in his Cotswold village pub, drinking a pint with the local bobby, so we can imagine Bingham in leisured retirement – as we would want for Smiley – chatting at a garden table, puffing at his pipe, taking time to plot his next book. For all the similarities, however, Smiley is a mere literary device. Bingham was flesh and blood.

CHAPTER 12

RETIREMENT, 1979–88

My father was offered a CBE [Commander of the British Empire medal].
He was very grateful that his work had merited such an honour but said that
he would prefer it be given to someone else in MI5 as he already had a title.
Simon, 8th Baron Clanmorris, to the author, 31 May 2011

Through his membership of the Crime Writers' Association, Bingham was friendly with Colin Dexter, who published his first Inspector Morse novel, *Last Bus to Woodstock*, in 1975. This was followed by four other bestsellers between 1976 and 1981. Inspector Morse became a well-known and much-loved figure on British television and a source of considerable fame for Dexter.

Madeleine was convinced that she and John could collaborate in the creation of a similar series for television. He would craft the plot; she would adapt the stories to create an alluring series; Charlotte and Terence would use their connections in television; John would at last receive the financial rewards he deserved.

Yielding to Madeleine's urgings, he began to work on that elusive character that would captivate the reading and viewing public. At the time of his retirement from the Security Service, his fourth Macmillan book was in production and was finally published, after editing disagreements between author and publisher, in June 1980. It contained the formula that Madeleine had argued for: in common with the Inspector Morse series, the book introduced a brace of detectives working together, Superintendent Harry King and Chief Inspector Owen.

Madeleine's editorial presence now became more prominent and she worked assiduously on the plot of *Deadly Picnic*. Uncomfortable with Bingham's plan to put drugs, a subject of which he knew nothing, at the centre, she suggested that gambling should be the central illegal activity as this was something that he could 'mug up on' more easily. John considered but ultimately rejected the suggestion.

Deadly Picnic, published in 1980, was a disaster. Macmillan had lowered their expectations; on this occasion their advance shrank to £350 on delivery. The two detectives are slotted into an unconvincing plot, punctuated by improbable dialogue in a setting that has only the slightest relationship to the book's title. Author and editor failed to reach agreement about either the story or the length of the book. Large portions were cut; the plot suffered; ultimately Bingham lost interest and referred to the book as 'Deadly Nightshade'.

Presented in a dustcover that, in its garishness, was the antithesis of a Gollancz volume, the book does not appear to have been reviewed by the major daily papers, with the exception of the *Financial Times*, who commented that 'the solution is slightly disappointing and not exactly unexpected'. Far more direct were the *Huddersfield Daily Examiner* reviewer, who wrote that 'John Bingham has come up with *Deadly Picnic*, a novel with all the bite of a toothless vampire', and the *Irish Press*, who 'thought it all rather tedious and the writing pedestrian, even though Mr Bingham has quite a reputation'.

Deadly Picnic disappointed not only the reviewers and the public but also, in the gravest possible way, its author; business dealings with Macmillan came to an abrupt conclusion. Macmillan have not kept records of the book's sales. It was a parting of the ways to which both parties were probably amenable; fifteen months before the book was published, Bingham had made the decision to find another publisher.

Unsurprisingly, he returned to Gollancz for his final effort to break into the burgeoning market for a detective series. The concept of a sustainable detective had been in existence long before television extended its reach: Agatha Christie's Hercule Poirot and Miss Marple, Simenon's Maigret, Chesterton's Father Brown – not to mention the great Sherlock Holmes – were iconic figures in the genre. Television, moreover, had raised the stakes; Madeleine continued to be acutely envious of John le Carré's success with *The Spy Who Came In from the Cold* and in 1979 insult was added to injury when the BBC aired a seven-part series of *Tinker, Tailor.*

. In the late 1970s Madeleine's name appears more frequently in the Gollancz correspondence files, at one point describing herself as 'the keeper of the archive'. She and her family – but not the viewing public – knew that the finely drawn character of George Smiley had, since *Call for the Dead* in 1961, owed its exist-ence to her husband, who, frustratingly, had not yet succeeded in creating an equally popular or financially rewarding fictional character. At this point she increasingly took matters into her own hands.

Possibly – but far from certainly, as he continued to lean more to espionage than crime as a subject – John shared her ambition and he dutifully threw himself into research to find the right setting for his hero, whom he named 'Badger' Brock. He settled on Salisbury as the centre of the action, dubbed the cathedral city 'Melford' in the fiction, and wrote to Livia Gollancz about his ideas for the developing project on 15 March 1979. The letter conveys his excitement with his new character, his hopes for the series and his contrition at having strayed from the Gollancz stable with his last four books:

As I may have mentioned to you last year, I am thinking of creating a new character for a continuing series, Superintendent Brock ('the badger'). His early police career was in a provincial town like, say, Salisbury. Having been seconded to Scotland Yard for a while, and then done a stint in N. Ireland, he has now returned to his old stomping ground for a nice, orderly, normal, peaceful existence. Or so he thinks.

I reckon the first book, establishing people and scenes, would take about six or seven months, or more. Thereafter, local research and geography, street layout etc. being done, I would aim at three books every two years, as a minimum, and hope for four every two years.

The response was positive. Livia Gollancz was attracted by the character and setting of Melford/Salisbury for the series, and proposed a three-book contract. Bingham applied himself to the task but was interrupted by the Anthony Blunt scandal of November 1979. On 3 December he wrote to Livia Gollancz to request more time to brush up the first book:

> There has been a certain amount of flak flying around – to put it bluntly – Anthony Bluntly – and I do hope you won't mind if my book is a month or two late. I suppose I could rush it through by January, but as I am creating a new and, I hope, continuing character, I want to get the 'first appearance' right. I am not usually late with my copy, as you know, and after December 31st, when I finally retire from MI5 – emergencies excepted – things should be easier.

By April 1980 he could see the end of the tunnel. He was satisfied with Badger Brock; Melford was taking shape in his head and, most importantly, he would soon be free of his obligation to Macmillan. 'The last of the Macmillon [*sic*] books comes out on April 24th,' he wrote, adding, 'I think it is a rotten book ... it should be called *Deadly Nightshade* in my view.'

The final stage of John Bingham's writing career, between 1980 and 1986, was not the crowning triumph that Madeleine had envisaged. A series of errors and finally incapacitating illness attended those years. There was an element of transference in his attributing the blame for *Deadly Picnic* wholly to Macmillan; the truth is that it was not a masterly piece of writing. Clearly, however, there was a symbolic quality to his return to Gollancz, where, he felt, he would resume where he had left off, where his best books had been written.

The first book featuring the detective whom Madeleine hoped would be an iconic figure, the key to riches, was titled simply *Brock*. Bingham was reasonably happy with the character and, with more time on his hands, despite sporadic requests for help from 'The Office', he soldiered on. Even so, it was September before he delivered the final manuscript. Its reception did not augur well, as Jon Evans's report makes clear:

> The last Bingham novels that came my way were a falling-off, and during his absence he hasn't regained any of his original form ... Altogether, a curiously unsatisfactory story, which ambles on with little sense of direction ... The next book, already in hand, is about a Russian KGB defector, sent (with characters from 'The Double Agent') to sleepy Melford for safe keeping – a some-what incongruous development from the present novel, but it sounds promising.

Brock was eventually published in April 1981 and was out of print by June 1982. Gollancz tried without success to sell the paperback rights. By the time that *Brock and the Defector*, the second book in the proposed three-part series, was published, it was impossible to find a copy of its predecessor on the shelves. There seems to have been a less than wholehearted confidence in the series on the part of the publisher.

Reviews of *Brock* were unenthusiastic and, one suspects, it was only Bingham's stature from his earlier work that restrained reviewers from the savagery that might have greeted a first novel. 'A promising new series, though this one a bit contrived,' commented the *Northern Echo*. 'Idiosyncratically told,' wrote the reviewer in *The Times* with some ambiguity. The *Daily Telegraph* commented simply and accurately that 'the writing is better than the story told'.

Jon Evans, as ever, was on target with his criticism that the story 'ambles on with little sense of direction'. Improbable scene follows improbable scene as Superintendent Brock attempts to solve a series of rapes that have shattered the calm of sleepy Melford. For added spice, sub-plots involve different characters contemplating – but not committing – murder. The resulting mixture is dysfunctional; a weak plot might have survived if the character of Brock had been sympathetic and compelling but, sadly, he is no Inspector Morse and he ultimately fails to convince.

On the dustcover for *Brock*, Gollancz gave advance notice of the next book in the series, which, as Evans had mentioned, was 'incongruous'. Its subject again suggests that it was espionage rather than crime that appealed to the author.

Bingham, clearly, was tired, very tired. He battled manfully to develop the series, but by now it was clear that a new book every eight months was an unrealistic goal. Matters were further complicated by his and Madeleine's decision to sell their house in Abingdon Villas and to move to Campden Street in January 1982.

It was a tragically false move. The house was too small; their furniture would barely fit through the front door. Although still in Madeleine's beloved W8 postal district, it was closer to Notting Hill Gate than Kensington High Street, her manor. North of that beat was uncharted territory.

On 16 January John noted that 'Madeleine is in a fit of deep depression, which is usual when she moves to a new place'. As for himself, he commented that having a patio instead of a garden at Campden Street was a good thing as one garden in the Cotswolds was enough. Even gardening, previously his principal hobby, was no longer giving pleasure.

Lowfield Cottage in Sarsden, the cottage that Terence and Charlotte had bought in 1968 with 'the not very huge proceeds of the highly successful BBC series *Take Three Girls*', was a refuge for him during his last years at MI5 after Madeleine bought it from Charlotte in February 1972. There was a small summer-house in the garden and he used this as his quiet place for writing. During the short period that he and Madeleine lived in Campden Street they spent most of their time in the Cotswolds rather than their new London home.

With some trepidation, Gollancz moved to publish the second book in the Brock series. Livia called for an analysis of sales of recent books; this revealed that a mere 1,781 copies of *Brock* had been sold on the home market. Alarm bells were now ringing about the future of the series.

Bingham was simply not writing as well as before. At first he recognised this, and he amended, edited, rewrote much more than hitherto. Underpinning all his efforts was his ambivalence about a detective series and his preference for spy stories.

His solution was pragmatic if not particularly promising: he would adapt partially finished ideas for spy stories and turn them into Brock novels. At MI5 he had begun to write a biography of Anatoli Golitsyn, the KGB defector. When Security Service officers were unable to agree as to the value of Golitsyn's intelligence, the biography had been abandoned amid controversy.

He had copious notes, however, and he used these to construct the character of Alexi Schorin in *Brock and the Defector*. Limiting Inspector Brock to appearances at the beginning and at the end of an insipid spy yarn, he topped and tailed a defector story to create the second book in the series. By 1982 his output was pedestrian compared with the felicity of expression of his earlier work. Nonetheless, he delivered a finished manuscript to Gollancz.

Jon Evans was very doubtful when he read the final manuscript of *Brock and the Defector*, commenting that:

> It's a feeble story, feebly told. The writing is slack and the development painfully repetitious. Moreover, it's a most incongruous episode in what's intended as a Melford series built around Brock, who certainly emerges with no distinction here. I wasn't greatly impressed by *Brock*, but this could certainly sink the series.

Evans was right. The fundamental problem at the heart of the book is that the author was unclear in his own mind what kind of story he was telling and how Badger Brock would fit into it. Essentially, it is an espionage story that plays out in Melford, where Brock happens to be. A prior understanding regarding a safe house in Melford has been worked out in advance between Ducane, the spymaster, and Brock. This provides the only real link between the central story and Superintendent Brock, the character after whom the series was named.

Despite Evans's concerns, *Brock and the Defector* was published in 1982 and Bingham began work on the third book in the series. By this point even Madeleine must have doubted that Badger

Brock would capture readers' imagination as she had hoped. By then it was also clear that John was unable to write a story from scratch and that he scrabbled through old manuscripts to find something that he could adapt to fit the bill.

The obvious candidate was *The Old Spy's Papers*, featuring his fictional agent runner Ducane, a manuscript that he had worked on a few years before. Madeleine now began to rewrite it. Heading her notes 'B's Best-Seller', she inserted his most sympathetic detective, Vandoran from *The Third Skin* and *God's Defector*, substituting his name for Ducane. Clearly, husband and wife did not have congruent views, as John systematically changed the name back again. There was, in short, total confusion as to how the series would emerge. The explanation is alarmingly simple: Madeleine wanted a detective series; John did not. He wanted to develop Ducane in the spy genre. The result was an unsatisfactory compromise.

The book was then renamed *Brock and the Old Spy's Papers*. It went through several different incarnations as the work to complete it, to discharge his obligation to Gollancz and, if possible, to satisfy Madeleine, became more and more difficult for John. He was suffering transient ischaemic attacks, brief stoppages of the flow of blood to the brain, which affected his clarity of thought and expression. He was beginning to lose his memory and he became increasingly confused as he wrote.

For the next three years he wrestled with the project. At different points he attempted to insert elements of his previous work, even reintroducing la Matholière, which had been such a powerful ingredient of *Five Roundabouts to Heaven*. Ingrid reappears, this time as Gerd, and the action moves from Melford to London to the Loire valley. That version of the plot was soon abandoned.

As it became clear that he was unable to combine the disparate elements of the uncertain and shifting plot, Tim Goodwin, a young writer, was brought in to work with him as editor. Among

Bingham's papers is a work of 231 foolscap pages called *The False Image* by John Bingham and Tim Goodwin. This features not Brock but Ducane, who had been reinserted into the series. It is undated but was certainly written between 1982 and 1985, after the publication of *Brock and the Defector*.

The work seems to have started life as *The Old Spy's Papers* and then to have been reworked as *The False Image*. Someone, presumably Madeleine, pointed out that this was hardly the third book in the Brock series for Gollancz, whereupon the book morphed back into *Brock and the Old Spy's Papers*. On 26 February 1986 David Higham Associates, Goodwin's literary agents, wrote, confirming an agreement that Goodwin should receive 50 per cent of the royalties of *Brock and the Old Spy's Papers*. The royalty was never forthcoming as the project never materialised in any of its three incarnations. After seven or eight rewrites, Madeleine and John were compelled to concede that there was nothing publishable in the material.

Bingham never completed the third novel he had been contracted to write and Gollancz did not press him to do so. His return to Henrietta Street had been accompanied by optimism about his new character, not to mention an unprecedented advance of £1,500. Six years later, the series unfinished, neither author nor publisher were unhappy to let the project die a natural death.

Having been instrumental in urging him to undertake the series, Madeleine probably continued to press him to write some time after he was equal to the task. He was still confident, even after the dismal results of *Brock*, that he had at least another two books in him. Sadly, the evidence is that physical and mental decline had already set in. His handwriting is less confident, and his typewritten letters between 1981 and early 1984 contain a host of crossings-out and alterations.

Livia Gollancz, recalling those difficult years, commented tactfully:

Did he not complete the contract for three books about Brock? Perhaps not, perhaps he simply became bored with it, with writing. We certainly wouldn't have enforced the contract; we weren't sticklers for that sort of thing. Now, if he'd taken the third book to another publisher, well, then we would have done something. But if he didn't write the third book, that was up to him.

It was a dismal end to their long professional relationship. What was to have been the crowning creation of his career instead brought that career to an end, tarnishing his reputation as a writer. The saddest part is that he almost certainly knew this would be so while he was writing *Brock and the Defector*.

Like many an actor, Bingham had delayed leaving the stage too long. He had wanted to recreate the success of *The Double Agent* from 1966 and, probably for that reason, kept reverting to the spy genre as he fashioned the Brock series. As, successively, his later books failed to measure up, he became increasingly desperate to redeem his reputation. By 1984 he knew the time had come to abandon his attempts to do so. Deciding against the third book was ultimately an easy decision.

The greatest frustration must have been that he had been unable to produce a book that he was truly proud of since 1966. When he wrote *The Double Agent* he had completed ten books, of which at least seven were of very high quality and four were outstanding. For nearly twenty years he strove to recreate that magic without success. He would, one suspects, have been content with just one new book of the high quality of *Michael Sibley* or *Five Roundabouts*. But with each successive book, certainly after 1971, he diminished rather than enhanced his reputation.

The single exception was *The Hunting Down of Peter Manuel*, and those critics who argue that his objectivity, sensitivity and balance made him a more accomplished journalist than novelist can point to that book to support their argument. As he would be the first to admit, he was not good at what he called 'the fluffy stuff'. It was that, above all, that accounted for his falling-off as a novelist, for when he came to write *Brock*, not only did he not complete the third novel in the series, but the whole notion of Brock had foundered. In truth, Brock's creator never seemed very fond of him: he was an indistinct character, never lovable, never quite real.

Bingham's writing career had been chequered with distinct successes and a few dismal failures; it had ranged from provincial journalism to popular columns in a national newspaper, from an insightful, autobiographical first novel to a sadly inferior work that did, as Jon Evans of Gollancz predicted, sink the Brock series.

What, we may ask, would Bingham himself have been most proud of? Without doubt, he would have wished to be most proud of his novels. From his earliest days of writing, that was the ambition that he had for himself. Yet, by the end, he was unable to complete a work of any length. This was, to a great extent, a matter of health, but one may reasonably ask whether he was at his best as a novelist.

Madeleine tells us that he wrote slowly and painstakingly. Simon recalls that he simply viewed writing as one of his two jobs. There is no suggestion of genius, yet he had a remarkable talent. Just as in life his easy good nature encouraged people to unburden themselves to him, so, when he dealt in fact, he had a deft and humorous touch. Facts were the bricks and mortar with which he constructed his written work. As a writer of fiction, he struggled for a variety of reasons. The journalist who could work with facts, interpreting them, applying a light flight of fancy here, satirising the ridiculous, deflating the pompous, darting nimbly between fact and fantasy, was less able to create a consistently credible fictional world.

His best and most successful works were *My Name Is Michael Sibley*, *Five Roundabouts to Heaven*, *A Fragment of Fear* and his first spy novel, *The Double Agent*. It is no accident that three of these were, in varying degrees, autobiographical. It is that personal content that grounds the books and allows him to embellish, to be objective when he chooses; to reminisce hauntingly when he takes a different direction. Nowhere do we encounter a character who captivates us as much, ironically, as Bingham himself, who continues to enchant readers as George Smiley.

Simon's wife Gizella, the present Lady Clanmorris, became very close to both John and Madeleine, albeit in different ways, and recalls how her father-in-law would enter the house in Abingdon Villas when she, Simon and their daughter Lucy were visiting:

When my daughter Lucy was quite young, before she went to school, he used to come in, pat her on the head and vanish upstairs. But he always came down for drinks. I said to him, 'You're happy to come downstairs for drinks but not to sit down for five minutes with Lucy.' He replied, 'Yes darling, but you're so interesting that I have to rush off immediately and make notes.' He did spend a lot of time in his study; whenever the family was there he was always in the house but appeared only for drinks and meals. I think this was his handicap: he had no problem with plots, segmenting his books from start to end, but he was no good at the 'fluffy stuff' so he had to observe people. He used to come home from work, at whatever time, then immediately go to his study to write because on his way home he'd seen people doing certain things: gestures, body language, the way people communicated and he felt that using these prompts in his book was more successful than anything he invented. He was not an imaginative person; he couldn't create, he couldn't start off with a tiny thing and make it this big. He manipulated a bit with that; he took personalities, problems, circumstances that he came across in real life, and he then manipulated them in his writing.

The result of this inability to create is that many of his characters are unconvincing. The most sympathetic and realistic characters who carry us through the narrative are different manifestations of himself. He possessed a rare objectivity and was able to observe himself, his strengths and weaknesses, and, given his skill at plotting a story, to make even a caricature of himself realistic.

In *Michael Sibley* he takes a pitiless look at himself in his youth, overemphasises his weaknesses, plays down his strengths and creates a deeply flawed character who is entirely credible. The combination of his self-analysis and his experience of inter-rogation allows him to chart the progression of Sibley's woeful behaviour with the police in an utterly convincing manner. To suggest that Sibley is himself is to oversimplify. He is a cocktail of the worst of him. Similarly, Philip Bartels in *Five Roundabouts to Heaven* represents some of his better features – kindness, deep consideration – overlaid with what he saw as the characteristics that hampered him: lack of material ambition, a tendency to withdraw rather than push himself forward.

Those two books were his first crime novels and the most convincing of his stories. They both, especially *Michael Sibley*, drew heavily on his own life. When he wrote his first spy story, *The Double Agent*, he modelled his hero Ducane on himself; physi-cally and intellectually, Ducane resembles him in many details.

It is in *Michael Sibley* and *The Double Agent*, his first crime story and his first spy novel, that we encounter variations on the theme of Bingham as the central character – and Bingham himself was finite. In other books, where he is not the basis for the central character, the plot needs to be so compelling – as in *A Fragment of Fear* and *A Case of Libel* – as to make the central character relatively unimportant, or the character fails to convince, as in the Brock series and *Deadly Picnic*.

So we return to the question: what would John Bingham himself have been most proud of? Ironically, the *métier* in which he excelled was as a humorist, a *métier* that he considered irrelevant and peripheral. Possessed of a sense of humour that ranged from delicate and sophisticated to exuberantly adolescent, he was able to turn a piece of news into a finely crafted piece of comic verse or to apply a *reductio ad absurdum* and make the reader roll about with laughter. When he turns to novel writing, however, it is as if he 'put away childish things', as if he viewed novel writing as a more serious business, in which there was no room for the humour that suffused his columns.

He had every right to be proud both of the volume of his output and of the quality of at least four of the novels he wrote. Apart from the four already mentioned, there are elements of greatness in others: *The Third Skin*, for example, is less than perfect because, as one reviewer pointed out, he wrote about a milieu of which he knew little. Yet it has qualities of compassion and understanding, a sensitive grasp of human weakness, that are haunting in their perception.

We know from his letters to Livia Gollancz that he was not proud of the three Macmillan books, *God's Defector*, *The Marriage Bureau Murders* and *Deadly Picnic*. In returning to Gollancz, he was attempting to put fire back in his own belly. The final attempts to edit and finish the third Brock book petered out, both through lack of interest and lack of energy. By 1985 he recognised that he was unable to write anything substantial and from that point on he wrote only short pieces for himself.

Both John and Madeleine were growing old. Beginning in 1981, John suffered from ischaemic attacks with increasing frequency, and when Madeleine was also admitted to hospital in 1985, it became clear that he needed, if not permanent help, then at least the proximity of family. Simon and Gizella, who had bought a flat in Battersea, were able to buy the flat next door for John and Madeleine. This achieved that goal, while maintaining privacy. In many ways it was an ideal arrangement.

Madeleine, for whom Kensington was home territory, was distressed at living south of the Thames, in SW11 rather than W8, and quite unjustly called the Battersea flat 'a Peabody home', comparing it with the social housing built by philanthropist George Peabody. She was, moreover, unable to give her husband the nursing attention that he was beginning to need. A tragic series of events was set in train.

Gizella had become a confidante of Madeleine and she speaks with deeply sympathetic insight about her mother-in-law. She concedes, however, that Madeleine was quite impractical:

> She wrote a cookery book actually, and a book on bringing up children and how to be a good wife. I don't know what she was talking about as she had no idea how to bring children up. I phoned her up when my daughter was quite young and said 'Mama, Simon and I want to go to the cinema. Can I drop Lucy in?' and she said 'Yes, darling, no problem.' So I knocked on the door and said 'Here's Lucy' and she looked out and said 'Where's the nanny?' so we ended up taking Lucy to another friend because she almost had convulsions at the notion that she had to look after Lucy without a nanny.

While Madeleine's father Clement was alive, she depended on him to solve problems. He was an irreplaceable anchor for her in a way that John never could be. Gizella describes how the loss of Clement affected not only Madeleine herself, but also her marriage:

> My mother-in-law was very close to her father and very happy being married and having her father sort everything out. There was marital friction once her father died, simply because Mama started wanting from her husband what she was used to from her father: his protection when she was distressed – and my mother-in-law was quite capable of being distressed – and my father-in-law was baffled when someone was distressed.

Now that John increasingly needed attention, Madeleine was simply unable to cope. Nurses were hired to give him day care; successively they proved unsatisfactory. One nurse was hired to come in and have tea and play chess with him and to take him for walks in Battersea Park. When she tried to 'take Jack over', Gizella became alarmed. While Madeleine was staying with the de Moncuits in Tigy for ten days, the nurse refused to allow Gizella into the flat. She was soon shown the door.

The arrangement in Battersea was, in many ways, ideal. Madeleine, however, missed Kensington and, according to Simon, when she went to the National Theatre she would drive from Battersea to Kensington and then proceed along the route she was familiar with. Simon pointed out that a short trip along the south bank of the river connected Battersea and the National Theatre complex, but that had no impact. For as long as her husband needed attention, however, she accepted the situation.

In February 1987 Simon and Gizella were on a skiing holiday when Bingham took a turn for the worse. Acting unilaterally, Madeleine arranged for him to be taken into Dowdeswell House, a private nursing home outside Cheltenham. Not far from the cottage at Sarsden, this was a newly opened home and, in its location at least, eminently suitable.

When Simon and Gizella returned to London, a crisis followed. They had not been consulted and they felt strongly that John should not have been committed to care without their views being heard. 'We don't think he was actually a nursing home candidate when he was put in,' said Gizella.

> We lived next door to them. We had a carer in and we went away for a week, and my mother-in-law got into a frightful panic. He needed care but he was still quite bright. Simon and I were not consulted; we were away and by the time we got back it was all decided and, because the system worked like that, that was it.

To commit his father to care, Simon argued, would be the beginning of the end. Madeleine, however, was adamant, maintaining that he needed permanent round-the-clock care that the family was unable to provide. He frequently needed to be carried and Madeleine was physically unable to support him.

Once that step had been taken, however reluctantly, the full force of Madeleine's dislike of Battersea became clear. The rationale for buying the second flat had been to bring John close to the family. Now that he was in Dowdeswell House, that need was removed.

Gizella came back to Battersea one afternoon to find her mother-in-law distraught. Simon and Gizella decided that the only logical course was for the three of them to move back to Kensington together. The arrangement worked reasonably well: their daughter Lucy was now twelve and away at school; Simon and Gizella were out at work all day; Madeleine had her own drawing room. As Gizella recalls:

So we moved back together, which was no problem as Simon and I were out to work all day, and when we had a dinner party she was an eminently cultured woman and she was quite suitable to sit on a chair and keep people chatting. And she did a very good job at that, chatting about the theatre, the theatre, nothing else. She always used to say to me 'Darling, you're so clever' because I knew about something other than the theatre.

At weekends Simon, Gizella and their daughter Lucy paid visits to Cheltenham. It became a fixture in Lucy's life that on weekends home from school she and any friend she brought home would play in the grounds of the nursing home. It was a routine that the family adapted to. As Simon had predicted when John was admitted to Dowdeswell House, it was now merely a matter of time.

For Gizella, the decline of her father-in-law was tragic and tragically mismanaged. She had seen as early as 1981 that his brain was not functioning as effectively as before. She noticed at Abingdon Villas that he sometimes remained rooted to the spot as if the command from his brain to walk was not reaching his feet. Madeleine, by contrast, appeared unaware for some time that there was anything wrong. Gizella comments on this period:

> She was no good at intimate things. I think I was the only person to be close to her on that level. Certainly not Simon, she would rather have died than show any emotion there. My mother-in-law was a tortured creature because she'd have a problem and instead of saying 'We'll do this or that' she would churn it over, making the problem even worse than when it started, and she found no release because she grew up with her father solving everything, even during her marriage until Clement died. She said that things weren't the same after her father died.

For Gizella to voice her concerns to Madeleine was far from easy. Her mother-in-law was able to become a *grande dame* in an instant – indeed, she was known by several friends of the family as 'The Duchess' – and Gizella hesitated to interfere: 'There was no marked point at which it got worse; it was a slow decline, very slow, over about seven years. I noticed very quickly. I don't know when [Madeleine] noticed or if she pretended. My mother-in-law was a very good pretender.'

Ironically, just as the family were coming to terms with the imminence of John's demise, on the morning of 16 February 1988 Gizella's mother found Madeleine dead in her bed. She had worked on her newest book during the morning and that evening, to Gizella's shocked surprise, had been watching *Boon*, a television programme featuring a stocky, leather-jacketed, motorcycle-riding detective.

As she wished her daughter-in-law good night, she called her back and asked for Gizella's signature dish of chicken paprika the following evening. Early the next morning, Gizella's mother, who was staying with Simon and Gizella and who had taken Madeleine a cup of tea, came into their room and told Gizella in Hungarian that something was wrong with Madeleine. During the night she had suffered a fatal aneurism.

Simon drove to Dowdeswell House to inform his father of Madeleine's death. He found him in a confused state, imparted the news, then returned to London, unsure whether his message had been understood. When he returned on the following day, John greeted him and told him, 'Your mother's in the kitchen.' There was little more to say. Simon didn't mention the matter again.

Less than six months later, John too died. His retirement had been a slow decline, a seven-year period in which he had derived little enjoyment from his leisure. He had remained at his desk at MI5 long past retirement age – Gizella believes that he was still performing jobs for the Service until he was seventy-two or seventy-three. He officially retired on 31 December 1979; whatever the exact date of his final retirement, the decline swiftly followed. After forty years of service in 'The Slaves' Galley', he had, at best, a scant year as a free man possessed of all his faculties.

His obituary in the *Daily Telegraph* captured much of the man, referring to his image among the 'Young Turks' of post-war MI5 as 'a little old-fashioned', commenting that: 'He had less faith than many of his colleagues in electronic methods ... saying "Nothing beats an agent in the right place. Bugs can't tell you who is sleeping with whom, who is jealous of his superiors and fed up with his job – and who is drinking."'

Those few sentences, combined with the comment that 'Clanmorris was a gentle man, almost benevolent looking, [who] gazed at the world with a slight air of puzzlement', captured in a few words the essence of their subject.

Since 1950 he had struggled to perform two jobs to the best of his ability and by and large, particularly during the 1960s, he had maintained an enviable output of writing while dealing with recurring crises at 'The Office'. Those jobs took him away from his family and made incursions into his favourite relaxation, the flowers, fruit and vegetable patch in his beloved garden.

For such a man, 'quiet, deceptively quiet', according to his son, 'comfortable in his own skin', a twilight period was no less than his due. That he was denied that graceful retirement, during which he could gaze benevolently at the world, poke fun at modern customs, indulge in a few stanzas of light verse pillorying the political villains of the day, enjoy his three grandchildren, was a grave injustice dealt him by fate.

From 1982 onwards his jottings are almost universally morose.

His 'autobiography', largely handwritten on scraps of paper, never ordered or completed, is a wistful reminiscence on his youth and on his parents' families. It takes the reader through his early years through anecdotes and long reflections on the eccentricities of his aunts. It is a ruminative and sentimentally selective document.

His other jottings return again and again to Tigy, to the nine months spent in Arcadian bliss after his public school upbringing in England. Time and again, in his last attempts at writing the third Brock novel, he strives to bring the château into the story. But it doesn't quite fit; the magic has gone. Try as he might, he had left Tigy behind for good.

Despite his deep and unshakeable love for England, his country puzzled him in his latter years. From his vantage point at MI5 he had seen plots to undermine the body politic from Right and Left; he had been on the scene when one after another of his well-born contemporaries had been unmasked as Soviet spies. Indeed, the scandal that retained him at his desk in 'The Slaves' Galley' concerned Anthony Blunt, the very man who, forty years before, Max Knight refused to have nosing around his section.

It is easy to imagine him happily ensconced in Kensington and the Cotswolds, revisiting his youth in France and Germany, perhaps a week in both countries each year, returning to enjoy his garden in Sarsden in those glorious English seasons, the spring and the autumn. Retirement is designed for such men.

Considerate, courteous, a man who shunned cocktail parties and his wife's salons until she imperiously called him to do his duty among her guests, he once more reminds us of George Smiley. The man whom John le Carré modelled on John Bingham talks of the retirement he yearned for but, like Bingham, never had.

With quiet detachment, he accepts his forthcoming retirement and, with London property prices rising to absurd levels, he proposes to become a mild, eccentric figure living in a quiet Cotswold village. Steeple Aston, he decides, will be his home. Yes, he admits, he is out of date, but that is not important. Better to retire now when one is still 'an oak of one's generation' rather than allowing one's values to be blown about by every change in fashion, every new policy of the intelligence service.

Once more, we find the original painted in bold strokes in the copied image.

John Bingham the writer has retained a solid group of aficionados who read his early work nostalgically, savouring the era in which they are set. Ironically, it is through le Carré, through Alec Guinness, and through the revival of the *Quest for Karla* trilogy on the big screen that a greatly wider public catches fleeting glimpses of the 'oak of one's own generation' that was John Bingham.

CHAPTER 13

THE SEVENTH LORD CLANMORRIS, 1908–88

This is a mood I cannot afford to miss – pain which is not pain. It is not a pain that longs for the past – yet it is a pain which is of the past. It is not a pain which laments the present and it is certainly not a pain which fears the future, and any pain it might or might not bring. It is just a pain which grips without reason, and will not leave me in peace. It grips and holds and will not let go. It agonises and yet it thrills; it holds the pain I have known so well in the past and will know again, if I live long enough, gripping the stomach and nearly choking the breath in the throat.

And yet, and yet ... it is rooted in the past. It is not a pain of lost opportunities; some of those lost chances there doubtless were – yet I cannot recall them, and therefore cannot be bounded by them.

What, then, is this strange pain – which is almost pleasurable? I wish I knew for then I could switch it on and wax redolent its welcome waves.

I look out of the window and see the friendly red bricks of the London I know so well. Yet I know I do not see them. I see something I should not see, though, God knows, the broad poplar-lined drive, leading to the French château, is dear enough to me, and I have seen it often enough in real life.

The château is quiet and empty and I could leave my car and walk towards the château and leave this London flat far, far behind, and in that flat I would also leave many of my old, old hopes and dreams – all safely packaged, and eligible for a label which says 'Not Wanted on the Voyage'.

But it would be incorrect. It is indeed wanted on the journey.

This piece of writing from 1985, headed 'Pain that is Not Pain', is a bittersweet piece of nostalgia. Bingham yearns for the days of innocence at Tigy in 1927–8 but wistfully accepts that the almost sixty intervening years also have meaning for him. They cannot simply be packed in a suitcase of memories and discarded.

Those intervening years had cast him in many roles: journalist, agent runner, novelist, husband and father. If he could have been selective in 1985, which memories would he have selected? In which role would he have judged himself a success?

Bingham's struggle at MI5, first against Nazism, later against communism, was rooted in his belief that Britain enjoyed a way of life that was sound, rational, founded on human decency and respect. Moderation, especially political moderation, was, he believed, the keystone of the British way of life.

As he looked in 1985 at the course of events in Britain, he must have wondered if it had all been worthwhile. In the very period that he strove to check malign outside influences on Britain, his country seemed to be doing a perfectly good job of destroying itself from within. The twelve months from March 1984 had witnessed a form of civil war in Britain as the National Union of Mineworkers challenged the authority of Margaret Thatcher and went on strike for a year. The Prime Minister echoed the thoughts of many in the country when she declared, 'We had to fight the enemy without in the Falklands. We always have to be aware of the enemy within, which is much more difficult to fight and more dangerous to liberty.'

This was not an isolated event but the latest in a series of crises that had plagued Britain since 1945. For Bingham, the war was a watershed; the country that emerged from the conflict was very different from the country that he had written so lovingly of in the *Sunday Dispatch* of 1938. Moreover, he would have argued, things had since gone steadily downhill.

The lurch to the Left and systematic nationalisation of industries in the 1940s, the spy scandals and decline of British influence in the 1950s, the prostitution of his hometown as 'Swinging London' in the 1960s, the industrial crises of the 1970s, for several years of which Britain was governed by a Prime Minister about whom there were strong suspicions that he was a KGB spy – all these undoubtedly made him question the efficacy of the ethical positions he had espoused.

Suspicions about Wilson and the fear that Britain was once more vulnerable to communist takeover had led to a right-wing conspiracy to install Earl Mountbatten as Prime Minister. This conspiracy, in turn, was linked to allegations of a dark South African plot to subvert the Wilson government and discredit the Left in Britain. Bingham had been familiar with all these conspiracies, real or imagined, from Left and from Right, during his last years at MI5.

His retirement had been delayed three times. Although committed to the work, he would have been insensitive or super-human if he had not asked himself if he and his colleagues were actually doing any good for a country that appeared bent on self-immolation.

In 1985 he regarded the country he loved almost brought to a standstill by a crippling labour dispute. Increasingly polarised, increasingly materialistic, increasingly disdainful of 'old' values, Britain had changed beyond recognition – and the destructive forces came not from Berlin, not from Moscow, but from within.

Of his career as a writer he will have had mixed feelings. With the exception of *A Fragment of Fear* and *The Double Agent*, none of his later books received the critical acclaim afforded to his first two novels. He wove elegant plots, was sensitive to human ambition and frailty, but he saw his protégé John le Carré eclipse him and establish himself as one of the twentieth century's most successful novelists. In his last twenty years of writing he never recovered the graceful facility of style that characterised his early work.

Regarding his life as husband and father, he would have been reticent. Not because he doubted his success but because such things fell into a category of emotions that one did not discuss. Towards his son he felt enormous affection, moderated by the restraints of his class and era. Gizella, a self-confessed hugger, was astonished at the lack of physical contact between father and son. Hugging a son was not something that came easily to John, but that in no way diminished the mutual respect and love between the two.

It is not uncommon for a father to be closer to his daughter than to his son and for a mother to sanctify her son. If Madeleine did so with Simon, it is understandable: she had seen him almost die as an infant, had home-schooled him during the war and, as he grew to manhood, had wished for him the life denied to her adored brother Mark when HMS *Vandal* sank. Simon would become what Mark had not had the opportunity to become. She had, she felt, some proprietary rights over her son. With her daughter Charlotte, by contrast, she had a generally thorny, frequently tempestuous relationship.

Naturally enough, it was to her father that Charlotte turned. The stranger who had walked into her nursery in 1948 became an idol for his daughter, encouraging her writing talent, throughout his life her most ardent supporter and friend. When Charlotte's writing of *Coronet* stalled, John wrote to her, 'Carry on kid, you could make a hundred pounds.' The estimate was, it transpired, on the low side. They shared a delightful joke aimed at Madeleine, a supposed nightmare for each of them – that one or the other would die before coming to the end of writing a book, and that Madeleine would be left to finish it. Charlotte shudders at the memory of the decline in her father's health in the 1980s. It is still too painful for her to discuss.

Which leaves us Madeleine, his companion of almost sixty years. When they met in 1929 Bingham was conducting an uncertain and long-distance friendship with 'Ingrid', whom he had met and loved at la Matholière. Choosing Madeleine because she was 'more patriotic' and 'had a better sense of history', he married her in 1934, not without reservations, as he had already witnessed her petulant side when she hurled her shoes at her former nanny.

Madeleine Bingham was not an easy woman in any sense of the word. Capable of harbouring an implacable grudge, irrationally jealous of the success of others, frequently condescending, given to a haughty imperiousness and known to her close friends and family as 'The Duchess', she maintained a powerful presence.

Four men dominated her life, each assuming an unassailable position in her hierarchy of mortals. Her father Clement, her brother Mark, her husband John and her son Simon were placed on pedestals. As daughter, sister, wife, mother, she was supremely confident that her emotions and sense of duty combined to make her the perfect incarnation of the role she played. She was not self-critical; instead, she tended to the self-righteous. A devotee of the theatre, she seemed, on occasion, to be playing, even overplaying a part.

The fixity of her positions could be chilling; her animosity towards different philosophies unyielding. Her studiously common-sense attitudes reflect not the result of intellectual search but rather a distillation of her world view, simplified for a less than cerebral audience. Neither shallow nor intellectually profound, her tendency to the glib invites the former description. She could, in short, be infuriating.

The daughter of a figure who filled whatever stage he strode onto, she adored her father with a passion, loved him with a dependence that intensified her deep sense of loss when he died. In two of her books, *Peers and Plebs* and *Cheapest in the End*, this magnificent and munificent Colossus bestrides her world, turning her childhood into an adventure. A demanding adventure to be sure, as Clement would pay the same attention to her school reports as he did to his choice of food, wine and furniture. Nothing but the best would do. Small wonder that a father so surefooted would be Madeleine's iconic notion of manhood.

While Clement was alive she was able to depend on both him and her husband for emotional and practical support. When Clement died, however, the entire responsibility shifted to Bingham. This new burden was neither to his liking nor fitted to his emotional makeup. Although deeply kind and sympathetic, he was not equipped to shake Madeleine from depression in the way her father would have done. He allowed her space in her life for her foibles and passions, but he did not share them. Increasingly, he withdrew his investment of emotion, even compassion, and concentrated on 'handling' his wife. Charlotte recalls that, soon after Clement's death, they 'began to live separate lives'.

Bingham never subscribed to his wife's rancour against le Carré and he never reveals to what extent that rancour affected him. As in many of his activities, he simply adjusted and soldiered on, maintaining his friendship with his former colleague, apparently without discussing it with Madeleine. When Madeleine pressed him to take a position and recorded the conversation between them, he was deft in avoiding passing judgement, even then finding plausible and generous explanations for le Carré's behaviour. Bingham had ambition, to be sure, but it was never as urgent as le Carré's determination to succeed. If he felt envy of le Carré, he never revealed it publicly. Far more likely, he was more concerned about what toll success would take on his friend. He surely regretted that Madeleine abandoned the friendship but he was able to function quite independently of his wife for, as Charlotte points out, emotionally at least, they were living separate lives.

Arthur Spencer, John's friend and colleague in the intelligence service, wrote to Simon Clanmorris in May 2011 with a story that he felt Simon should know:

Like most old men (I am now 94) I recall interesting events in my life. One which I record below will, I am sure, interest you in particular. It is an account of your father's long love for a Norwegian lady. When the Eire republic was founded the Clanmorrises lost their ancestral fishing rights there. So at least once before the war they rented a good stretch of a river in S.W. Norway to fish. When there your father fell in love with a Norwegian lady living nearby, a passion which, as you will see was returned.

Under German occupation for 6 years they couldn't write to each other. But on the assumption that she hadn't moved home John wrote to her old address and she replied. I don't know whether they previously discussed marriage but by that time your father had married your mother and stopped writing to the Norwegian lady.

One day in the mid-1970s your father asked me to meet him near St. James's Park tube station to discuss something which couldn't be discussed in the office where colleagues could hear what was being said. He told me of his old love for the Norwegian, saying that she had just written a sad and desperate letter saying that she was slowly dying (probably of cancer) and implored him to come to see her for one last time – which he intended to do. If anybody asked why he was not in his office I was to say that he had joined me in a special operation which was expected to take about a week. In the event nobody showed any interest and John went to Norway to see the lady for one last time.

Apart from thanking me for my help and despite our close friendship he never referred to the incident again. Did you know anything about this? I'm sure your mother didn't.

Bingham had covered his tracks carefully when speaking to Spencer. He was careful not to confide that he had known 'Ingrid' since 1927, two years before he met Madeleine. He had also visited Ingrid on at least two occasions while ostensibly on a fishing holiday. He was equally economical with the truth concerning Ingrid's health, as she was still alive and was visited by him in London ten years later.

In fact, Madeleine did know of 'Ingrid', whom she referred to in the family as 'Jack's girlfriend', and later, when John was in decline, corresponded with her, telling her of his condition. When she learned of this, 'Ingrid' – whose real name was Gerd Strand – came to London and invited John to visit her at her hotel.

By that time his short-term memory had failed him completely. He and Madeleine had moved to Battersea in March 1984 and, to help him remember his new address, Madeleine had sewn a sheet of paper with the address written on it inside his jacket. When he went to take a taxi home from the hotel, he unfortunately forgot not only his new address but also that there was a sheet of paper sewn inside his jacket with that information. The only address he could remember was Abingdon Villas and so the taxi went there first, subsequently circling around west London in case John should see and remember where he lived. After two or three hours of this, the driver regretfully took him back to the hotel as that was the only contact point of which he was aware and where he could reasonably leave his fare. Fortunately by then Simon and Gizella, who were living next door in Battersea, had become concerned and had ascertained from Madeleine where he had gone. They went to the hotel, found him and took him home.

Soon after this John wrote his nostalgic 'Pain that is not Pain'. He also strove to introduce Gerd and Tigy into *Brock and the Old Spy's Papers* but succeeded only in burdening the story with his own nostalgia. While it is not good writing, it illustrates the emotional triangle and the gulf that separated him from Madeleine.

As John looked back over his life towards its end, he was justified in taking pride in his secret work, however much subsequent events had undermined the body politic. A ruthlessly objective man, he will have recognised the good and the less good in his writing. He had been brutally realistic about *Deadly Picnic* and, as he struggled with his third Brock novel, he must have recognised that the Brock series did not measure up to the brilliance of his early work.

When he considered his career as a writer, he had no regrets at not having written a novel of the stature of *War and Peace*. When Richard Adams published *Watership Down* in 1972, he was enchanted by the 'Lapine' epic. It was, he maintained, the one book that he would like to have written.

With his children, as well as with Gizella and Terence, he had firm and deeply affectionate relationships. There was no reason to feel regret or failure, wishing that things had been otherwise.

Towards the end of his life he said to Simon, 'You should have been Norwegian.' There can be little doubt that when he wrote, 'The château is quiet and empty and I could leave my car and walk towards the château and leave this London flat far, far behind', the château was not quite empty, as Gerd/Ingrid, in his mind, would still be there. The château at Tigy was symbolic for him, representing the close friendships of his youth and, tantalisingly, the first love that stayed with him all his life.

It is too simple to say that he was unhappy with Madeleine. It was a marriage that worked as well as most. But it was not the grand passion that he had wanted for himself. If the piece of writing that opened this chapter reflects regret, then that regret is to be found in the lack of mutual passion in the union.

Once more we stumble on a Smiley-ism. Before Smiley leaves London on his epic journey to ensnare Karla, Oliver Lacon lectures him, applauding his patriotism, reflecting that if Ann had been Smiley's agent rather than his wife, then Smiley might have handled her better.

Lacon's words resonate in the case of Smiley, accomplished agent runner, disappointed husband. One can only speculate whether in le Carré's mind John Bingham too handled women better at arm's length.

If so, it is a sad but fitting epitaph.

BIBLIOGRAPHY

Books by John Bingham

My Name Is Michael Sibley (London: Victor Gollancz, 1952)

Five Roundabouts to Heaven (London: Victor Gollancz, 1953)

The Third Skin: A Story of Crime (London: Victor Gollancz, 1954)

The Paton Street Case (London: Victor Gollancz, 1955)

Marion (London: Victor Gollancz, 1957)

Murder Plan Six (London: Victor Gollancz, 1958)

Night's Black Agent (London: Victor Gollancz, 1961)

A Case of Libel (London: Victor Gollancz, 1963)

A Fragment of Fear (London: Victor Gollancz, 1965)

The Double Agent (London: Victor Gollancz, 1966)

I Love, I Kill (London: Victor Gollancz, 1968)

Vulture in the Sun (London: Victor Gollancz, 1971)

The Hunting Down of Peter Manuel: Glasgow Multiple Murderer (London: Macmillan, 1973) [In association with William Muncie]

God's Defector: The Case of the Missing Priest (London: Macmillan, 1976)

The Marriage Bureau Murders (London: Macmillan, 1977)

Deadly Picnic (London: Macmillan, 1980)

Brock (London: Victor Gollancz, 1981)

Brock and the Defector (London: Victor Gollancz, 1982)

Relevant books by John le Carré

Call for the Dead (London: Victor Gollancz, 1961)

A Murder of Quality (London: Victor Gollancz, 1962)

The Spy Who Came in from the Cold (London: Victor Gollancz, 1963)

The Looking-Glass War (London: Heinemann, 1965)

Tinker, Tailor, Soldier, Spy (London: Hodder & Stoughton, 1974)

The Honourable Schoolboy (London: Hodder & Stoughton, 1977)

Smiley's People (London: Hodder & Stoughton, 1980)

A Perfect Spy (London: Hodder & Stoughton, 1986)

The Secret Pilgrim (London: Hodder & Stoughton, 1991)

Absolute Friends (London: Hodder & Stoughton, 2004)

General bibliography

Adams, Richard, *Watership Down* (London: Rex Collings, 1972)

Andrew, Christopher, *Defend the Realm: The Authorized History of MI5* (New York: Alfred A. Knopf, 2009)

Aronoff, Myron, *The Spy Novels of John le Carré: Balancing Ethics and Politics* (Basingstoke: Macmillan, 1999)

Barley, Tony, *Taking Sides: The Fiction of John le Carré* (Milton Keynes: Open University Press, 1986)

Beene, LynnDianne, *John le Carré* (New York: Twayne, 1992)

Bingham, Barry, *Falklands, Jutland and The Bight* (London: John Murray, 1919)

Bingham, Charlotte, *Coronet Among the Weeds* (London: Heinemann, 1963)

— —, *Daughters of Eden* (New York: Bantam Books, 2004)

Bingham, Madeleine, *Cheapest in the End* (New York: Dodd, Mead, 1963)

— —, *Peers and Plebs: Two Families in a Changing World* (London: George Allen & Unwin, 1975)

Boyle, Andrew, *The Climate of Treason: Five Who Spied for Russia* (London: Hutchinson, 1979)

Bruccoli, Matthew and Judith Baughman (eds), *Conversations with John le Carré* (Jackson: University Press of Mississippi, 2005)

Carter, Miranda, *Anthony Blunt: His Lives* (London: Macmillan, 2001)

Cave Brown, Anthony, *Treason in the Blood: H. St. John Philby, Kim Philby and the Spy Case of the Century* (London: Robert Hale, 1995)

Churchill, Sir Winston, *The Second World War, Vol. 4: The Hinge of Fate* (London: Cassell, 1951)

Clark, Alan, *Barbarossa: The Russian–German Conflict, 1941–1945* (London: Hutchinson, 1965)

Clay, Lucius, *Decision in Germany* (Garden City, NY: Doubleday, 1950)

Colvin, Ian, *Flight 777* (London: Evans Brothers, 1957)

Cook, Andrew, *M: MI5's First Spymaster* (Stroud: Tempus, 2004)

Cookridge, Edward Henry, *The Third Man: The Truth about 'Kim' Philby, Double Agent* (London: Arthur Barker, 1968)

Cudlipp, Hugh, *Walking on the Water* (London: Bodley Head, 1976)

Ffrench Papers: Rahasane, County Galway, 1765–1831 (Galway: Galway County Council, 2006)

Gaulle, Charles de, *Mémoires de Guerre* (Paris: Plon, 1954)

Golitsyn, Anatoli, *New Lies for Old: The Communist Strategy of Deception and Disinformation* (New York: Dodd, Mead, 1984)

Herwarth von Bittenfeld, Hans-Heidrich, *Against Two Evils* (New York: Rawson, Wade, 1981)

Horn, Adrian, *Juke Box Britain: Americanisation and Youth Culture, 1945–60* (Manchester: Manchester University Press, 2009)

Hough, Richard, *Mountbatten: Hero of Our Time* (London: Weidenfeld & Nicolson, 1980)

Hyde, Douglas, *I Believed: The Autobiography of a Former British Communist* (London: Heinemann, 1951)

Keating, H. R. F. (ed.), *Whodunit: A Guide to Crime, Suspense and Spy Fiction* (London: Windward, 1982)

Khrushchev, Nikita, *Khrushchev Remembers* (London: André Deutsch, 1971)

Knight, Maxwell, *Report on the Work of MS Agents During the War 1939-1945* (1945). London: Public Record Office, KV/4/227

Liddell, Guy, *The Diaries of Guy Liddell* (1945). London: Public Record Office, KV/4/185 *et seq.*

McCalmont, Rose, *Memoirs of the Binghams* (London: Spottiswoode & Co., 1915)

Macintyre, Ben, *Operation Mincemeat: The True Spy Story that Changed the Course of World War II* (London: Bloomsbury, 2010)

— —, *Double Cross: The True Story of D-Day Spies* (London: Bloomsbury, 2012)

Marnham, Patrick, *Trail of Havoc: In the Steps of Lord Lucan* (London: Viking, 1987)

Masterman, Sir John, *The Double Cross System in the War of 1939 to 1945* (New Haven: Yale University Press, 1972)

Masters, Anthony, *The Man Who Was M: The Life of Maxwell Knight* (Oxford: Basil Blackwell, 1984)

Miller, Joan, *One Girl's War: Personal Exploits in MI5's Most Secret Station* (Dingle, Co. Kerry: Brandon, 1986)

Monaghan, David, *The Novels of John le Carré: The Art of Survival* (Oxford: Blackwell, 1985)

— —, *Smiley's Circus: A Guide to the Secret World of John le Carré* (London: Orbis, 1986)

Newton, Verne, *The Butcher's Embrace: The Philby Conspirators in Washington* (London: MacDonald, 1991)

Page, Bruce, David Leitch and Philip Knightley, *Philby: The Spy Who Betrayed a Generation* (London: André Deutsch, 1968)

Penrose, Barrie and Simon Freeman, *Conspiracy of Silence: The Secret Life of Anthony Blunt* (London: Grafton, 1987)

— —, and Roger Courtiour, *The Pencourt File* (London: Secker & Warburg, 1978)

Philby, Kim, *My Silent War* (London: MacGibbon & Kee, 1968)

Public Record Office, *Camp 020, MI5 and the Nazi Spies* (2000), London: Public Record Office

Public Record Office of Northern Ireland, *Clanmorris Papers* (2007), Belfast: P.R.O.N.I.

Public Record Office of Northern Ireland, *Ward Papers* (2007), Belfast: P.R.O.N.I.

Rimington, Stella, *Open Secret: The Autobiography of the Former Director-General of MI5* (London: Hutchinson, 2001)

Sauerberg, Lars Ole, *Secret Agents in Fiction: Ian Fleming, John le Carré and Len Deighton* (London: Macmillan, 1984)

Seale, Patrick and Maureen McConville, *Philby: The Long Road to Moscow* (London: Hamish Hamilton, 1973)

Shawcross, William, *Dubček* (London: Weidenfeld & Nicolson, 1970)

Sillitoe, Sir Percy, *Cloak Without Dagger* (London: Cassell, 1955)

Smith, Jean Edward (ed.), *The Papers of General Lucius D. Clay: Germany, 1945–1949, Vol. II* (Bloomington: Indiana University Press, 1974)

Tangye, Derek, *The Way to Minack* (London: Michael Joseph, 1968)

Trevor-Roper, Hugh, *The Philby Affair: Espionage, Treason, and Secret Services* (London: William Kimber, 1968)

West, Nigel (ed.), *A Matter of Trust: MI5, 1945–72* (London: Weidenfeld & Nicolson, 1982)

— —, *Molehunt: The Full Story of the Soviet Spy in MI5* (London: Weidenfeld & Nicolson, 1987)

— —, *The Faber Book of Espionage* (London: Faber & Faber, 1993)

Wheatley, Ronald, *Operation Sea Lion: German Plans for the Invasion of England, 1939–1942* (Oxford: Clarendon Press, 1958)

Wolfe, Peter, *Corridors of Deceit: The World of John le Carré* (Bowling Green, OH: Bowling Green State University Popular Press, 1987)

Woodham Smith, Cecil, *The Great Hunger: Ireland, 1845–49* (London: Hamish Hamilton, 1962)

Wright, Peter, *Spycatcher: The Candid Autobiography of a Senior Intelligence Officer* (Melbourne: William Heinemann Australia, 1987)

Ziegler, Philip, *Mountbatten: The Official Biography* (London: Collins, 1985)

INDEX

PICTURE CREDITS

Denis Arthur Bingham, third Lord Clanmorris of Newbrook; John Bingham, first Lord Clanmorris of Newbrook; Madeleine Bingham on her wedding day; the Hon. Simon Bingham; the Hon. Charlotte Bingham and Terence Brady © The Hon. Charlotte Bingham

A triptych of John Bingham; the Hon. John and Madeleine Bingham at their wedding, 28 July 1934; John and Madeleine attending the wedding of Madeleine's sister Suzanne, 1936; presentation at court, July 1938; a self-portrait of John Bingham © Lord Clanmorris

John Bingham and his goddaughter Rosy Denaro at Abingdon Villas © Rosy Burke (née Denaro)

Château de la Matholière © Author's own